The First Mythology

A Book by

Alfred W. Sylvester Jr.

Being a work of those lost things that made us as we are!
By finding we may change and with understanding become more!

The Serpent

Drawn by

Micah

The Serpent is the path of the stone. The astrological times and colors are shown as they come and go! By understanding the stones can be made!

Order this book online at www.trafford.com
or email orders@trafford.com

Most Trafford titles are also available at major online book retailers.

Print information available on the last page.

ISBN: 978-1-4251-6469-0 (sc)
ISBN: 978-1-4269-6217-2 (e)

Trafford rev. 06/08/2015

 www.trafford.com

North America & international
toll-free: 1 888 232 4444 (USA & Canada)
fax: 812 355 4082

Contents

This Book is dedicated with many feelings to my late friend, Richard. Only his friendship and drive caused me to become interested. For some reason, he believed we could do this. Also, to those alchemists of the past that risked their lives to pass on hidden information- - -

I would like also to thank my wife for all she did to help with this work. Few would put up with those smells and other things that went on for years!

As this is a work about things lost for many reasons, I have included here at the start a list of my understanding of terms I will use. The reader should become familiar with this way of using those terms. It would be more correct to say these understanding have been hidden from the common man! All of the lost mysteries of the past will come alive and united with this explanation. Much in your life will be seen in a different way. In alchemy we say that each must walk his own path. I consider my words and I am hopeful that the information here will open your path, and cause you to have a greater understanding of your surroundings.

To Give an understanding of natural alchemy.   Because it is about nature and understood in its own way, tied to Genesis and our 'All' outside. These understanding should be known upfront.

Alchemy:

A term used to describe forces in and the way nature creates substance (salt) with those forces. An understanding of how nature (outside) works. Alchemy natural is seen from the viewpoint of a philosopher.

Alchemical Process:

The way Man uses different natural forces to control and recycle matter. The work is done within a pyramid glass oven.

Alchemical Forces:

Energy and conditions we work with and consider in our Process being sun, moon, moisture, cold, warmth, hot, dry, wet, air, time, shape, and their connections to the yearly cycle.

Waters:

All parts of the creation, (what is found outside) being those term mentioned in forces.

Shape:

Any seed, shell, shuck, seed arrangement, anything having to do with PHI. Called sands by the ancients. Also the firmament and heaven.

PHI:

A mathematical principle found throughout nature and tied to sands.

Ouroborous:

A sign showing the serpent biting his tail, In alchemy it is used to understand matter being recycled.
Consider a compost pile.

Androgynous:

Matter that has been recycled by nature, it is both male and female as the work was done by both lights above. This comes from an ancient understanding of the sun being male, the moon female. There are two stages of androgynous material in alchemy.

Sun:

Masculine, perfect, gold, spirit, hot and dry, sulfurous.

Sulfurous:

Being a combination of sunlight and vapor.

Moon:

Female, wet, cool, silver, a lesser light than the sun, mercurious.

Mercurious:

A substance made of vapor and moonlight, a combination.

Oven:	A Place to work alchemical processes. In natural alchemy we work with a glass pyramid shaped oven built so as to contain PHI.
Primordial matter:	Matter that has been recycled by nature in a pyramid oven. The only matter that will collect the above to create the stone. Believed to be like the original waters of the creation. Dead matter.
Prime matter:	A substance that has been augmented by nature within an oven.
First Matter	My understanding, matter we would refer to as mercury. It is the first matter of all things found in nature. It is the first matter made and is of moisture and light combinations.
Mercury:	Matter that has been recycled and augmented in the oven. Mercury is the first matter of the metals. It becomes the base matter of the two stones of alchemy. It would be similar to the earth created in the creation. Alchemically it is known as Septembers Child.
Vulgar:	A term used to describe any substance found in its natural state. Vulgar terms do not apply to their use in alchemy when concerning substance. Example, The mercury of the philosophers is not the same material as the vulgar mercury. Lead is not as the lead you buy downtown.
Times of year:	The months through spring, summer, winter, fall. They are connected to the movement of the sun. They will be shown alchemically by astrological signs.
Times of the Stone:	Found during the times of the year, pointed out by astrological signs. Astrology: Used in alchemy to show steps of the alchemical process. They are from the finding of the stone, or a result of that found process. Astrological word definitions are those of and connected to the stones process.
December 21st:	Start of the alchemical process.
May-Day:	Bull in ram, time of change in the alchemical process. Related to the third day of creation described in Genesis as, "letting the waters come together."
Septembers Child:	A description of the substance and connected to the time of year. In natural alchemy will also be mercury. Very important to alchemy , also to ancient religious beliefs. Septembers Child

of alchemy becomes the rebirth of Osiris. Many connections that need to be understood.

Conjunction:

The step after Septembers Child, connected to time of year (October). A time to turn the wheel again, Genesis repeated . An ancient time of celebration.

Crowned Androgynyn:

A term used in natural Alchemy to define substance worked on for 13 months. Is finished the second January, a part of which is then the white tone. Also this is the matters to produce the red stone from or the beginning of the last step. Tied to Osiris and the 'Eye of God' (Horus). The second androgynyn.

January 21:

A time the matters are taken to an oven, and divided from natural forces found outside. The start of the Ouroborous and done in darkness. Anciently, Osiris in his tomb, then called envelope.

April:

A Time of the stone, achievement of the stone that is found 16 months After the start. Osiris resurrected. Completion of the stone.

Cycle of nature:

One year. Cycle of the stone, 16 months thus causing the overlap. Genesis repeated in each hemisphere or 12 days of creation.

The Overlap:

A way that the alchemists (some) used to hide the process. The final steps were hidden in the first steps. Sometimes with pictorial allegories That had two meanings. Connected to the times of Osiris originally.

Process Steps:

Shown in as little as seven steps to more than 150 steps in different pictorial allegories.

Genesis:

A cycle of the year, As Genesis is described as being six days, the time, times are concerned with both the northern and southern hemisphere. Each hemisphere is seen to rest when the sun is active in the other. From the ancient understanding of, 'Two Earths.'

Day:

An alchemical day. One month long approximately. Based on the cycle of the moon. Also one cycle of the moon is one day of the creation. Consider the morning and evening as the cycle of the moon.

Days of the stone:

Based on the days of the creation according to Genesis. In Genesis one day was a month long, in alchemy and the process of the stone, a day may be and is several to more days long, most but not all steps. We can do the work, but not as God did! We adapt to nature.

Day in Genesis: One month long based on the cycle of the moon.

Genesis: The process of creation concerning the world and the stone of the philosophers, said by many masters. Found by a long study of nature.

Natural Alchemy: Follows the path of Genesis but conceived and finished by Man, therefore done by adaptation.

Sulfurous: A substance that can be collected by vapor only by being in sunlight.

Mercurious: A substance that can be collected by vapor being in the moonlight.

Salt: Concerning natural alchemy, a substance collected from the sun and moon by vapor. There is only one receptacle being primordial matter, or matter being augmented by this process.

Spirit: Something in the below gained from the sun. Can be understood as the good we collect from the above. Found in man more than in other things in the below. As believed by the Ancients.

Soul: Something in the below gained from the moon. A lesser good as is a reflection from the sun. Found more in man than in anything else in the below as believed by the ancients.

Red Stone: Primary object of alchemy. Contains spirit in maximum amount possible in the below. An exalted substance found by substance and good of the light joined.

White Stone: Secondary object of alchemy, contains the maximum amount of soul in the below, Not a natural substance. substance and lesser light joined.

Sun: Represented in alchemy by any pointed object. obelisk, unicorn horn. Time should be considered, thus a trident means sun for three (alchemical) days.

Moon: Represented by pointed objects (plural) or hair disheveled, examples, deer horns, woman with hair messed up, anything female.

Fixing:	A term used to describe the collection of substance from the above by a process change. Augmentation of the below substance.
Waters Above:	Understood as the sun and moon used in the creation.
Waters Below:	Understood as waters and matter with process in the creation.
Air:	Understood as a water of creation. Makes natural alchemy possible Allows a place where the above (light) can mix and become a substance.
Isis:	From mythology. Becomes linked to the moon, female and to Virgo the Virgin as the explanation proceeds.
Two Sisters:	From Mythology. Female being moon and Virgo the constellation.
Osiris:	From Mythology. Male being linked to the sun eventually. Also linked to the stone. The mythology of Isis and Osiris becomes the process of the stone.
Djed Piller:	Tied to Septembers Child in alchemy and Osiris in mythology.
Tat Cross:	Tied to alchemy in September, and to Osiris.
Times of Osiris:	Same as the times of the stone of Alchemy.
Astrology:	Like Osiris, is a result of the stone of alchemy.
Firmament:	The design found in nature containing PHI. The one oven of the philosophers. It is designed by this mathematical principle.
Pyramid Shape:	The design of the firmament used in the creation. The oven. Always repeats when the time of year is considered.
Egg Shell:	Contains PHI and so is the same as a pyramid shaped oven. All shapes containing PHI are mathematically the same.
Sands:	An ancient term meaning shape.
Envelope:	An ancient term connected to tomb.
Alchemy as Art:	Controlling matters by forces controlled in nature was considered art.

The Great Work:	Man controlling those forces found in nature to perfect matter. Genesis understood!
The Stone of Alchemy:	Can be made only by nature, but only by nature controlled by man.
Pictorial allegories:	A way to hide alchemical information in pictures.
Written allegories:	A way to hide alchemical information in the written sayings. The pictorial and written will with this work become understood.
Mythology of Osiris:	Will be known and understood with this work. Will be seen as the result of the search of nature for the stone of alchemy.
Gold:	Considered perfect in the below. All things in the below tend toward gold over time. Gold was perfection and so a result of the perfect stone being mixed with anything inferior.
Like:	A term needed to be understood alchemically. Like reproduced like! How to understand, the sun was the seed for gold, and so would reproduce like, or gold. This needs to be understood to know why the alchemical stone was possible as it is a work of the sun. The white stone was possible because it is a work of both lights, but finished by the moon. The stone is not gold, but is perfection. That perfection is linked to God who is the only perfection, and is captured with the good in the light. The ancients who knew never worshipped the sun, but the good that it contained. The perfection of the matters creates the medicine that cures all ills! We always knew the light was good according to Genesis. Now you will learn why.

Prologue

The First Mythology.

The First Mythology is a work about alchemy and what is needed to finally understand this subject. Not many know of the term or what it means. Many though can understand the desire to turn lead to gold, combined with eternal youth!

Alchemy you will find is from our very distant past. Ancient Egypt needs be visited again, but this time in depth. Finally to know and understand what it was about and how still today it rules our lives. By Ancient Egypt, I point to a time 5,000 BC, perhaps as you understand, even further back.

What is involved? Genesis needs be understood. The six days are of the two earths of the Egyptians, and so the twelve days (Genesis repeated) make up our twelve months and a year. The earth created in the beginning, (according to Genesis) is as the base matter of what we desire to find. The base of the Philosophers Stone. Genesis is an on going cycle, one started a long time ago and still continuing. One if Darwin knew, would have made him realize, his theory was just forgotten knowledge of the past. A forgotten knowledge about nature that was and still is a working process. One we have always known, but misunderstood.

Isis and Osiris, their times which cover the overlap are connected to the same times of our year (holidays), and of the times of the philosophers stone. An so, and ancient religion is from the process of the stone. Easter as we know it becomes a time of resurrection of Osiris, and is the same for the stone of alchemy and of that messiah, Jesus Christ.

The Overlap! 16 months of time which it takes for Osiris to live, die and to become resurrected as a God. The Mystery of Amenta, 'The Mystery of the Stone, The Mystery of the Djed Pillar, The Mystery of the Tat and Tau Cross, all tied to Genesis and finally explained. The 16 months, Genesis repeated, and of course all the work is done within a glass pyramid oven known as the firmament.

The First Mythology is a work about the original religion of the Egyptians. That religion is a result of man searching for God, and knowledge found of him. All of nature was studied, from the creeping things to the stars overhead. It in time was known as 'The All.' This system of forces was studied, and from design, shape, sands as they called it, a place (the pyramid) was found where these forces could be brought together. Matter, as our matters after death, they found could be transformed and purified and changed into something perfect. This perfection could only come from God! Thus man found God. Man could know of God, and from this study an organized religion was born. That religion had to do with Isis and Osiris. Today we know little of it and consider it a forgotten ancient mythology.

But I would ask, why is it we know little? Why has it been buried and hidden from us? I ask because this knowledge is our heritage, where we come from. Our lives even today is so entwined I stand all amazed. There are libraries of this material around the world (alchemy). All information not known or understood. But now that will change. Soon the stone of the philosophers will be made by anyone wishing to do so. Genesis will be known. The mythology and the 'All' known and understood and how it works together. It's your world, you live here, shouldn't you know how it works? If there is a medicine that cures all, shouldn't you have it?

What you're about to find is a world of secret knowledge! Never was it permissible for the common man to know this material. With this work all that will change. The near time man will know. As it was said in the past that all had this medicine, now all will again. This information was never lost. Hidden yes, but not from all, the alchemists always knew it.

From Mr. E. A. Wallis Budge, author "The Book of the Dead," here the preface of "Egyptian Religion."

PREFACE.

"THE following pages are intended to place before the reader in a handy form an account of the principal ideas and beliefs held by the ancient Egyptians concerning the resurrection and the future life, which is derived wholly from native religious works. The literature of Egypt which deals with these subjects is large and, as was to be expected, the product of different periods which, taken together, cover several thousands of years; and it is exceedingly difficult at times to reconcile the statements and beliefs of a writer of one period with those of a writer of another. Up to the present no systematic account of the doctrine of the , resurrection and of the future life has been discovered and there is no reason for hoping that such a thing will ever be found."

The material in this book will answer and prove, the information looked for by so many has been found! Of ancient Egypt, of alchemy and the so many mysteries they conceal. The stone gave them (the ancients), a process #1, astrology #2, and a religion #3. Because of what it was about it became hidden. Not by them, but by those of today who wish it so. Slowly, the understanding, where from, the celebrations, the holidays, were changed and taken away. A new order and a new method of control was established. Today we live with what they found, but we never knew! Now that will change and as a society we move forward.

It took many years for me to know enough to start to understand this material. Some things, over 20. Much of the material still needs further reference to the past, if the material can be found and gathered.

Several years ago I felt that I had solved alchemy. To me it was just the 16 months and the steps that cover that time period. It was Genesis used and again repeated. In the last few years, I was referred to a work that connected Jesus to Osiris. All the times and facts are there, the two are the same, the material unquestionable. Can you imagine the surprise to me when I saw that all that was mentioned tied exactly to what I had found concerning alchemy and the process of making the stone? Wow! A thousand facts, all tied together, unlimited when understood! How could it be? What did it mean? I said, alchemy #1, Astrology #2, Religion #3. We live in a system based on how early man found how to use and remake matter through natural methods! Another way to say it is, I believe the only God man ever found is this God of generation and regeneration. For many reasons man has made him into many things. Quite a statement. You will see and many will understand it when you know what is here. I really can't express how this finding makes me feel, and it may be the same for you.

Beginning

A long time ago while at work a friend came up to me with a book in his hand. He mentioned alchemy and said something about us doing it, and that we could. I didn't know what alchemy was at the time but with a quick explanation I found the book was about some gentleman and his ability to change bad gem stones to good ones, and that he could turn lead to gold. It got my attention, I can't remember now if I was amused or doubtful, but said I would read the book.

I was doubtful because I had spent time in the U.S. Navy in the nuclear power program. The changing of one substance to another (lead to gold) is something that can't be done, at least with the knowledge we had at that time.   As far as I know it is still something we as a society can't do, but I like to read and so I read the book. It was titled "We are not the First." The work had many parts to it that were about different things that had been done down through time. Things that we at the present date would like to take credit for, but the evidence showed that the subject being talked about had been done in the past. The part I was supposed to read was about alchemy and a person called St. Germain. In the work the person did say that he had a science whereby he could remove the imperfections found in gemstones making them perfect and that he could change lead to gold. After reading and contemplating I concluded that perhaps there was something to it, alchemy, only because I found the science had been known for a very long time. A history going back thousand of years actually. Being fair to my friend I said so, that perhaps there was something to find because I didn't think the science could exist for such a long time if there wasn't some truth to it. I considered greed as a factor as I felt anyone saying they could turn lead to gold would get much attention, but that if there wasn't something there in time it would be discredited and forgotten. From what I knew about things, I concluded that the only possibility was that perhaps something had been overlooked by our scientists. I was willing to spend some time investigating to see if there was something, something that gave the possibility of the science. Something that maybe we as a society had overlooked. I don't know why really that I started all this, it was interesting reading. The lure of gold was there, and maybe it was just because I didn't want to dismiss my friend. At any rate I started to collect books. At the time, a hard job! Not only was it unknown, the science, there were few books about it available.

The information on alchemy was scarce at best. It was also old information from old books. I found alchemy was believed by some to be purely a spiritual aspect and the science was about purifying oneself through religious understanding and self enlightenment. Another more popular understanding and one followed today by many was the practical method. This is about a combination of the spiritual being combined with lab work. The lab work is very extensive with many medicines and remedies being produced. Books are written about the alchemical processes run and found in the lab.. Much of the alchemical allegories and metaphors can be connected to these lab processes, and many are the students of these processes that believe they are modern day alchemist's. Their lab work is of a great and wonderful knowledge, that of searching for the philosophers stone. There is a great history connected with the lab work along with great tradition.

In time I did get a collection of information. What a puzzle, alchemy, what a mess. Never in my life did I ever read such material. I was so totally confused that I was lost before I even started. Alchemy is not just information, it is a collection of allegories, puzzles, and metaphors. In other words no information is just given to you, if not in a hidden fashion. They, the alchemist's, have their own language and I dare say that few on this planet can understand it. I used to say I liked puzzles. I really liked to spend time with things just figuring them out. I felt I was good at it but I had never run into anything like this material before. If there was something overlooked I could see why. I spent time, I spent months, I spent a year. I threw the books into a locker where they couldn't bother me and forgot about them. I did say that it was interesting though didn't I? It was.

In the first years there was many times I threw my books into a locker, many times I gave up and tried to forget, but each time I eventually came back and tried again, I don't know why, was it the allure of gold? was it because it was a challenge to my mentality? What or why I don't know. I returned and somewhere I decided that if I was to spend time with alchemy I needed a plan, some way to proceed, and some way to organize all this material I misunderstood. I chose Genesis, I chose The Emerald Tablet and a work by an alchemist called Flamel. I also considered the pyramids of Egypt. A strange combination wouldn't you say? Genesis was something mentioned occasionally in my books. I wondered what Genesis had to do with alchemy. Whatever the reason Genesis was something I could understand I thought- something solid that I could follow. The Tablet I chose because I had somehow concluded it also was a type of creation process. Flamel was really two processes or works combined. Part was a work from a gentleman called Abraham the Jew. Flamel's discussion of Abraham's work was combined with his own work, and so I really had two works or something that I could compare. It gave me something to study or actually I had Genesis, the tablet, Abraham and Flamel The pyramid, was just there because I saw the design in some of the work from St Germain, and I noted the design again in the Flamel Abraham work. I didn't know where it fit in, but it is a mystery isn't it? Perhaps the explanation of the pyramid had to do with alchemy, It came from Egypt, Genesis came from Egypt, and maybe alchemy also came.

Having a plan, Everything I read I referred back to these subjects, Genesis, Flamel, and Egypt. Somehow there was a connection, and every month or two I would find a little tidbit hidden, something that perhaps connected. I am not kidding, only a little and only every month or two. Now it is thirty some years later, and I am still looking. This book, as you read and pay attention is about that time, about my hobby and about alchemy. Briefly I believe Genesis is the way of perfection. What I mean is if I could repeat Genesis and understand it perfectly I would have a process that resulted in the creation of a perfect substance. I have found that if I could make that substance and if it was perfect I would have the Philosopher's Stone. The Philosopher's Stone would give me the ability to change lead to gold. That process is about the yearly cycle or just nature as we see it pass us by, or Genesis is about our yearly cycle. A repeated cycle started long ago. You see, Genesis didn't end. The process, the cycle, the days of creation are still with us today. The days of Genesis are really about the months of the year, and are based on the light of the moon. The work of Flamel and Abraham and many other alchemists is about the same cycle and about the same process that can be found there. What makes it so interesting is art. We use the yearly cycle, but to find the perfection we have to pick and choose what and which forces we use throughout. In Genesis, God made the world near perfect as the work was perfect. The message of alchemy is this, we by art can pick and choose how to use the forces in this process. We use the light and the dark, we use the sun and the moon but we have to discriminate. What I mean by that is we will work on a substance. What nature provides is the sunlight but perhaps not for a long enough period, or perhaps in a way where we need more heat. Nature provides us with moonlight, but not enough. Because of art, we need moonlight for a longer period than what comes to us naturally. We then allow our substance to be in moonlight, but hide it away from the sun. What all this means is there is a way to change an imperfect substance to a perfect one using those same forces found in nature that God used.

The object of Alchemy is to make the philosophers stone. We do this using nature and we do it by controlling what I have come to call, "the nothings." We use the sun, the moon, shape, humidity, a substance and time. I call them the nothings because I know they are there and I use each but I can't see the light, or the humidity or the warmth or the coldness. I use shape, but again I can't see what it does. I just use all the forces I find in nature, or perhaps I should say…all the forces found in Genesis.

The pyramid is involved and is the shape. In Genesis it is called the "Firmament". In nature everything starts out as a seed or is in an egg, discounting of course people, animals, etc. The shape is another of the nothings. I see it but I don't know what it does, I only know it is necessary for the process to work. God used the firmament called heaven. In alchemy it is my belief that the pyramid shape duplicates the work of that firmament that was used in Genesis.

Egypt and much of the old religion from Egypt is involved. They had the pyramid, they also had the Obelisk that stood for a single ray of sunlight. They had religious beliefs we will visit. They had astrology and holidays. They had many things that needed to be found and understood. What I found connects with nature and connects with Genesis, connects with alchemy, and when you put it all together you can have that perfection. You can make a perfect substance. Part of it can be used to make a medicine that will forever keep you well for as long as you are supposed to live. Another part is a substance that will change lead to gold and perhaps, remove impurities from gemstones. Have I done this ? No, I've made the medicine but I never tried it on myself or on anything else, no nerve I guess. Of course, it is only my opinion that I have, had this medicine. I like to say I have completed all the work except the last step, and I have now decided to finish that. I am writing this because in all my life I have found nothing that compares to alchemy. It is not an easy work to understand but if you will look you will find as I have that there is the possibility of perfection in nature. What that means is there is a way to manipulate nature, a way to use the cycle and forces. To combine them in such a way as to achieve perfection in your work. I always originally saw Genesis as a creation process, one misunderstood, or something not able to be understood. Something from God to man that was not a part of anything we could use or really understand. Now that has changed. Perhaps like myself you will see the whole world is the garden created and maintained by Genesis. We are living in it, and destroying it. The point is alchemy will change you and make you see things differently. It has me, and maybe that is the only reason I am writing this. It may raise questions, but it will answer all those questions you have if you will spend the time with it to understand. I said I haven't done this. I as of yet haven't tried to change a metal. I haven't eaten any of the material. Have I made the stone? Yes, I believe I have. I will include with this work pictures, and tell you what I have done, and also will say what needs to be done. Research! My work needs to be researched. If it is a medicine that cures all ills, then all now with this publication can make and have it. Don't think though all that needs to be known is easily understood. You will have to learn this material! Like me you will have to live with the process to understand. Sorry, there is no easy way to do it. 16 months is a long time to baby sit an oven outside. Outside I might add where those forces will destroy as quickly as they will build. This book also gets the information to those persons like myself, people, common. Always this was secretive information, and for only the select few! Also, I want to tell you, I am a mechanic… not a writer, not gifted in the Art of telling a story. I am presenting the material as best I can, and hopefully in a way to allow all others that read a way to understand. As you understand, you will know this is information people in Egypt had in the distant past. I don't know why it was lost, or perhaps hidden, but I conclude it may be because of religious ties and for control.

I believe, that this material will produce the stone, and it will work. You decide with what you will learn. If it changes metals to gold, then I guess we will have to learn as a society to live with that. I think we will survive. The hard part, will be the understanding of it all, and what it may mean to you. It is a truth, one from our past and I call it our heritage. There are libraries of this material in many places of the world. Time to know and understand what it was all about.

Where am I with this work? I have completed all but the last step. I haven't taken it, I haven't tried to transmute. I stopped working on the process some years ago. Why? It is hard to explain. I felt I knew and understood and that was all I needed. Maybe I was afraid to finish. Maybe after 30 years it was because of the prospect of failure. Somehow I was satisfied and a finish didn't seem important. I don't know, I just know I stopped working on the process. I now want to finish the work. Some have told me I will have nothing when I finish and perhaps that is true, but I will always have the understanding. That can't be taken away, that is what I want to share. You can decide if I have solved the puzzle. I told you alchemy will change you, it changed my desires and me. Yes, I wanted to change lead to gold and as I saw changes in my work as it progressed I started wanting it very bad. Understanding the work though makes you see yourself in a different way. You not only think about your work, you really start to ask if what you are doing is ok, is it something I should be doing? Is it something I should talk about? Is it something I should show people? What if it does work? You see, I have talked about it to many alchemists like myself but they are all on a different path. I wondered if I should because I haven't completed the work and if you understand that it somehow made it OK for me to speak about. . Why do I speak about it? I do so because of the things I mentioned, the time I spent and the confusion, and I mean the years of puzzlement. I told God many times I would tell the world if I ever totally understood it. I am not saying that I do, but for a long time I was mad about it all. I don't want anybody else to have to go through what I did, and frankly, I don't think many people could ever figure it out. Not that I am so smart, I just had the time to spend where few could ever come up with the time it would take to understand. I also have a library now where in the past collecting books was a hard thing to do. So, where does that leave us? Whether or not I ever finish my work, and if I do, if it does or doesn't work. I can say this, it is a most wonderful explanation about you and your surroundings and by that I mean nature and the yearly cycle and how so much of our surroundings can come together. It will explain Genesis and connect it to the pyramids, and to our yearly cycle. It does explain most all the allegories and metaphors found in alchemy, all those little sayings that are dismissed as meaning nothing by many that practice the art. It will bring together the past and the present. And perhaps you like myself will contemplate others that had no library, and studied nature as it was their only teacher. Not taken for granted, the explanation will make you note your surroundings in a different way. You will see the nothings and outdoors differently, perhaps never the same as you see them now. You will find an explanation not found anywhere in other books. Others more qualified to speak on certain parts of this material, than myself I am sure will see things differently. You will have to decide it's worth, just remember I have spent over 30 years by myself with this material, I think that makes me some kind of expert. I didn't learn anything at the foot of a teacher or from some practiced art, my information is from nature herself, and from the thousands of hours spent in contemplation of the given material. Last, Genesis, or the creation is something that should be explained in our schools. I am not sure how this explanation will effect that. I believe it was written as the process of nature was understood. You see if there was perfection in the work and man could find it then it proved something to those that searched. I feel they searched not to find perfection but to find if there was a God The perfection would become the proof, and as Genesis was written it would seem to mean they found it. Consider that when you wonder about the philosophers stone, and if it was or could be made. Just what does it prove if it works, and if Genesis is the way.

Presently I have no stone, and I can't change lead to gold. I and several others are working again the process, and that I will hopefully soon change. There are many changes to the matters, beautiful colors I might add, and they will not appear unless you are doing the process right. The color changes I have are those of Flamel as he has shown them in his work. Other alchemists have said that the only way you can know your right, is to have these correct color changes as they come and go. I have completed all the work, and I have seen all these colors. The last color took several years just in itself to figure and find. I had it, I saw it, and I lost it. I stopped working just to think about and to wonder just what should I do. To me it didn't matter. Knowing as I felt I then did, was as good to me as having. Some years ago, I again started where I had left off. There are answers. Sometimes they come, sometimes not. I had finally received what I thought was the correct finish, the multiplication. So I tried again, and successfully again saw the last color. I found to my great surprise another wonderful secret about Genesis, and more of an understanding about the creation. The information is somewhere within this book. I will show you that everything I touched alchemically fit to what I was doing, and I knew, know it can't be just a coincidence. Perhaps you like myself will contemplate the others that had no library, and studied nature. Not one man, but many and many lifetimes had to be involved with this work. The result shows that Genesis works. Every year our planet is renewed by the process. It has been going on since the beginning, and there is an attempt by nature to make perfection in the work. What that means is Genesis is an evolving process. The waters still come together, and we know by the result studied over many millions of years, those forces produce changes. Some will always call it evolution, I like to say that Genesis when understood, is a work in progress!

My own conclusion about Genesis is that it was first a nature study conducted for several reasons. It was about early man wondering if he was just another animal, perhaps a little smarter than the rest, or something special. There was only one way to find out, and only one teacher and that was nature. Genesis was written as the process of nature was understood. I don't think man was looking for the philosophers stone when he began, only for God. In time he found a way of understanding nature, and of using nature and with a process he made something he felt was perfect. The perfection proved two things, one that man was special because only he in all of nature could find what he had searched for, and two, because it was perfect he knew he had found a way to know something of God! Genesis is the result of that search, and the beginning IMO of organized religion. We still live that religion today. Then is was about Osiris. today, it is about Jesus! However you see it, it is about the generative principle of nature found in the light. That will never change.

There are many things I cannot explain about my substances at present. I can take matter and make it pass through the stages mentioned in alchemy. And I do so only with the help of nature, and only by working outside. I am not sure if what I found is perfect, or that it will change lead to gold, but I know that now it will be further investigated and explained. If a medicine is found there that will cure all ills, then it belongs to mankind. I can say that it is a substance made extremely pure as nature would have it if she could. However, nature cannot make this substance, only man can make this substance. The way is through nature, and because it is man and nature combined it is art.

The finish of this work, my book, the understanding, is from a very near time. But the information is from the ancient past. That is how it had to be. What is found at the end of this book, information that ties it all together, I would have read and not known in the past. What is at the start of this book, is the path I had to walk to understand what is written at the end. For you to see and understand, you may have to consider it several times. You may have to compare it to the outside, and all that happens there with our yearly cycle. Many have touched on this information in many ways, somehow, I found this path. I could never express it as one being easy. If you think what follows is hard to see and understand, that perhaps will show you what it was for me to find.

Lastly here, this is not a book written for the understanding of Genesis. It is a book written about nature and the ways of understanding and how shown, so that others may make the philosophers stone. It is about early man, and how he saw and tried to understand the All. The All is expressed not as law, but as Principle. As there was no written way to express, nature was not only the teacher, nature was the book of definitions to explain the results. As time passed, the traditions of the past seemed to be the way of carrying on the information. Today we would express the terms and things needed to be known differently. That is ok, that is us. What is here is them. With what is written here you will be able to duplicate my work, and all wanting to will be able to read the alchemical material. The ways it has been kept alive with allegory and metaphor to me is beautiful. You will be able to duplicate my work, but not for some time. You will have to learn this material, and with that understood, you may someday have. This still gives me time to do those things I need to. My today training and education still tells me transmutation is impossible. That same training tells me I have found at the least, an extremely pure material. From what I have learned, it can be no more pure worked on by nature. It is finished by the sun alone, and so has become like the sun. By the old definitions, that means that within it is, "the seed for Gold", is "gold", and will "reproduce gold"! It also means that it should be the medicine! Whatever it is, as I find out, you will know. This work is about what I originally looked for, things overlooked by our society! To me that could be the only answer to the stone!

A Journey into Alchemy and Early Mans Thoughts

For some time I have been explaining to those I have spoken with about Alchemy, that it was necessary to take oneself back to understand. What do I mean by that? One must try to think of terms and surroundings as early man did. Not from what you know today. Your way of understanding lets say, early man is just taking his first steps. You have a life of education, he had the rudiments of a simple life. You cannot understand him, unless you place yourself at his level. I have come to this conclusion based on my own path trying to understand. It probably took me about 5 years to realize that I had to go back. I know that in the first few years of my work, there was no understanding, only frustration. We today live in a world where information is easily available. What do you want to know, where you come from, where you live, what type of country do you live in? Whatever question you want to ask there are answers. In a quest to understand alchemy, one has to consider originally that there were no answers. There was no library to go to, no elders with the information you sought. Perhaps all there was, was an inquisitive mind. A desire for answers to your questions, but no place to go for the answers. The questions were different, more along the lines of who is Man? Is life and the world an accident ? Are we just a smarter animal, or is there more to all we know, all we see? What makes us different, if we are, and is there a reason for living. Perhaps, one important question, is there a God? Think and consider, not the Gods they had, Gods for everything, but a true God. If there was one, how do we find him? Did he know of man? Can man know of him?

There were no answers for man, none written at any rate, and so how would he find the answers to his questions? He must have advanced to the stage of having ways of communicating, had some laws, and a way of life. Probably was a farmer and a hunter gatherer. The first organized society, and for the purpose of this book, found somewhere along the Nile River. There may have been (I believe) something further back but it would seem lost. At any rate, I have found the answers I sought, in Egypt, and so my explanation starts there.

Early man needed a place to seek answers and so where could he look? All he had was nature. His surroundings, those things he touched, those he could not, those he could feel, and some he could only see. Some were hot, some were cold, some grew, some were wet and others dry. There was day and night, and there was a repetition of the yearly cycle. There was movement in the sky of the stars, and there was a great light, and a lesser light. In time all this had to be organized in some sort of pattern, some way of meaning where answers could be found.

I have several books on the beginnings of scientific thought. They say that all of it started in ancient Greece. Plato and many other Philosophers spoke of earth, air, fire, and water. Earth was the condensed material at our feet. Air was the kind of place where fire and water could mix. Fire was related to the sun, and water was something needed by everything alive. There was great discussion of all this and it went on for many years, with many great different philosophical viewpoints. I found, and it is easily available, that many years before this, the discussions were held by the Egyptians, and the answer to this was found there. The understanding and the organization of earth, air, fire and water had already been accomplished into a working system and the answers had told man he was special. Why, it was because he had found how to organize and understand nature. He found perfection, and believed it could only come from God. The perfection meant he had found something of God, and it meant to him, God was aware of man.

We need to know how man came to these conclusions, and how he found the truths he was looking for. To do this we need to discuss his surroundings and try to understand. First, the reader needs to know the conclusions of the study, then as we go on with the explanation, it will seem to fit and be understood. Finally, knowing what we call mythology, and from the ancient times, you will know all this is truth.

Alchemy today is the search for the philosophers stone. In our time we believe the stone to be a perfect substance that has the ability to lend its perfection to what it touches. It is said that if mixed with lead, it will turn it to gold, and if mixed with mercury, it will turn it to silver. It also is a medicine, one said to cure any disease, and to confer long life onto the one who takes it. These are descriptions and understandings, based on what we have read of the stone. Conclusions based on what the masters have said. By masters, I mean those people that have professed ownership of the stone.

You will find as we continue, all of alchemy is about substance, matter, and changing it by natural methods. I said it was a nature study, and so all we work with is nature and with the forces we find there. The natural forces can be controlled to an extent. It is by the controlling that nature can perfect matter as it was believed by those masters of the past. Alchemy is called by some, "The Great Work" and is done so, in my opinion, because I believe that man felt he had found how God had created the world. It was created near perfect, and by the same process we will use to make the stone. If man could copy it, Gods ways and work, then man could do and understand who, what and how he fit into his surroundings. If he could find perfection, he believed he had found God and he had found his place in things.

Early man also found that there was earth, air, fire and water to work with. Let's say that he had already noted the passing of time and had some sort of yearly cycle. He knew there was a start to his year, and that the sun and moon moved in a certain way and created the seasons of the year. The moon also had an effect, not as great an effect as it was understood as a lesser light. It was not like the great fire in the sky, but an effect. He noted that the stars also had a pattern. When the sun came back to a time of the year, there were certain stars that always returned to the same place they had been before. So, nature had a cycle. Man found other things that went with the yearly cycle. As the sun returned, the rains came and that part of the year was wet and went from a cold condition to a warmer condition. He found the hot part of the year was dryer, and the later part of the year was again returning to being cool. The world had a cycle, perhaps it was alive? If it lived, parts of it died and again returned to life. All parts of the mystery. All parts of what he must study and know for the answer to his questions.

In my many years of contemplation of the mystery of alchemy, I have at times done many things, trying to understand. A study of nature by you would cause you to do similar things. Alchemy was said to be about the joining of the above and the below. A part of it raises and falls. For some reason I was to

"learn about the egg and its parts." The sun, moon, rain, dew, hot, cold, wet and dry, I cut tree limbs and watched the sap run back to the ground. I sat in trees when I was hunting in the fall, and looked at the buds that had formed. I wondered why a flower closed up at night, was it because of the moonlight? Was there a detrimental effect? Or, was it something to do with the shape, and the tiny seeds inside the bud that were forming? I looked at the seeds inside of an apple, like a flower in ways. What was the purpose naturally for the part I ate? I found I was always staring at the moon if it was out. It was considered the "second eye of God," and so what place did it have in all of this? I wondered at all the things early man could have thought about it.

My first Great discovery had to do with the pyramid. We will discuss it later in depth. In the start of my work, I suspected it had a part. I could see it in many places in the alchemical drawings I had. Just an outline, or some mention in a vague way, it was always there. Strange, what would a pyramid have to do with alchemy? I couldn't dismiss it. It was from Egypt, kind of a mystery, and it seemed connected with nature. Being a great philosopher myself, I had eventually figured that the pyramid shape had to do with the shape of an egg. And the shape of an egg had to do with the shape of a seed, and I found that all mathematically were identical. I found that the flowers that closed at night returned to that same type of shape, and I believed it had to do with the seeds forming inside. An apple had to do with the seeds forming inside. I found the egg yolk was connected to the shell and that it was held in the middle of the shell. I found that shape was an important part of nature, and that all of nature was mathematically the same as the egg shell and the pyramid shape. I found all this changed through the year, first there were no seeds, then they came and developed, and then the flower, they died, but the seeds dried and fell to the ground, only to repeat the cycle again next year.

I am sure that early man found all that I did, and I know even more. I say this because I have found that alchemy and the process of perfection must have taken many years, perhaps many lifetimes to understand. And if you contemplate, you also will know this took early man a long time to know.

I mentioned the pyramid, and its shape. I mentioned the egg, and said they were the same mathematically. It seems all of nature is the same, mathematically. If a pyramid is built correctly to be a true pyramid. It incorporates what we call the PHI Factor. The great pyramid in Egypt, called the Cheops Pyramid, is a true pyramid. Most of the others found there, the "Bent" pyramid, or the "Step" pyramid are not. I found this was the same with an egg shell, or an acorn nut, or any seed, or the tip of a blade of grass, the arrangement of seeds, say in a pine cone, or the PHI Factor is found throughout nature. For, as reason for my understanding, I concluded there is an energy force here. It works with all we find here, and shape somehow captures this force. I call it "Creation Energy." Why not? It, being involved with nature, creates everything.

My understanding, is that all nature works with this energy force. All growth has to do with PHI! We today could say that for anything to happen, it takes energy. Nature also works with energy, and PHI is the shape that uses this energy. More here than sunlight and warmth and cold with water, there is also PHI. The true pyramid is built so that it will use this force somehow, yet to use PHI, all has to be involved, light, water, warmth, day and night, obviously the pyramid needed to work with is made of something besides stone, one made of glass. I don't know all this force can do. I think the early Egyptians knew much more about it, and perhaps in time we today can also. I leave it up to you to figure how long it took the Egyptians to discover this fact by observing nature. Seriously, think about it. The idea would never have occurred to me, much time and many lives must be involved. And so, when you think of this time period, remember the Egyptians were building pyramids at the start of their society? What this means to me is that those at the beginning there, must have been from another place and time. If not from another place, what we know is perhaps not exactly correct. As you will find, those forces and of the All connected to this study, many thousands of years must be missing from what we have known, or been told. I am including information that will show the true time of the past, consider what is shown is the result of alchemy, my opinion and so is even a further time away than has been known.

But what does it mean, PHI, and how would we use the force. Further study was needed, and more understanding. I think I had worn myself out with what I had been looking at, time had been passing and I was getting nowhere with my understanding. I started to work more with my egg. "Learn about the egg and its parts." Why? I had found out about the position of the yolk, it was connected and held in the middle of the shell, and I found out about the shell. Was there more? Alchemy in part is about matter, or substance. I had looked at time, position, wet, dry, hot, cold, raising and falling water, light and dark. All parts of the creation, all spoken of with alchemy. On the other hand, I might add, things one would never really consider to be important or consider in today's world. It took me a long time to realize, what wasn't important is really all that is important.

In my study I found it was about the waters inside of the shell. I read in my books about prime matter, primordial matter, first matter? What are they talking about? I found primordial matter had to do with, like a compost pile. If I rot a matter back to what it was originally, I have returned the substance it was back to primordial matter. Primordial matter is a base substance or what things are made of. I refer to a compost pile, and if you understand the end point, that good black substance would be called "primordial matter", or like primordial matter. It makes it easy to understand how things are made from it if you understand how nature works. Thing is though, this is how nature makes a type of primordial matter when she is left on her own with a pile of leaves lets say. But it is not the primordial matter we must make and use for the stone. Earth, air, fire and water made everything. With compost, fire and water do most of the work. Fire is the above, sun and moon, and water is needed for the process to go on. Earth is made, the black substance over time. Air is needed more than you would think, as it needs to be within the matter also for it to do as it must. We all know it is good (compost) to add to the soil of anything growing and it turns into the plant, or it is used by the plant as food. By itself it can be nothing, as it has no seed within it. Consider our world, and all that has lived and died? All has been recycled and is now being used to give life to that which we see outside today. I jokingly say, " I know where the dinosaurs went, they are in the trees."

Prime matter would be something like a compost pile that we made better than it could be done by nature. This is important in the understanding of the stone. Nature can produce perfection, but only with help. It is a work of art. It is from nature, yet it takes man, art and nature to bring it about. Prime matter is what the earth was when finished in the creation we might say. Not compost, yet similar. It wasn't perfect matter, but prime matter. I had to make primordial into prime matter. I had to work with matter and augment it to or nearer perfection. How do I do this? I had no books that said how! I only had nature, and so I looked further and deeper. I checked eggs I found in a birds nest and left by the mother bird. Nothing left usually, maybe a trace of yellow within the hollow shell. Or just a hollow shell, all dried up. I mention the color yellow and that is obvious, the yolk is a yellowish. I was looking for black, as black was the first color. I needed to make a black compost, and improve it to something better, how? The first color of the stone was black, and somehow I felt the egg would rot, and turn black. I studied nature. I noted that the leaves under a pile were black, anything buried was black. I noted the bark of a tree that had fallen, was black underneath. It seems when air doesn't get to the rotting substance it can turn black. I returned to early man, and with seeds and substance and compost pile, I considered a garden, and early man and what he could learn there.

In his search for answers, did a garden help him? Did he note that where the pile of garbage was, now stood his best plants? Did he find out about compost? Did he bury fish, lets say, and wonder why they turned into corn, and the best corn! What did he conclude when he realized one thing could change into another in the garden? Was this a part of some of the answers he was looking for? Perhaps he wondered what else could matter become, is there any limit? The compost pile could be made from many things but the most important thing is what all compost can become. If a fish could rot and become corn, what else could it become? Everything man studied had to do with matter, growing it, maintaining it, drying it, using it as food, and recycling it to use again. More had to be known about matter. Easy enough to make compost, how do we make something better than that compost? Can nature controlled make something better?

I said in man's plan to find himself by understanding nature, he had to organize all that he knew. The movement of the stars, sun, moon, the growing of a plant, the hot and cold and what each did, the wet and dry and how to use, the whole system. How it worked, and could the system give him answers? How could the system give him answers? How could he use the system to give him answers, or, could he use the system to cause other things to happen with matter, and why would he do this? The study was coming to be more than just about nature, the study was for man to find himself, what he was, and if there was more to man and to the world than he seemed to know. If all man wanted was a better garden, the compost would have given that to him. It seemed the more he knew, the more he needed to know, and yet all he had was nature. The gardener, hopefully by now you realize was more than just a gardener, he was the tribe's priest, perhaps an early philosopher. Someone with more and deeper questions. Finding only meant a deeper search to find more. If the fish in his garden became corn, what happened to man after he died?

We have to go to Egypt now, and search there to see and know the connections, to see how man was successful in his quest. Consider though, as we go back, how easy it is for us to learn something today. We hear the word Heaven! You know what it is, right? a place where we hopefully go when we die because we have been "good!" You know earth, firmament, air, water, all these terms. How did they come about, what from? Where from? Spirit? Soul? Are we to believe God came down and walked with those early men, and explained things to them? Or do we search and try to understand based on a study of nature? Using what they said and believed, how they lived, and what they wrote down on their temple walls. Always place yourself back to beginnings for your understandings, or you will miss what it was really all about. And when you have time, go outside and look around. See the sun shining through the clouds? See the rain as it waters the below. Is there something special within those drops? The light mixed with the vapor while above! Look at your compost as it lies at your feet everywhere. What it was is gone. What it is to become, only nature can say. The Dinosaurs once roamed the land, now as I said they are a part of the trees. The water you drink today, who can say what else and who else drank it in another time, another place, see the world, and look to how you fit into it all. Your just a part of it, early man found for you most of what you know about it today, what you think, and how you live. As we proceed with an in depth study. Consider, where did it lead man, what was the conclusions? Perfection in the work, did man find it, and if so, what did it mean to him, and what will it mean to you? With again finding the stone, if this leads to that, what will it mean today? What early man found, you will be surprised how much of it is connected to you and today. Perhaps you will wonder, why is it you never knew?

As we proceed, I have chosen to write in a series of books. Why is because each is of an understanding, and of information not generally known or understood. Genesis as you will see is explained and used as the process of the stone. Genesis I had to find is really about the yearly cycle, and the days are really the months. Alchemy is hidden knowledge, again about how to use Genesis to process the stone. However, Genesis is used in a hidden fashion, with different terms and ways of showing information, all different and all in a hidden fashion. Each alchemist did this as a means of passing on information, but did it in a way that could only be understood by those knowledgeable in the Art. To understand alchemy then is to understand how nature works according to the time of year. To understand alchemy, one must understand the language of the alchemists, and to know the process. If you know the process, then you can relate the step to what is happening outside, to Genesis, and to matter being effected by those forces we deal with. If you know the steps of the stone, here I explain the works of Flamel, then one can compare those steps he knows to steps of another master, and so read that it is the same process. There is ten steps that you must learn to make the Philosophers Stone. Flamel showed this process that way. Some of the other masters used many steps, some over a hundred. I could say, some were a person of few words, others of many! The process covers 16 months of time, and the important days of changing the process are in part linked to holidays of ours today. This 16 months of time you will find is linked to a very ancient religion, that of the past Egyptians. Isis and Osiris, many today have heard the names. The religion you will see and understand means the ancients found the stone or to them proof of God. This religion went on for a very long time, and from it we received much of our religious beliefs of today. As you come to see and understand, it will answer many of the questions you have had about the past. I know I had many, I now have few. They say that "The Truth Shall Set You Free." Each must decide just what that truth is.

Finally, this is a book one should read and think about, and then read some more. It is not easy to explain all these so called mysteries in a way that is clear for a novice to understand. Consider myself, I started this in the early 70's! Still today I have very much to learn.

I have found so many things with the All, as the ancients called it. It is my wish that you may also see and find this understanding. Those connections to you and the system that created what is found outside your window. The system and understanding that Created you over a period of time. We have this huge battle within our society, Darwin, Genesis, who is right? Here you will learn Genesis which has never been explained or understood was known by the ancients. All here is about what is out there, outside. They didn't make things up, they used and tried to understand what is! You didn't have to accept unexplainable things, you worked to understand what was. The ancients knew about evolution, in fact mentioned and studied it. They had to. Had Darwin known what was in this book, there would be no theory of his, and no controversy. There would be only Genesis, the working program and it would be known and connected to the Creator God!

The Book On Tools

For you to understand me and my explanation of alchemy you will need to understand certain things. I called them tools. Some would call them word definitions, explanations of alchemical terms. What it is exactly is how I came to find my way or path. Observations of nature we might say, actually my stumbling around with it all trying to see and understand. Truthfully, I was totally lost to it, but nature was their teacher, and so it became mine. I had no where else to look, and no other ideas as to what it could be all about. All of alchemy is given to you in a hidden fashion. Nothing it seems, even the simplest of terms could ever be just given to the seeker of wisdom in an open way. Thus we have allegories, information given in a hidden fashion. We also have metaphors, information given where something we know and understand needs to be understood in a philosophical manner. Now, today I can give an example. The Bull is a term used in astrology, and is connected with May we can say and spring. A bull we understand for what it is, alchemically, it is a time of the year when the influences from above is strongest. As the Bull is very big and strong, it is a good "metaphor." The ancients used nature in this way to express "Principles." Principles to us today would be an understanding of how to understand a law or fact about something. We have a developed way of expressing, they did not and so linked things in nature to the facts they observe.

In alchemy there are many word and pictorial allegories. Many of the pictorial allegories are given in a series and it would seem that for each alchemist' there was a series of allegories to give as a gift from himself. All different from anything ever put down before. And, though there are many series allegories, and as I have come to see them as all saying the same thing, all are written and drawn completely different. Why is simple. We will use Genesis as an example. If you wrote it and I understood it, for you to know me as a "brother" so to speak all of what I write had to be drawn and shown in a completely different way. You, when you saw what I had done, would of course be able to understand it with some study. You would know I knew what you knew, and that it was Ok for us to speak of these things. Those the masses, the common and the king would not know or understand either, and so we were safe from any persecution.

Along with the pictorial allegories were the explanations. They were of course all in allegory. This is the reason I needed a plan if I were to continue with alchemy. Even today on the Internet where I visit other alchemist's, these allegories for the most part are dismissed. It still can't be understood, even by those practicing the art. I have seen where parts of series allegories are used in process by these other practicing alchemists, and I have read word definition of some of the alchemical terms. Those explanations don't mesh with what I do. They are very vague and really could mean about anything you wish for them to mean. What this means to you as to my information and explanation and what is given here is, it's only my path. Those things I have come to understand in my study. You as you come to see and know all I have done and written here will have to decide as to if it is truth.

I said "with what I do." I need to explain that. I used to call alchemy a very lonely hobby. I started with a friend. I didn't know there were alchemical groups around the world, or other alchemist practitioners. I didn't know there were schools of thought about it. This means that what you are about to read is different from what you will find in other books. I have said to others that what I found is natural, and perhaps something they also would have found had they worked by themselves. As soon as you find or look for schooling from others you find what has been passed down for hundreds of years as alchemy. It doesn't mean it is the right way, only that they have process and tradition from those that have gone before. The point would be to say that alchemy is still a mystery! There are those that profess to have the stone, and I would tend to believe there are some that do. However, I see no evidence that it has been found and believe until now, it is a lost art. To be brief, there is what is called practical alchemy. This is concerned with what is called lab work. This is the path that most modern alchemists have chosen. Best guess is that it has been extensively practiced for maybe 500 years. My opinion, based on what is written. There has been established tradition and process with it and it is what most know. Also there is spiritual alchemy. This is understood as man being the object of alchemy, and it is to be understood as a way of improving and perfecting man . To me both are relatively new, and not the old alchemy I am attempting to learn and practice. It is not the alchemy I wish to try and explain. Remember, alchemy always has been for the few. Those somehow initiated into the art. It is not for the masses and to teach it too the masses has been considered as some type of sin with eternal damnation the resulting punishment. I don't of course believe this. I don't see my God as a God with chosen people, or one that plays favorites. I see us as all equal, and if this is a gift of God for mankind, or man, I see it for all. To compliment this idea, in several places in this world tablets have been dug up that say, "we had a universal medicine, this medicine made all well." "We lived a long and a happy Life." To me this is the stone I seek. If all had it in the past, and this information leads to it again, then I believe it is OK for all of us to have it again now. I may fear for my life, but not my immortal soul. It also I want to point out it doesn't mean I am right in what I do. There are many, those that see and study alchemy with a different way of understanding. I am only me.

When first starting to collect books, I had come up with several thoughts on alchemy. As I mentioned, something overlooked, was the thought that caused me to go on. I became interested in the pyramid. Why was because it is something perhaps not understood. "It does wonderful things, but it doesn't repeat." The gentleman that had the science that started all this with me was called St. Germain. I found a book that he had written and it was called "The Most Holy Trinopsia." It was a three-fold wisdom kind of book all written into one. There are wonderful explanations of what he could do with alchemy. It turns out, this book to be something about his initiation into the arts. I read this book for a long time. I studied it, and I looked for codes, turned it upside down, inside out so to speak and found nothing. However in one paragraph he mentioned that during his initiation he was lifted up unto a high place, so high that all he could recognize below him were some triangular objects. As he was above the Mediterranean Sea, I felt he must have been indicating the pyramids of Egypt. Why not just say so? If he was so smart surely he knew of them... Was he mentioning them this way to point them out? I noted that on the cover of the book there was a drawing of the pyramid also. Somehow it must be part of what is hidden. Somehow the pyramid was a part of Alchemy. For what it is worth, even today if I read his work, I find nothing. However, I had the pyramid and that was a possibility to me. We know it is mysterious and unexplained and that it seems to do unusual things with different materials.

Also, I was reading Genesis all the time, (after my plan was conceived) and comparing to The Emerald Tablet. In the creation epic, God created the firmament. In the tablet something rose again and again within heaven. Eventually I wondered about the firmament that was called heaven in Genesis. Also the heaven that was mentioned in the tablet. As I said, they both seemed to be the same to me. Genesis is about the creation, why would something about alchemy be about the creation ? If the Emerald tablet was alchemy and at the end of the tablet it said that it was all that you needed to understand alchemy, and to have the philosophers stone, what was that saying about Genesis? There had to be something about the creation process. There had to be something about heaven, the term used in both. What about the firmament, why would it be called heaven? The firmament had a design, was it the same as the design of the Pyramid? I was convinced that pyramid was something I would really check out. Along with my books about alchemy I would also collect books on the pyramid, and Egypt, why not?

During these first few months that turned to years, I started to study nature. In the allegories I will bring to you it will be evident that nature seemed to be much of what the alchemist's talked about. "Follow in natures footsteps," "Let nature be your guide," the sun, the moon, water. Everything about nature. I noted one allegory where an alchemist's was using a looking glass to concentrate sunlight. It was termed something about the secret fire. There was something, I thought, what do we know about concentrated sunlight? I looked for something in nature that rose and fell again and again. And as funny as it may seem I stared at trees for a while watching the sap raise and fall as moisture from the leave. I even peeled the bark from a tree so that I could see just how much sap did raise and fall. I noted flowers and how they opened in the daytime, and how they closed up at night and made that shape. I looked at buds and remembered once when hunting how I stared at the buds in the tree and wondered how they could survive the coming winter through the freezing. Again there was that shape, does a flower close at night to make the firmament shape? Are the buds of trees made that way or shaped that way for a reason. I found all seeds had this shape. They didn't all look the same, but all mathematically I found that through PHI, they were the same.

It should be evident shape was getting important to me. I read an allegory about the egg, "Study the egg and its parts." Why would an alchemist's say that, what is there about an egg? What does an egg have to do with Genesis and creation? I found that the yolk was held in place within the shell. Maybe known by many, but not by me. I wondered about the shell. It had a shape and it also was of a material that was transparent. Light could pass through it. Was that important? Was it important that the yolk was held in place? Was the shape of the egg important? It seemed that anything about seeds became important to me. One alchemist mentioned that grape seeds could be a part of alchemy. What he said was something about the grapes being better if the garden was irrigated. I checked out grape seeds. It seems they like to absorb gold if it was in the soil. We are trying to make gold aren't we? Must be grape seeds have a part in alchemy!

I found after a while that what I was doing was looking for a 'base substance.' It seems that was a big part of alchemy, finding the base substance. What is a base substance, it would be the substance that all things are made of. I read about puffers in alchemy. People like myself looking for the Philosophers Stone, and doing so by trying to find this base substance. I believe they were called puffers because it is how they sometimes maintained their fire. The richer ones had labs and spent great amounts of time working there looking for something, I am not sure what. It seems they left few things unturned in their quest for knowledge. The alchemists, or those I call the old masters laughed at the puffers, and I think there's a message there, but it has to be thought about. All worked in a lab of some sort I thought, and a puffer may not know as much, but wasn't he on the right track so to speak? And so why laugh at them? I wanted to experiment myself, but wasn't sure just how to go about it.

A lot of time was starting to pass and my friend that had started all this was a busy man, and he kind of fell by the way side. I spoke with him, we discussed all the strange things I came up with. He was interested in as far as listening but as far as working he was finished. He continued to be my rock for a long time, the one and only person I would speak to about alchemy. Every time I found something out that to me was a great secret, I confided in him. That went on for over 20 years.

I wanted to experiment! How could I do it? I was convinced that the pyramid was a part of alchemy. I found what I call the Norton oven. We will spend a considerable amount of time with this oven in another place. It was a glass pyramid shaped circulating oven that sat over a water base. In alchemy there is talk always about a fountain, never ending fountain that never dries up. There is talk about mountains and little mountains, and many mentions of glass. It seemed to me the oven used by the philosophers must look like mountains or little mountains and be made of glass. It somehow had to be full of water and to be able to circulate it. Remember the again and again word from the Emerald Tablet. The Norton oven filled all the descriptions, and so I built one. It was wrong, but I had no place to work and so I used it anyhow. I just didn't at the time understand how to make a true pyramid and so had made a mistake in the angle. After time and after much reading I built another with the correction and was on my way, at least I now had a place to work that I knew was correct. There is an interesting story that even this lesson taught me. The correct oven, as I will explain as we go on, will cause an egg to rot correctly. Rot correctly? What does that mean, how many ways are there to rot an egg? I don't know why, but in the oven that is designed wrong, I never have been able to do this part of the work and finish it as it had to be. Perhaps, as they said, one oven, (an allegory of the alchemists) really did mean something. We don't know much about shape, and so I had found and proved to myself, shape could be a part, and there was only one oven to do it in. I used this oven on the roof of my house, I had an eggshell in it and a diamond with a flaw.

I was going to remove it and I tried. St Germain did it! This was a part of his science, and a thing he said he could do. Naturally it didn't work. I learned though that I had found a wonderful circulating oven. With water in my glass pyramid oven, within a few minutes of being in sunlight it is covered within with moisture, and it starts to circulate. I could not remove the imperfection of the diamond, but found within the egg shell red bacteria growing in it. Red was a finish color of alchemy. Who knew, maybe it was something and at that time and with that small amount of knowledge it was something to me. I placed the eggshell in the work area. I later found there were two areas of work within the oven , a high area for winter time, another for the summer. I filled the egg with water and then placed the diamond in the water and covered it. Why, was simple. The shell is a kind of filter for light and it made the light move in one direction. Sunlight and moonlight would pass through the shell. But this made the sunlight kind of like the moonlight? It seemed a possibility that the light could have an effect, and it was inside of the firmament wasn't it?

I was learning more about Genesis and more about the creation process. I found that the eggshell and the design of the pyramid were the same mathematically. That is why the firmament was called heaven. I found that in Genesis what made it work and what was special is that it was an oven within an oven! This is the same as the egg shell within the glass oven I made. I also had found that the length of a day in the creation epic was based on the light of the moon and so was really a month long. That is the time period of one day of the creation! But there was six days in the creation. It was a long time before I realized there are two hemispheres in our world, and the process of creation is repeated in each! The six days of creation became the twelve months of the year, very important to know and understand. Genesis wasn't something we could not know and use, Genesis was here today, always here, always has been, and always will be !! It seemed that nature and or the yearly cycle was tied into Genesis as Genesis was really about the year and the process of growth and death, the recycling that we have. The six days of creation covered the six months of the year, and as the six were ending in the Northern Hemisphere where I live, they were starting in the southern.

A lot of things were coming together, I was developing a process, and I was still looking for a base material. I as of yet didn't have it but it seemed to me that the whole year was tied into alchemy somehow, that is why I was to study and follow nature. It became the sun and moon and seasons to me, it was the wet and the dry. Most of all it was the rotting process or what we today would call recycling. All I had to do was to put it all together in the right fashion. I was further convinced that my Norton oven was the correct oven as I watched the water rise and fall again and again inside. There was more, in the Emerald Tablet it did say that it rose and fell again, but it also said; "it raises from earth." What I needed to know was what was earth? It had to be the same base substance that I mentioned, the ones the puffers were looking for, and the one that is still searched for today. It was the base substance that was used to create the earth in the beginning. If I was correct, it was the same base substance that was used somehow to make my medicine and my stone.

The alchemist's tell us that all things are made of earth, air, fire and water. Earth was a part of everything, and if understood it could be or was the base substance. The alchemist's also said earth was only condensed water, or a condensed liquid. As we read Genesis we find that first all were waters, and the dry land that was formed was called earth. This matched and again reinforced that Genesis was a part of alchemy. I wondered how do I make earth? How do I change a liquid into a solid? If I was to find the answer, I had to know more about Genesis, more about earth, air, fire and water, and this raising and falling in the Emerald Tablet.

Earth as I said was just condensed liquid, and was water in the beginning. Earth was without form in Genesis when created. This meant there was no ordered process connected with it. Earth ended up being dry land, and so the process I looked for was within Genesis. As time went by earth in the process became alchemically an androgynous material. What this means and why is that the substance is both male and female combined. Why was so that as seed was made by the commandment of God, whatever it was, male or female it would find its mating part within the earth and be able to grow. As we get further into the alchemical understanding, you will learn the sun is male, the moon female so to speak. As they were the lights used to make the earth, the material below was to absorb some of each light, and so was both male and female, or androgynous. In a compost pile outside, this process still goes on today . I considered at one time, and still believed today this was the reason why Eve was made from Adams rib. He also was made of this androgynous earth! He was both male and female so to speak, and so within him was the possibility of female. His substance could be used to make the women! Alchemically what this means is it is both male and female, all here in the below! All made from the sun and moon with water over time. Time was another of those things we don't seem to know much about. Time to me was becoming very important to understanding alchemy.

Air, what was air? Air it seems is just a go between. It can be dry or moist. It can be hot or cold. Air you will find is a substance you use to control what is in your oven. You can keep your substance wet by the moisture the air carries, or you can dry your substance, as it will carry away the moisture within if you let your oven dry up. The air though is important for another reason. The air holds the moisture within itself. As the air circulates, so does the moisture. The moisture and air circulates within the oven which is in the lights, and so the mixing of the above and below happens. Look outside your window, see those clouds in the sky? Consider from a philosophical point of view what is happening. The alchemists mention a water, "that does not wet the hands." We call it humidity, a vapor in the air, lots or little, it is a water that we know is there and today can even measure. It does not wet your hands.

Fire, What is fire? What is the secret fire alluded to by the alchemist's. Always and forever the practicing alchemist's have been searching for the secret fire. And I wanted something we don't know about! To me it is the sun. It was used to make the earth in the creation, it is hot and dry, but with the combinations of air and water it is hot and moist. It can dry your substance in the oven, it can burn your substance. It can impart a masculine effect to your substance, and it can impart perfection to your substance. Why, the sun is said to be a perfect thing in creation by the alchemist's. It is perfection and it is gold, and it is also the seed of gold. The sun is called spirit in many places in alchemy. From Egypt I found the Obelisk represented the sun. The Obelisk was made to represent a single ray of sunshine. When we are dealing with alchemy the sun will be indicated by a single pointed object. That single pointed object is a representation of the Obelisk. For example, in alchemy a Unicorn (single horn) would or could represent the sun. Remember the information is an allegory and is given in a hidden fashion. This example also links Egypt with Alchemy. The fire is also the moon. There were two light created in Genesis, the sun and the moon. This was done on the first day with the creation of light. The moon is the reflection of the sun and is cool and moist. The moon is female and can impart a feminine aspect to your substance. The moon is soul, and is portrayed in alchemy the opposite of the sun. The sun was the unicorn the moon is a deer (check horns), and remember it is an allegory. As I said different alchemists used different ways of saying the same thing, or to make the same point. A gentleman by the name of Flamel used his wife, her hair to indicate the moon by saying; "her hair all disheveled." Compare disheveled hair and the horns of the deer and again remember it is an allegory. The sun is gold, and so the moon is silver. If perfection were a straight line, the sun would be what was found at the end of the line. The moon would be found on the same line, but only about ¾ of the way toward the end, and it is never perfect. The reason is because of perfection; the moon is not as perfect a light as the sun but close. Another reason is like. Like is important to remember as it is an alchemical term we need to know and understand. The sun is like gold; the moon is like silver. It is said that there are two stones in alchemy, one is made from the moon, actually finished by the moon and changes base materials into silver. You should see the connection; the other is finished by the sun and changes base materials to gold. That also is because of the same reason and helps you to understand like. The medicine we will eventually mentioned is what both stones are made from. The material or substance is first a medicine and is until you further augment by light when working for either of those stones. I have made the medicine, it is a very pure material, and looks crystalline. I did not use or try the medicine but will the next time I am successful at producing it. It is easy to make and you will be able to make it also from what I say here. All of this needs to be researched, then as we know more we can say what it will do. Lastly, about the light is something most important, and something never explained to me or even considered. I will mention it again in another part of this work. "The Light is Good." Now I have described the light, the sun as spirit, gold, perfection, masculine. Also it is good, what does this mean. The ancients found by process and by experimentation that within the light was something that could make wonderful changes in the matter here in the below. They believed God had put something of himself into the light! This something could be captured by this circulation of the moisture here in the below within the oven. The word again now consider. Again and again the moisture raises in the light, and absorbs something from the light, and adds it to our earth below. If this be true, what is happening? I said I wanted to find out about something we as a society know nothing about didn't I. Well consider material within a pyramid glass oven and setting out in the light for a year and longer. What does the light that was thought to be in part perfect do to the material below? There is nowhere you can read about what may happen, except here.

I still needed to find my base substance, I needed something to make earth. I studied seeds for a long time. I watched them being produced by a plant, I even grew wheat. I watched the seeds fall to the ground, to be covered and to lie there all winter long to bury themselves somehow, and to spring forth in the springtime. They repeated the process. I learned that nature renews all things, and I considered again, again. Genesis wasn't something that happened along time ago, it was something going on today, I became very close to my surroundings, and I now see all things outside in a different way. I know I am a part of a system, and I see it and feel it everywhere. It is a system that I know brought me forth as it did all things. If there is perfection in the work, what does it mean? I wonder what it was that drove early man to find these things and to write them down as a legacy for all mankind today.

I say to myself I know what happened to the dinosaurs, they are the trees we now enjoy, and the grass and all other things now in existence. Long ago, Cleopatra drank the same water, perhaps, that I drink today. I found that on all seeds and all eggs there was a firmament, call it the shell or husk or covering of the seed, it was the same thing. I found that everything is just the end product of nature, but more, how Nature works together.

Still I wondered how do I find earth? The alchemist's referred to the dung heap or pile a lot, and I spent time there. It was the product of nature, but it was recycling. It was nothing really, could be nothing and was good to make black dirt or to be used as fertilizer. It had characteristics, but could be nothing by itself. It was a substance, earth, I found I could make it by using the sun and moon, remember I said that each imparted either male or female aspects. Well if I used both they would make an androgynous substance for me. The dung heap was such a product. It was rotting material and it set out in the sun and was changed. A seed is different and different material. A seed is going to be something; a dung heap can become a part of something by being a fertilizer, but can be nothing by itself. It is male and female so that this blending with another material is possible. The earth that was formed in Genesis was androgyny, it was both male and female as the two lights formed it. It needed to be so that it also could join with every seed that God produced and commanded to grow on the androgynous earth. If you understand that, you can see that I can make earth. I can take any substance and rot it and take away what it was and at the same time, make it also the same type of base substance. I needed something that was liquid; earth was condensed liquid, and something that would rot. I had it all the time and didn't know it. I knew why the alchemist's had said to "learn about the egg." Within the eggshell are two liquids, one the yolk the other the white. I found that by rotting an egg the white left as water and the yolk became a black stinking mess. I had my earth! And in Genesis, wasn't there waters below that needed to be divided? This meant the earth was originally a combination of liquids somehow. And the egg fits the description and my way of understanding it all. I only needed to find the right way to convert it into a perfect substance and a medicine. One to turn lead to gold, the other to make me well for all of my natural life.

I want also to explain another connection of alchemy. As it will help you to understand what and why of what I do. There is in alchemy what is called the sulfur, mercury, and salt theory. From sulfur and mercury we get salt. Salt is then the residue. Salt we might say is the earth to be made by this theory. We need to know what sulfur is and what mercury is and how we produce them or how we use them. We need to know how to get this salt, as the salt is really the earth I mentioned. The sun as I told you is masculine, another aspect is that it is sulfur or hot and dry and in alchemy that is sulfur or sulfurous. The moon is mercury, female or cool and moist, and to me mercurious. With the lights above, I have what is needed to work this theory. From the sun a sulfur, from the moon a mercury, and the combination is the salt, the earth. Not known, but with the understanding of Genesis, and those terms and definitions we find in alchemy, we have a process that will lead us to the stone.

I said, the alchemist's taught that all things are made of earth, air, fire and water. How is this done? It is easy for you to consider your garden. You plant a seed and nature does the rest. The sun shines, it rain, the moon is there at night, all of it comes together for you according to Gods plan and your garden produces for you. In alchemy we have what we term as Art. What does this mean? When we work for the stone for changing substance to gold, you should understand now it is primarily a work of the sun, it needs more sulfur. If working for the stone for silver more mercury and you will see it is a work of the moon.

When we speak of Genesis and try to understand it and relate it to the yearly cycle you will see that the waters coming together is a sulfur, mercury combination. The waters above were the sun and the moon, and as dry land was produced it was because of the work of the combinations of sulfur from the sun, and mercury from the moon that produced it. As we look at the Emerald Tablet, part of what is said is "it receives power from the superior and inferior things." They again are the sun and moon, and what they are receiving are those same materials. When you look to the sky each day and you see the clouds with the sun shining on them consider the reaction. Call it what you will just remember something is going on. Remember also that those same clouds are there during the night and the moon is shining on them. Art is from alchemy. You know your garden would be much better if you could control the sunlight and the water it receives. When I run my process in my oven that is just what I do. If I want moonlight that is all that I bring to the oven and is so with also if I want more of the sun. I control the moisture and the dryness and also the darkness. I control the amount of heat and I limit the cold. Nature cannot produce the perfection of the creation unless controlled. It did when it was controlled by God in the creation, now again it can if you control it in the proper fashion. I have called these forces the nothings, now perhaps you can better understand. I control darkness, light, humidity, temperature and time within a shape! The only thing that you can touch is the oven and if you open it the substance inside. I point this out because all these things are going on around you every day but you can't see them or touch them. What I want you to know is they are there and we can control them and we will. And to know how they work together. When an alchemist's say's, "his water is a water that doesn't wet the hands," I want you to consider the humidity in your oven. Consider the sunlight, or the moonlight. None can you grasp, but they are there. It is there but you can't see it or touch it. Sure you can see the sun and the moon, but you can't see what is sent down but you can learn to capture it and use it. If he mentions sulfur, then you should know it is either a work about the sun or some aspect of the sun, beaming on and into your oven. The moisture is within, the sun is shining into it and you are producing the sulfurous aspect of alchemy. You can't see it being produced, but the earth (salt) is receiving the power of the sun. If it is at night then the salt is receiving the power of the moon, then female and mercury is what we are receiving. If we control this process it is art, but in alchemy it also is known as The Great

Work. As we go on you will see why it was described in that way. How else could you ever describe the Creation Process?

I want to mention also at this time primordial and prime matter. Primordial is what you might find in your dung heap. Prime is what we will make in the oven and is what was called earth on the third day of Genesis. Even in the creation process the material made on the first day, earth, had to be prepared for the process of becoming earth prime. It is the same thing we do today if I want to grow something. I can't take a bunch of any fresh product and place it on your garden and expect results. If I take that same product and rot it first and then use it I can, as it becomes a perfect fertilizer and base substance for growth. Just remember though that even what is found in the dung heap has to be processed before it is any good to you. The proper way to do things is to recycle that material until it becomes a good usable product and then use it and expect the results you want. In our oven and if we used an egg, it started out as a fresh egg. We first take it back to primordial matter by the rotting process and then we bring it forward to something we can use, prime matter. Another way this has been said is to take it away from the Light! Any time we move from the light we move toward death. Death returns matter back to the base matter I needed and searched for, for many years. It's another easy way of understanding alchemy and most of the allegories that I will bring to you. Compare to nature, look outside of your window and see what is going on. The alchemist's mentioned a secret fire as I said and many have looked for it for many hundreds of years, all they had to do was just stand in the sunlight and see it. So simple and yet so well hidden. I guess that is why alchemy was for so long such a lost art, it was always right in front of us where we couldn't see.

I have covered enough to let you know what your going to find within this book. I include with the front a list of my definitions. How to understand terms we will always be dealing with. I understand them a little differently as you see. By reading them, and understanding it will make it easier to bring together the other following material connected.

All of it is about things not explained or connected in this way. It is about the known things, but about so many different unexplained subjects. Alchemy is about nature, but seen by a Philosopher. You need to know the cycle of the year as it pertains to Genesis. I refer to a seed, as you can connect the life and cycle of a seed to nature, a nature your familiar with. Alchemy is a hidden science, I include a section about how they spoke in riddles describing it. They called them metaphor. They drew it in pictures, we call them pictorial allegories. Each is very complicated, and it will take you a long time to know how to read them. I have collected many metaphors and explained them, and have shown many pictorial allegories. All of it, pertains to Genesis, the process of the stone, and to nature and how described by them. Also, time is shown differently. A day in the creation is one month long. This is also explained as a step in the process of the creation of the earth. Now we use those same steps, but the time is different. God could do as he wished, and so did a step in a day. We might need two, or three or more of these days, (month), to do the same work. Thus, in alchemical pictorial allegories, count! If there is one flower, or five, or seven, that means something connected with time. I have given several examples so that you can, (when you count), know and understand.

It had to be done in a hidden fashion, alchemy, as a way to stay alive and also a way to pass hidden information. You will find too that Astrology is involved. The times of they stone, the times of your garden, the times of Genesis all have to be blended so that you see each as a same time for the things that need to be done in the alchemical process. Where possible, and with Flamel, I point out the astrological signs so that you will know the time of the year for the step. Lastly, where is all of this information from originally? I have called this work, The First Mythology. To me the first mythology is about the creation of the earth by the Egyptian gods, and that story. The mythology I use contains the story of Isis and Osiris and Horus, along with the destroyer Set. The work will be very indepth, and as you read and know, all of it was based on something. It had to be based on something, and that something is what we call The Philosophers Stone. The stone is very ancient. First, it was found by a long study of nature. From that study it was believed man was special because he had the ability to find. From that study man believed he had found the One True God, and how to know of him. From that study Astrology was developed, as was the first Religion. The belief of Osiris and Isis, of the resurrection of the body, of an eternal life and all that man could know and see tied to it in nature. Life, death, resurrection, heaven, matters, nature, Genesis, time, shape, hot, dry, wet, cold, all tied together from this very ancient understanding   With knowing what is written here, you will have the ability to make the stone. All alive, it has been said, had the stone in the past. Perhaps all will have it again. This work, of how the All ties in together, and is how man can know this all, and use it to keep himself well. It is an understanding of how Nature works outside Philosophically, and how if controlled by man as he can, can produce something said to be wonderful and a medicine. I have produced this one time. Whatever it is, I know it is a very pure substance. It is a very beautiful process to work and behold and understand. I don't know yet, and won't for a time know what it really will do. I have tried to give this away to several organizations in the past, and I have spoken openly about it to many. Most think I have a misunderstanding of the facts, and without saying so, many others think, well, you know what they think! All remains to be seen. This information was but will not again be lost to mankind. I have shown much of it to others around the world. I realize it is tied to many things we hold dear. It will cause some of us to see some of them in a different way. I rely on the words, "The Truth Shall Set You free." I have tried to show the Truth as best I can. I try to see things with an open mind, and so with me there is only understanding. This has become for me very important in my now understanding. I actually carried with me all my life guilt feelings from things I was taught and told in the past. I didn't live as I was told I had to. I did things all children do, but not all carry the guilt. Some persons grow and so break away from those vices of the past used to control, but even those that do carry on with them a burden because of not knowing. And so, I have become to myself a happy free person. Yes, I had a hobby that lasted all my life. Always though the past will be there, but now for me, I see it as what it was, a method of control.

I can say now, the easy part is now done. We proceed now with information. If you will always try to connect to Nature, the understanding will simply be outside. The compost pile, the life of a seed, the times of the year, always connect. Bring them together. There is a reason a plant springs from the ground in, spring. Nature is in tune, all the ancients did was observe and understand and connect. Many things around you will be pointed out. There is wonderment in looking the first time at a constellation, and knowing why it was named. To be able to connect it to the time and the below from what is happening all around you. There is a reason as to why a seed is shaped that way! It is nice to know why the light is good, and it all goes on with a total understanding of the whole system. You're a part of and from that system, learn it, Love it and help to take care of it in your way. It is important.

A quick way of the Steps of the Stone

Step one.
Selecting matter or an Egg to work on. See it as organic matter in a perfect oven.
All nature works in this fashion.

Step two
Selecting a place of work. Consider Genesis and the firmament. Consider PHI and the pyramid design and connections to nature. Our Galaxy is designed after PHI. From the greatest to the smallest!

Step Three.
Work the process according to nature and Genesis. Returning matter to a base! Consider a compost pile, a seeds cycle, the yearly cycle! All lives, dies to be recycled.

Step four.
Work the process. Joining matter with the All! Consider spring and Genesis Third Day. Consider all outside starting to grow and reproduce.

Step five.
Work the process. Achieve results of process, consider dry land of Genesis. Consider Septembers Child. Consider a seed that has reproduced a seed!

Step six.
Work the process. Divide substance and work two ways for two stones. Two ways to consider. Now going beyond what nature produces naturally.

Step seven.
Work the process for White Stone and consider like. Two Stones, one from the moon.

Step eight.
Work the process for Red Stone and join All again for further augmentation. Primary way of work, here for the Red.

Step nine.
Work the process for further like augmentation of matters with sun. Consider sun is good, gold and perfection. Consider the below becoming like the above good light.

There are other things to consider as we work these steps. This is a short understanding of 16 months of work. Note at end of each, selected augmentation for each stone. During each phase, combinations and conditions change.

In our process we cover 16 months of Time. Nine months to remake matter into a base substance. That substance will be like the matters the Earth was believed made originally. Nature cannot make this substance naturally by itself. It does not exist in nature but is a possibility of nature and man working together. The base substance is divided to make two stones. For three more months, the moon and only matter and vapor are joined for the White Stone. During that same three months, the substance we work for the Red Stone are further augmented as we did before. Then the white is finished, the substance for red is augmented. The last four months the substance for red and the sun are joined in a certain way to produce the Red Stone. The good of the sun is captured!

Genesis

Prior to explaining Genesis and what it has become to me, I need to say a few things as to why I have come to these conclusions. Like with many, and originally with myself, Genesis was a few short lines at the start of my bible. You accepted them, or you did not. To me they were something God Like, and what that means is I am not supposed to understand, that there is not and never will be an explanation. Now, for me that has changed. Those changes are from the many years I have thought about, but also used and tried to work from and with the mentioned conditions. For me the way to explain is to express some of the thoughts I have come to concerning Genesis, as a Creation Epic. Also as The Great Work as it is known alchemically, and as just understanding how nature works to the common man, you and I! You must understand what is happening naturally outside, every day, each month of the year. Why is that? The alchemical process needs to be understood as this process of outside, controlled so that I am always moving toward the light. Because it is nature, but controlled as you shall see, it becomes Art.

I never really get there though (when moving toward the light) until the end. Always I am making my light of the sun stronger, but never does the matters see the light of the sun directly. Always I am creating conditions where the light is stronger. How to do this is what makes the stone possible. You'll see also that the ancients never worshipped the sun. This was always a misunderstanding. Yes, there were at times groups of people that did, but that also was because of misunderstanding of past beliefs. Our society today does not understand. We move toward the light with process. The ancients worshipped something in the light. The ancients believed God had put something of himself there and that is the part they worshipped. Also, in alchemy that is the part of the good Light we must slowly capture. The process is long, Genesis repeated I call it. The ancient alchemists said, "To turn the wheel again." Our process then becomes one of slow purification of the matters, slowly turning compost into what was believed a perfect Substance. Their beliefs, which have become our beliefs will tend to make you know and understand that they accomplished their task. It becomes nature controlled, (understanding Genesis) which gives this process and way of perfection.

They found the light was good! They worshipped this good that they found. Why is it we never asked what it meant, why is the light good? What does it mean that the light is good? Genesis won't tell you. Man won't tell you, and neither will the Bible. Alchemy will though, and show you how to use it. How to capture it, and finally, when you can unite with it with matter then you will understand why it is good. Alchemy is not a bad word, Alchemy is just a word describing a short term for the study of Nature. Alchemy is what the ancient beliefs system became. A way of passing on information in a hidden fashion. Always in the past, information was for only the hidden… those in the Temples, those who would be King, and those we would call Philosophers. Never was this information known by the common man! It seems though from records dug up that all may have at different ancient times, shared this substance. They had a medicine that cured all ills! If this is true it remains to be seen. I know enough to know I have found how to make a wonderfully pure substance.

Will it lend it's perfection to what it touches? Only a short time remains to be seen if that is true! The process seems true, all here in the below can be seen as a product of that Good Light the sun. If I make a substance using that light, would it not be good for me?

It was written, Genesis, and so what does that mean? The author has two ways of discussion. This is something he knows because it is something he has done, or knows that it has been done. The second explanation is this is how he might think it was done, but again based on reasons why. Many will say and argue that this is information coming from Moses, as he is the supposed author. And from God to him. We can as many do accept this. Now after the many years of work with and through the study of nature, I disagree. Genesis I believe came to Moses from the temples of ancient Egypt. I would say though that Moses perhaps didn't understand the text he found there. If he did, why wasn't it explained, and if it was, where is the understanding? Moses either didn't know, or knew the great secret that those few lines held, and so kept it secret at least from the masses. I say this because over the many years that I have spent with Genesis, I often wondered why there was no further explanation? I have looked in many places, surly not all. I have been unable to find explanations based on my conclusions and so to me a mystery as to why. In the near time, (present day) new evidence suggests that the information, actually Egypt herself was lost. I believe that the time was within a few hundred years of Mosses time. Evidently there was a small Ice Age that effected Egypt, and the Nile flow and all was lost to the point survivors forgot the past understanding of information in their temples. This may be why no explanation. But then, it also could be no explanation because information always was hidden from the masses in the past, Moses only continued this method of secrecy. Some questions we never will be able to answer. I have to say right here, much of what I have found is from many years of contemplation, over 35 now. If there is an expert of Genesis on this earth, I surly can speak with him. I have studied, and worked the process many times. Not always successful, but always learning. As I proceed, you also will come to see how easy it is to understand, and as I present the process, you also can now work it. Is it Ok to do so? Myself I don't believe God plays favorites. God Created man equal all say, and so all information is for all men. It seems to me that only some men might not agree with this statement, those who want to know and control.

Genesis was written. It is a process of just Nature and seasons as concerned with the yearly cycle. It is a process concerning matter and how the forces were controlled as it was believed by God in the original creation. Man found and understood this process, and found he could do the work as he thought God did it. Not in the same way as God did it, but he could do the same work with the same forces with the same outcome. Not that Man created man, man found this process, found he could make earth as God did originally, and found he could go further with the work and actually find perfection. It must be understood that it was the perfection man found that proved to himself that he had found and understood the work of God. Only God is perfect, and so finding perfection meant finding God. Again we are left with two choices. Did early man find perfection? Did early man find something he thought was perfect, and would we agree and think so today. If he found that perfection with the lights above, can you now understand why the light was good? The matters raised by again become divine. That understanding is where

Heaven came from, and what we know of as resurrection.

Genesis was written. It is just learning how nature works throughout the year. Again we have several ways we can look at what early man found. Did he assume that there were things about the creation he couldn't know? Was there something special about the creation, and if so how could man duplicate the work? Our thoughts today because of misunderstanding has us believing that we couldn't do the work. Why? Special lights and or forces were thought to have been used. If this was true, early man could not have found Genesis as he would not have those special forces, and so could not do the work. Therefore he could never know how it was done, and could never explain or duplicate. We would be left with a few lines that would have to remain God Like, and a few lines we either accept or reject as people do. Man could not, perhaps would not write something he believed unless he believed because it was something he had done. However, Genesis works! The matter I work on is changed, and I would say Perfected. I would agree with early man. They found something they could not explain. They could write it down, they could use it, but it still remains God like. Something they accept as coming from him. It was perfect matter! He knew he could not make it except by controlling nature and the forces he found there. To say it another way, it is beyond the ability of man to make the matter, but not beyond the ability of nature controlled by man. This is how man thought and believed the world was made, and so how early man found God. Yes, always before there were Gods, but now with the work, man had the proof of many things concerning God, the one true God. Through an understanding of nature, man could know of God. Because he worked with living and death of matters, man linked this process to himself and his eternal existence. If Man could perfect matter, God could surly perfect matter, and so man after death could be resurrected and his matters perfected by God.

As you read the explanation, I explain it as a process and a play with words. Line one is explained by line two. This is what is happening outside, and so this is how and why it was expressed that way. As I mentioned, I have worked this process now for over 35 years. I still believe I have much to learn. I have to see it and explain it as a process we all can know and understand. If there is perfection in the work, it leads us to what we know as The Philosophers Stone, alchemically. This gets us into magic, and the unexplained. It concerns the occult, but all that really means is that it concerns things we don't know about. That is actually what the word means, things unknown! It does not mean they are evil, or connected to evil. Nothing is evil unless man uses it that way, or tires to use it in that fashion. All of this became the start of the first True religion. Perhaps the first real true religion based on a fact, not on the rustling wind, or lightning or loud noises. It is about early man wanting to know more about himself, and about his surroundings and how it all worked together. In the "Book of the Dead," by Mr. Budge, he stated a fact we need to point out. "The early Egyptians were always puzzled and always were trying to figure out the creation." I explain it as such. Lets say they are the first civilization. What else could teach them except nature? We today can easily pick up a book and learn about anything we want to. Consider the far past. No books, no libraries, just you and what you could observe through the study of nature. Man had questions about himself as much as he did about all else he knew.

What is Man? A question we have heard many times during our life. See it or try to see it from the view point of early man who had no answers and you will do much better with my explanation. What I am showing is not new information, but comes from the understanding that the early Egyptians had. Originally the understanding and the information comes from their temples. Moses was educated in those same Temples.

SUMMARY – GENESIS, The 1st Day

The First Day. "In the beginning God created the Heaven and the Earth, and the Earth was without form, and void, and the Spirit of God moved upon the waters "And God said, Let there be Light, and there was Light. And God saw the light, that it was Good! And God divided the light from the darkness, and God called the light day, the darkness he called Night. And the evening and the morning was the first day."

The creation of heaven and earth, and for an understanding, the creation of something similar to an egg. Why? In ancient Egypt, it was believed "all came from an egg." If we look to nature, does not all come from an egg or a seed originally? Could it be any different for the earth? The heaven is the shell and the contents of the egg would be earth. Heaven is the space within a shell or firmament, the space within any design that is based on PHI and it causes the creation energy to be concentrated within.

This creation energy is found everywhere within the universe. The earth was also created and was considered to be like the contents of the egg, without form and void, meaning no ordered process. It was in chaos so to speak, and we will call it primordial matter. This process would be given to matter by the creation of light. As we consider the words, we will find there were two lights as there are today. The sun and moon were those lights. An important point, and my alchemical understanding is that the light will only work with a base matter. Here we will find the earth created had to undergo a process before the light was brought to it! Light creates our world on a yearly basis, but light can do more. Perfection is within the light, and it can be collected, but only with matter returned to what it was believed to be in the creation process. As I will say in different places with this work, consider the compost pile. all matter is recycled, and that was a lesson learned long ago and I think had much to do with the process of Genesis.

The Light was good. What does this mean? The ancients through experimentation found this perfection and they did so with the light. They after much consideration concluded that God had put something of himself into the light. Genesis only says, "God saw the Light, and it was good." We never knew what that meant, at least I never knew or had the explanation. It comes from ancient

Egypt where when mentioning the Lights, (sun and moon) a sign for good was placed between them to show this point. Why and how could they know that God had done this? Evidently they had a reason for showing the light in this fashion. As they studied nature, this means they studied the lights! They used the lights and found this Good. The process produced for them perfection! Only God is perfect, and so with nature and the light, something was there that caused that effect. It could only be a part of God as he is the only and all perfect that man could ever know or find. This answered for them a question I am sure that they had asked for a long time. Now for the reasons you will come to understand as we go on, they found an answer. Consider perfection! There is none in the world! If you found a way through nature to produce, what would you feel you had found? Also here, let us understand just what the first day was time wise or in length. It was described as the morning and the evening. The light came on slowly and went slowly away as it does outside every day! The day of creation was based to the ancients on the cycle of the moon. It was dark, it started to grow or get light, waxing, it became full, it started to wane, evening and a new moon came, and so ended the first day. In all of alchemy, many times an alchemical day is mentioned in some way. You will see that all alchemical days are of a month long, and all based on the cycle of the moon.

Waters

It was believed there was a great mass of waters. God had created a heaven and earth, considering them also to be waters. All parts of the creation could and is called waters, be it light, earth, or heaven, and the hot and cold, wet or dry. Everything was a water or part called a water. These waters also we can know as base substances, and with alchemy they are the only true base Substance. Water also to the ancients was any liquid! This means for example, the contents of an egg were considered water. I think from process they found that most of these substances, especially those they had to work with in those times were composed of water. As we use the rotting process, all organics are composed of mostly water, and by process almost all the substance can be taken away. To them, all came from water The seed for all was believed to be in water, and they grew and made things with just water. An example of this is they grew a tree, say in a bucket. All they ever added was water, and so believed all of it came from water. Today we know more of the process, but they did not know of the air and what happened with a tree and natural gasses used by a tree from the air. We have to see things as they did, with what they knew to understand what they said and to learn how they accomplished things.

Light

In our process we will work it with light. It has within it something special, believed by the Ancients to be a part of God. Something of God put there to cause all in the below to happen. We will be concerned with collecting the good of the light with our process. The lights in Genesis and in alchemy/art is the sun and moon called or known by waters Above. They cause everything to happen over time. The Constellations also we must learn, as they become times of the year. The alchemists hid the parts of the alchemical process, but in many of the allegories, times of the part are shown somehow by an astrological sign. Our process is a copy of the yearly cycle, but by art (alchemy), we control nature (the waters) in such a way as nature by herself cannot do. Nature can, and by observation we see that there is little she cannot make. Our search for the stone is a search for perfection, Nature controlled can also give to us what was believed the perfection of the original creation. In alchemy though, we will take the matters we work on to a point beyond what was done in the creation. We will do this by selecting which light, and how we use that light. You will see it is a slow mixture, described as again and again. That means that within our little copy of the creation, we again and again circulate the waters always collecting and adding to the substance this good of the above light.

Time

We also have the time of day, We will have shown that the day of creation is based on the moon and if you will consider the morning as the start of the moon going through its cycle, and the evening as the moon finishing its cycle. Then you will understand how a day based on the moon is one month long in our alchemical understanding. Also, you then can understand the six days of the creation as being needed for the yearly process in each hemisphere. This will be easily understood when we discuss information from ancient Egypt. Though the times are different, the alchemical process can be used anywhere on the earth.

Knowing the times are important depending where you live on the planet. You will find as we visit later ancient Egypt, they understood the earth to be 'Two' earths. I have come to understand and connect this to the northern hemisphere, and the southern. With those times or "Days," the first day as winter, and that it is one month long. The 3rd day is spring, when the waters come together. The 6th day as summer and that all in our garden is finished. And the heaven and earth were being subject to the light and form and process being established. If this is said to be in the northern hemisphere, then the next day is really the start of the same process in the southern hemisphere. In other words, the creation process was a thing started long ago, and still exists for man today. See it as six days in each hemisphere, and so 12 days or one year long. Always December is the start for the northern hemisphere, and always the sixth day is the finish. It is easy to see the third day as spring, look outside as all things start to grow and understand it as "The waters coming together." See to the sixth and your garden. It is full of or near to being full of product! That is why the man was understood to have been created on that day, the garden was finished, and the man had plenty to eat! Realize though, this was not the end of the creation process. It was a time of rest for God, but the cycle is ever ongoing... always sustaining the below with it's forces. It was not a thing stopped, but a continuing cycle. We live with those same forces today, and with the same light and water and times. We though, may be changing those conditions.

Process:

It was necessary to start the process before creating the firmament because the firmament tends to perfection over time and the process that is involved is a type of rotting or recycling process.

Another way to say this is with the light, we are always moving in the forward direction or toward the light. As all material on the earth is recycled by a rotting process. It was believed, whatever the waters within the heaven were, they also by this same type of process had to be made primordial before they could be made into something called earth, the finished earth that is. So, our first day is for us a way to start this recycling of matter before it goes into it's firmament to be completed. Then to be brought forth by the light. In nature if you would consider a compost pile, you would have the best understanding that can be given. Nature recycles, compost is our modern term for this understanding. What is different about our process of art in the alchemical understanding, as compared to nature is compost. It can never be anything by itself! Compost is only a food for other things, and by that way becomes other things. In our process, the matter we will work with is the same as it also has no seed. However, nature and the light over time will try to make something of this material. By collecting the good in the light, in time we make the Philosophers Stone. Those lights you will find have seed within, and become the seed of the new material they can make. The seed knows when and how to grow to survive. It slept through the winter, the waters came together for it in the spring and about the 6th day it has reproduced a seed. To better understand this consider a seed produced in our cycle. Consider it falling to the ground, being covered in its way, and lying there until the following spring. The light and warmth and water cause it to grow and reproduce. The cycle is in tune with nature. This is the natural cycle. It works and reproduces the seed. However, it is not perfection. So, the first day, earth was created, heaven was created, light was created and a day was started and given a time period. Process was started.

The Second Day

And God said, "Let there be a Firmament in the Middle of the waters, and let it divide the waters from the waters. And God made the firmament and divided the waters that were below the firmament from the waters that were above the firmament and it was so. And God called the firmament heaven, and the morning and the evening was the second day".

Firmament! It was believed to be the arch of the sky, but there is an older belief and the design of the Firmament can be shown to have the shape of what we call the pyramid shape. What is very important about this pyramid shape is that the design incorporates within it what we have come to call PHI. PHI is in everything found living and growing on the earth. The heaven created in the beginning was thought to be like an egg shell, and contained PHI. PHI is a mathematical principle, and though the shape may look different, if it contains PHI, it is the same. There is an energy here I call it creation energy as it is linked to all things living. This design containing PHI somehow uses this energy. So, firmament and heaven are the same. From Genesis, "And God called the firmament Heaven." This explains why heaven, pyramid, egg, shell and shuck are all the same. They all had the same something (principle) in common. They could look different but they were the same mathematically, or all had PHI in the design.   The creation process had to have a place where the process of creation could work.   It was a place like an oven, a place where the earth could complete the process.   This place or oven can also be called a pyramid as the true pyramid incorporates the PHI shape, and so a pyramid could be called heaven. It would be correct to call a pyramid a shell, as long as one considered PHI.   In our process it means it is time for our egg to be put into a pyramid shaped oven. The first part of the process is to return the substance within the shell back to what is primordial matter. The good of the light, for the process of the stone, can only work this way.

Matter

All matter before it can become something else has to return to what it was in the beginning, and that something is primordial matter. In Nature that is the compost pile. To the alchemists, this substance was called a base. Those substances you put into your compost pile are not dead, they are just matters being recycled. When the process is accomplished, then you have returned those substances back into what it was believed to be. The same as or similar to those used in the creation, a base matter. What is important alchemically, is to know that we work with nature, and nature must do the work controlled. We cannot make by any chemical means a base matter. Only nature knows how to do this in the proper fashion. Lets say it differently. Only nature can make a base she has made into something else. If you are going to use and control nature, all of your process and material has to come from nature. All the substance was has to be removed, or nature cannot make it into something else. Consider this, if you put to nature a substance, she has to make something out of it! All you need know is how to present the matters to nature in the right way. That is called alchemy/art.

Egg: consider the earth in the creation to the ancients as similar to an egg! The heaven was the shell, the contents was as of an egg. Now this is how they chose to understand it. It doesn't mean to me the original earth was a giant egg, it just means that is how the ancients choose to understand and explain what they found.

Now, in the process of Genesis, the only thing that I found that turned my egg black correctly (the first color of alchemy), was a sealed pyramid shaped oven. As an egg is returned to primordial matter, the moisture within the egg will be removed and what you will find is an oven full of moisture, and a hollow shell with a little black ball within it. It will still be moist. The waters below were divided. The substance was returned to a base. Believe me when I say, I used plastic bags, jars, everything and anything if it would hold moisture. This is when I was trying to learn. Even in my pictures, (which are included), if you look close in one of them you will see the black ball next to a similar pyramid shaped oven, within a substance that is orange. Now, if the shape is not true, it hasn't turned black? The one oven is true, the other is not. I can't explain this. If the ratio (more later) is wrong, it won't work! All things connected have to be exactly right for it to work. It is nature, but it also seems to be what we might call, an exact science. If it is not controlled and done in the proper fashion, it won't work! Nature has to be right to work. They say that some seeds will not germinate unless it is the right time of year- something is going on we don't know about, but the matters do. As we go on with the explanation, old texts from Egypt will tell you that, It will only happen if the time is right.

Time:

Evening and morning were the second day. Two steps have been covered, the first day the creation of what God needed to produce the earth and all on it and eventually all within it. The second day was the start of the process that would give to God what he desired in the creation. The first day in alchemy is one day or one month long. The second day in alchemy is four months long (art). It takes four months for the egg to process and return to primordial matter in the pyramid glass shaped sealed oven. Waters being divided means sealed The ancients found the process whereby God had created the earth. They understood they could not do it as God did it but by art, alchemy, and control of the forces involved, they could. Forces in nature are controlled, and times of the control periods are very necessary to know. "May-Day, a time that is an alchemical term, as it is called is the finish of the second day in our process. Also it becomes the start of the third day when the waters come together. It also is shown astrologically by the terms, "Bull in Ram." Now bull in ram simply pointed out the power of nature at that time of year. The ancients in their study so used things found in nature to explain what they were doing at that time. They called them principles, and springtime (May-Day) was the time the above seems to be most powerful, thus a Bull!

The oven, will be divided from the light above, or will be kept warm and in the darkness. This is during the second day of four alchemical months. In the northern hemisphere the first day would be Dec. 21st. The time when the sun begins to move north from its southern position. This 1st day would last one month. Or one period of the moon. The 2nd day in the alchemical process is for four months in length and ends in May. It takes this long for the process to return the contents of the egg to primordial matter. This is considered death in the process, and its color is black. Another way of understanding this is separation from the light, and so the matter reverts to primordial. This is very important to note. From another alchemist, and writer, Adiramled. He stated that the only hell was when we move away from the light. Connect this to alchemy and always moving toward the light after the substance is made a base.

It is important to note the size of your oven is in line with what is inside of it. The reason for this is that the process causes the oven to run out of oxygen. And so what is inside of the shell of the egg goes to a type of hydrocarbon. If there is too much air in the sealed oven or it is too big the process won't work correctly. Remember the eggs left in a birds nest outside? Very little if anything is ever left. I use an oven with a base of 6 inches for this part of the process. The oven has to be kept warm, I try to stay around 98 degrees. If it is too warm the process will work too fast, too cold and the opposite happens. It is hard to correctly accomplish, though it sounds a simple task, nature and conditions will defeat you if you are not very near correct in your work. Under my oven, is a two inch base that is for air originally, and a water supply later. It is necessary. Many things need be found out or you fail each time. If you fail, you start again.

The 3rd Day

And God said, "Let the waters under the heaven come together in one place, and let the dry land appear, and it was so. And God called the dry land earth, and the gathering together of the waters he called seas, and God saw that it was good. And God said, let the earth bring forth grass, the herb yielding seed, the fruit tree yielding fruit after his kind whose seed is within itself, upon the earth, and it was so. And the earth brought forth grass, and herb yielding seed after his kind, and the tree yielding fruit after his kind, and God saw that it was good. And the evening and the morning was the third day." "Let the waters under the heaven come together in one place and let the dry land appear, and it was so." The and word in Genesis actually denotes more than one step in a day. This first part lasts for three months from May until the end of August. What this means is that from the start of the May-Day until August, we process the substance. In alchemy this is the creation of the first androgynous material. The May-Day is a time for letting the waters come together. The water we divided from the egg in the first step, and additional water we will add now come together with the substance in the shell and is processed in the full sun and moonlight for the three months mentioned. In one place is also very important, the egg is within the oven and the oven is of glass as it has to let the light shine through it. The inner oven or egg shell must also let the light pass through it so that the light is within the egg, processing the substance. Consider the words, within one place. This shows that the inner oven must be of a substance that allows light to penetrate. The creation energy is concentrated within the pyramid shaped oven and perhaps again within the shell of the egg. For the process to work it is that an oven within the oven is needed. This is different from what is found in nature. A seed has only one husk, an egg only one shell. In the process there are two. How we do this is the lower and upper half of the egg are separated, hard to do, so a couple of egg shells will be needed. The circulating water within the oven will enter the egg shell where you have parted the shell, the light will just shine through the top of the shell that is there. Remember, within one place. In the alchemical allegories a rainbow is indicated in this process, being of the colors green, blue, yellow and back to clear. It is to be found between the colors of black and white (next step) and is found when the waters come together. The field or water that your black substance is now floating in will turn a brilliant lime green, within 24 hours, it will turn to a sky blue, and again within 24 hours, it will turn a bright yellow then finally clear up to look just like water. This is the alchemical rainbow. The water and the substance will mix automatically and become the substance that has to be processed for three months. All that is necessary is for you to add water for the proper circulation and to "clean" the substance as some vile material will be on the top. Always be careful to not remove any more material than is necessary as there is not much to work with. Also, the matters at this stage are not to see the lights directly, so always work so the sun is not shining on them. This matter will be of a greenish color if correct. It will stay that way until the next step. The rainbow colors are very brilliant, and beautiful to behold. I as of yet cannot explain them, but picture's of this are included. The water circulates within the oven, I will show you how as we proceed, and vapor raises and falls as condensation. As it raises in the day time it absorbs energy from the sun and deposits it to the below, and it does this at night and gains energy from the moon and again deposits it below.

Substance cannot see the sun or the moon or it will be ruined. When you can understand the whole process that it is about the light and the substance, the light never sees the substance directly until the finish. This is done very cleverly with the oven, the shell and the amounts of water, always getting to the next step where the light is because of the conditions you set, get stronger.

"And let the dry land appear."

In the creation the earth was basically finished at this point. Note that we now have dry land and shows that first we did not have dry land in the creation epic. All were waters and as far as the earth is concerned, it was a type of water or believed to be so originally. To the ancients, all liquids were called a water. This helps to show how an egg substance can be the substance of the stone. Now, God could put the above into the below in one day, we cannot. In our process of alchemy we also will let the dry land appear, but to do so we must dry it for one month and the drying is done in moonlight only. The second day had the oven sealed, divide the waters and it is necessary for the process to work. During the third day, the oven is vented, as air is a part of nature and as the oven is vented there will be a loss of moisture and so moisture will always be added. Be careful to add only the purest water you can find. Never well or spring water, only condensed dew or some type of pure water only. In our process we will have produced (the dry land) what is known alchemically as Mercury. Now the alchemists use this term in many places, but it is not the true mercury until it is like the finished earth. I said the substance had to be dried in moonlight. This is because alchemically there are two stones to make, and like is what we must consider here. We can always add the sun. If we do add the sun, we cannot make the White Stone as the white stone is tied to the moon, and addition of the sun is not like for the white stone. This will be explained in detail as we proceed. Also, as we cover the mythology of Osiris, you will find this dry land, this earth, was known to them as Osiris in a new birth. In alchemy it is known as Septembers Child. Our three days of work have covered nine months of process. This substance we produce in September is really just the base material of the stone. I said that making the stone, we take the matters further than God did in the Creation. Here, Septembers Child is the same material the ancients believed the earth was when created. It is not a perfect material. This is the material Adam was created from. Again, not a perfect material. Man was not created perfect! In alchemy, this material is androgynous material, that means it is part male and part female. This is the reason the ancients felt Adam was different, and a reason I believe Eve could be made from Adam. He was both male and female as was the earth. The earth had to be created this way, (ancient understanding) so that all things be they male or female would unite and grow from the earthly substance.

The Sun.

Is considered male, sulfurous, the seed for gold, and gold, hot and dry. What we receive from the sun was called Spirit. It can burn the substance and your product will be useless. In alchemy the Sun is known for the same reasons. The sun is spirit, male and considered perfect and is called gold, and is the seed for gold and is like gold as gold was thought to be the only perfect thing in nature. The sun is hot and dry and thought to be sulfurous. The good in the light is from the sun or was believed placed in the sun and is the perfection like the gold found in the below. When we collect it, we collect a sulfurous material. We can only collect this gold or sulfurous material through water vapor within our oven! In nature, this happens outside when the sun shines on clouds.

The Moon.

Is considered to be female, to be silver, not perfect but more so than many things found on earth, thought to be connected with moisture and coolness and her substance was considered to be mercurious She was known to be a reflection of the sun. We have sulfur from the sun and mercury from the moon. These are the names for those energies I mentioned that the circulation picked up from the lights above as water circulates within the oven. Later as we discuss the sulfur- salt theory, you will see that salt is just a collection of these substances of the sun and moon. Salt is the same as the earth created.

September's Child.

This is done during the month of September and the substance produced in alchemy is called Septembers Child. In Egypt it was celebrated as being a time when life overcame death. In our process it is to be considered as the same thing, the substance was first divided away and death was the result. Now the waters have come together and life is the result, death was overcome. At the end of September you will have a very pure white substance that you must grind into a powder, because we alchemically are not finished yet. In Genesis the earth was basically finished, but in alchemy and Art there is still much to do. We dry in moonlight, we gain the white substance and what we have is a base substance that has within it the possibility of all things. This is according to the alchemists, and remains to be seen. Mercury is what it is and was known as to the alchemists. In the ancient Egypt, this Septembers Child you will find is linked to Osiris and his rebirth. This white substance is said to be cared for by Two Sisters. This also is linked to Osiris, and the Two Sisters are actually, the constellation Virgo (one sister), and the Goddess Isis. The goddess (one sister) is the moon in nature. This will be explained as we go on. For time of the stone, we have moved through nine months of process. The first day one month, the second day four months, the third day three months, and finally one month of drying in moonlight.

There are said to be two stones in alchemy, one for silver and one for gold and they are from this substance.   For silver the white substances never again sees the sun,   For gold and the red stone, you will see the process has to be done again and further augmentation is needed.

"And God called the dry land earth and the gathering together of the waters he called seas, and God saw that it was good. And God said, let the earth bring forth grass, the herb yielding seed, the fruit tree yielding fruit after his kind whose seed is within itself, upon the earth, and it was so.
And the earth brought forth grass and herb yielding seed after his kind and the tree yielding fruit after his kind and God saw that it was good. And the evening and the morning was the third day."

During our yearly cycle this is the start of Spring, and lasts from the start of the growth of plants and fruit until the summer when they are basically finished. In the creation it was still being done on a months or "day" basis, based on the cycle of the moon. The 4th Day, and God said, "let there be lights in the firmament of the heaven to divide the day from the night, and let them be for signs and for seasons, and for days and years, and let them be for lights in the firmament of the heaven to give light upon the earth." And God made two great lights. The greater light to rule the day, and the lesser light to rule the night, he made the stars also. And God set them in the firmament of the heaven to give light upon the earth and to rule over the day and over the night and to divide the light from the darkness. And God saw that it was good And the morning and the evening was the forth day.

Process:

The process (of nature) is here changed, and the light is changed. The lights in the creation now can shine upon the earth, they are placed in the firmament when before they were outside of the firmament, and they will determine the day and the seasons and the times of the year, or the creation process was changed into the yearly cycle we now have. Note that though the waters came together before or the lights (waters above) came together they did not before this time shine directly on the earth. The sun and moon are used differently on this day in that they are moved into the firmament and our present cycle was established. Many today see the light of creation as a special light and believe that it was not until this time that the sun and moon were created. This is wrong. The lights we now have are the same lights used in the creation, just that God used them differently than they are now being used. We can copy this creation process, but cannot do it as was believed God did it. Time and control will give us the same results. If there was a special light of and for the Creation we could not do this work. The perfection is still available from the proper use and understanding. I have yet to know what the substance produced will do. I am only telling you how to make it and how to understand. It was considered to be something perfect, like the sun and because it was finished by the sun. What it will do and how we will consider it today may be quite differently than in the past. Early man felt that if there was a God and a creation, it must have been originally near perfect, that man and the earth must have been near perfectly made, and the long study produced Genesis. To me what has been known as the Philosophers Stone. Alchemy, or the study of nature combined with Art, gives us perfection of the substance. The perfection comes from process and how to use the lights that are good. The stone is a product of nature, mostly from the sun. I am sure that the process will teach man something about how matter and nature works together. I hope that whatever that something is will be of benefit to mankind. This is not the end of the processes for the stone, and is not the end to Genesis. however it is all I wish to explain with this part at this time.

The Emerald Tablet

Translation of Isacc Newton . 1680.

1) Tis true without lying, certain & most true.
2) That wch is below is like that wch is above & that wch is above is like yt wch is below to do ye miracles of one only thing.
3) And as all things have been & arose from one by ye mediation of one: so all things have their birth from this one thing by adaptation.
4) The Sun is its father, the moon its mother,
5) the wind hath carried it in its belly, the earth its nourse.
6) The father of all perfection in ye whole world is here.
7) Its force or power is entire if it be converted into earth.
7a) Seperate thou ye earth from ye fire, ye subtile from the gross sweetly wth great indoustry.
8) It ascends from ye earth to ye heaven & again it desends to ye earth and receives ye force of things superior & inferior.
9) By this means you shall have ye glory of ye whole world & thereby all obscurity shall fly from you.
10) Its force is above all force. ffor it vanquishes every subtile thing & penetrates every solid thing.
11a) So was ye world created.
12) From this are & do come admirable adaptaions whereof ye means (Or process) is here in this.
13) Hence I am called Hermes Trismegist, having the three parts of ye philosophy of ye whole world.
14) That wch I have said of ye operation of ye Sun is accomplished & ended.

Authors Note: As I have stated, when trying to find an understanding of alchemy, I choose this tablet as a text to work with. What follows now is how I understand what is said. This follows Genesis as to me it is also a creation Epic. I always tried to understand the one by comparison of the two!

My explanation.

"Tis true without lying, certain & most true.
That wch is below is like that wch is above & that wch is above is like yt wch is below to do ye miracles of one only thing".

This is a description of the all. The above air moisture and light combinations are the same as the dry and solid substances, and water below. The below is a result of the above. The below was believed to be a result of these combinations of the below with the above by circulation and mixing of the forces with substance.

"And as all things have been & arose from one by ye mediation of one: so all things have their birth from this one thing by adaptation."

Authors Note: This shows the ancients believed that all here in the below was from The Meditations of God! By adaptation means that the substances had a way of joining to become something else other than what they were as basic substances. This refers to Genesis (The meditation) as that process that allowed this adaptation to occur.

"The Sun is its father, the Moon its mother."

Authors Note: This teaches us that the ancients believed that the sun and the moon were the lights above in this creation epic. That it was not a special light used only for the creation.

"the wind hath carried it in its belly, the earth its nourse."

Authors Note: This shows us that circulation of air and moisture (earth) are a part of the process. One needs to know air is just a carrier of moisture, and thus become a place where the above forces can join to the earth which in this part is vapor. This mixture in air produce earth. which is added to the below substances. The below substance is also known as earth as it was considered a type of water. This earth below (water) supplies the vapor that raises to the above by the movement of the air.

"The father of all perfection in ye whole world is here."

Authors Note: By this process, perfection can be the result. By saying or using the term father he is referring to a male principle or to the sun.

"Its force or power is entire if it be converted into earth."

Authors Note: Here again he is referring to the sun, and saying that if we can capture this force, we can have all we need for this perfection. We capture this force by the circulation with an oven as I have described it.

"Seperate thou ye earth from ye fire, ye subtile from the gross sweetly wth great industry"

Authors Note: He is here telling us how to proceed with the process to accomplish this perfection. By separating, it is the same as the second day of Genesis where we divide the waters. This allows the below substance to return to a base matter The subtule (above lights) from the gross (below waters) 'With great industry' means there is more to it than just setting a substance into the dark. We need a place, and that place is within the firmament which is within a pyramid shaped oven. This is within heaven in Genesis.

"It ascends from ye earth to ye heaven & again it desends to ye earth and receives ye force of things superior & inferior."

This speaks of the process of circulating within the oven. Again is the key word here, and means we keep up the process for a long time. Why? To receive the force from things superior and inferior. They are the stars, sun and moon. The moon was considered inferior as it was known to be a lesser light, and a reflection. Also, he uses the term heaven. The firmament was called heaven in Genesis, and shows the oven that the substance is within is linked to the process of Genesis, and to that design of the firmament called heaven. Because it ascends from earth, this shows the earth was at the earlier stages a liquid.

"By this means you shall have ye glory of ye whole world & thereby all obscurity shall fly from you."

Authors Note: By this process within this oven, you shall have the only perfection man ever has found! With this find, one will understand that there is a God, that he created the world, and by this process man has found and can know something of God. This is what makes man special. Of all things created, only the man could find this and find something of God!

"Its force is above all force. for it vanquishes every subtile thing & penetrates every solid thing."

Authors Note: Here he is speaking of the perfect substance by those means you can make. In alchemy, we call it the (Philosophers Stone). This substance will penetrate all things, and is said to perfect all that it touches.

"So was ye world created."

Authors Note: This shows us that the process of the stone is a copy of the process of the Creation of the Earth by God. This is why it is known as The Great Work in alchemy.

"From this are & do come admirable adaptaions whereof ye means (Or process) is here in this."

Authors Note: What he is speaking of here is that there is more than one substance that can be made by this means. We know them in alchemy as a Red Stone, a White Stone, and a medicine of good health.

"Hence I am called Hermes Trismegist, having the three parts of ye philosophy of ye whole world."

Authors Note: The three parts are the substance, the process, and the oven. As he has them , he is considered a threefold wise person.

"That which I have said of ye operation of ye Sun is accomplished & ended."

Authors Note: The operation, the perfection, the process, all comes from knowing how to use the sun! I point to outside for all to look and see. What is impossible for nature to make?

Introduction to Flamel's oven, and the
One oven of the Philosophers.

You will see an outline in the oven design with the Flamel fresco. The line is to make it easier to see the different crosses and designs hidden there, very important to the alchemical explanation. The outline of this oven is shown in a hidden fashion in many of the Pictorial allegories of the alchemists. Also, you will see that it contains a Big Mountain, and Small Mountains. In many places of alchemical written allegories, mountains or small mountains are mentioned. There are two places of work within this oven. One of them at Homo. One of them at the number 5. Homo is used in the colder months, and when vapor and substance need to be mixed. At number 5, the ovens or small mountains are set back so that an egg shell is placed there for a work area. This would then be between the four small mountains, and the design forms four small rivers that feed the substance in the oven. This is I believe the River Lost, mentioned in Genesis with four heads. That river only ever existed in man's concept of the Creation, and not in reality.

Probably one of the statements I use the most to remind myself and also others, one way, one substance, and one oven. These are words I had read but with little meaning attached. In time you realize one way means a certain procedure, and you know from chemistry things usually work only one way. H2O means just that, two parts hydrogen and one part oxygen makes water, nothing else. When dealing with alchemical matters, one would hardly suspect or believe that also applies. The year passes us by, the temperature of each day varies, what in nature is so close that it matters? Well, I have found, and I mean in a hard way. One substance means just that, one substance. I have formed many black eggs, only one of them works.

One oven. I have now used many different ovens, pint jars, quart jars, plastic containers, nothing works except the true oven. In a way I was lucky. I quickly found the pyramid and connected it possibly to alchemy. Yet, what I had was not correct. It has to be made as is shown in the following drawings. If not, again like H3O, it doesn't work. What can I say, the oven design with four small pyramid shapes evidently focuses energy in a certain fashion that causes the reaction we must have. When I saw this design, being a mechanic, I quickly seen a never failing fountain. Just put holes where the numbers are, and it will circulate water. The larger the better it works. That is because there is more space for the different needed temperatures. Cool in the top, warm in the base. Also, the base and the a cross with four equal arms. Read the mythology of Osiris, and this is a part of the explanation. This is a world scheme of the creation. Because of that, I believe there is more to it than is said. With Osiris, the cross with equal arms is only connected to equilibrium. A time period when the sun crosses the equator. All is equal, days and nights the same. To us, with some changes in the creation epic, this cross becomes the river with four heads.

    I had the design of this oven for many years and called it on the forums I visit, The Norton Oven. This oven was with his work in that book I was reading. And so the Norton oven. I have received a lot of laughs because of it. Now with the drawing of the oven, I have included here the fresco of Flamel. Flamel said in his written work, that he had hid the oven in his fresco, but, it was the oven like that used by the philosophers. In other words, it was not the oven used by the friendly puffers in the local alchemist shop! I really looked for this oven for, let me say, over 15 years before I finally saw the design hidden in the way Flamel drew his fresco, and how he described things we must know. I have mentioned these things in other places. This oven has been shown in many of the pictorial allegories, and I will include some of them. It has been shown as a metaphor in some allegorical pictures, as a spider web, and I will also include some of those. However, the writings of Flamel are from the time period, 1400's, and so that time is before many of these included drawings. To me, all of them is just a way that an alchemist carried on information as he could, when he could. Considering ancient Egypt, They built pyramids, I think one doesn't have to consider for long to realize there was a reason. One also can consider they must have had a working model which the oven could be called. I have been asked if they in the distant past could make the flat glass? Well, in one of their ancient tombs, there is on the wall carved in stone pictures of, What looks like a helicopter, a parachute, a type of automobile, an airplane and many other designs that can only mean they had much of what we have today. Surly they had flat glass. One of the alchemists I read said, "that he knew a glass cutter that could cut glass so well that a hair could not be put between the seams." One might consider, why would he say this? The ancient obelisk, a pyramid on the top. They could cut the hardest stone somehow, and any shape, which they called sands. The other thing one must consider. PHI! It is the principle we must know! They used the pyramid design to show they knew of it. What other shape could they have used and built on the desert? An egg shaped building? A shuck shaped building? A seed type of building? You see, the pyramid design is beautiful, and practical. Another thing. The design. It has become my understanding that it originated by light refraction in the sky. We can see this design in the clouds and light mixtures during the day time hours under many conditions. Is it not natural to design the firmament after the design they seemed to see there naturally? Also, when considering the oven, as it is tied to the creation, and what they thought about how the earth was formed. The shape was from the sun raising in a straight line, and then descending again in a straight line. This also gives that shape. The earth was originally thought flat, and considering straight lines, it was square. That square was divided into four sections. This gave us originally the four armed cross which became a river with four heads. In time, the rest of the design came about by work with the oven! As it is a natural design, and works with PHI, it worked for them to accomplish what it was their goal. A dark base filled with water, an upper condensing chamber, and a place where the forces of nature can mix and be controlled. If you want to understand and know the creation, this is the way and the oven to use for many reasons. Matter within with light and moisture! Who can say what will happen over time? Consider the good light as it shines and is controlled by man, the artist at work. Consider nature and what she does. She has to do something with the matters does she not? There is just matter and nature, when is it she reaches an end point? Is compost all that nature can make? If the light is good, can we not over time capture that good? If we can, what will we have? Can you see how it will perfect matter over time? Can you see how this can become a perfect medicine as nature would have it if she could?

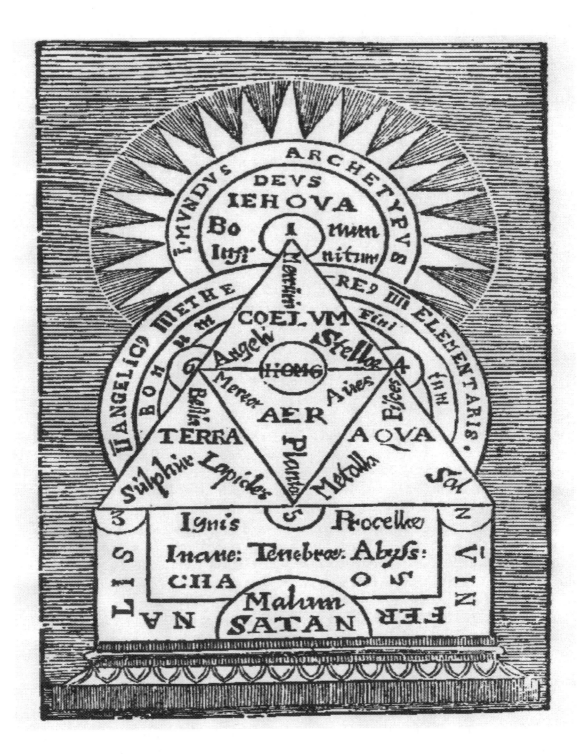

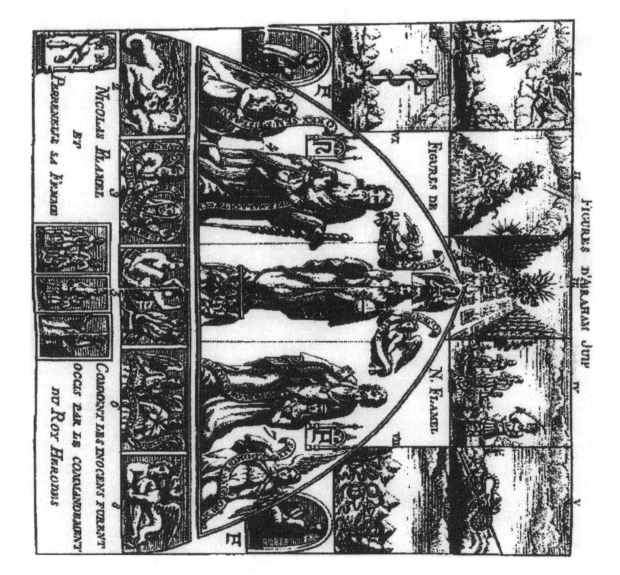

Flamels Hidden oven.

Flamel said that he had hidden the oven of the philosophers within his drawing. But, "one like that used by the Philosophers." The first of these three pictures is from where I first found the oven. It is a geometrical configuration of the Universe according to a gentleman by the name 0f Heliseaus Rosiln, (the operation of the Creation). To me it is a way to show ancient knowledge. I searched Flamels drawing for many years before I realized that the hidden oven was found by the way he drew his fresco. Flamel said it was necessary to know why he and Paranella was in heaven! They are because the drawing places them within the small mountains or small ovens or pyramids within the one large oven. The firmament, heaven is the name for the design. It is a place where God, the good of the light can be collected. The process also puts them there during the cold months as it is a warmer area. Also, when it is necessary to collect direct light in the process. In the Cheop's pyramid, it was believed a place of resurrection for the pharaoh. Now you know why.

Introduction to Flamel

The information to follow has to do with my understanding of Flamel. This information is about what alchemy has brought to me as far as an understanding and explanation. There is no easy way to say it all in one short sentence and so I will begin by saying that many things will be connected in the total explanation.

To start with Flamel. Why is because he speaks as any alchemist and you may appreciate what is there to try and solve or understand or connect. I will as is needed interject what he is saying and what it means in terms you and I can understand. It will slowly bring you an understanding. Sometimes it will seem I am bouncing around but I must. Flamel like many alchemists will discuss day one, and in the same paragraph, day 2 or 4 or 6! It is hidden material and that is just one way to confuse you. Some of what he said, I can't explain! I compare and use information from many, or several alchemists. Always they will say some things you can never understand. At least that is how it is for me. The imagination of man is a wonderful thing. As an alchemist it was necessary for you to present the material in a way the same, but shown differently. As you consider all the material, remember this. It is the product of that person's imagination. The same but different. Find those things you can see and understand, then the rest will slowly be understood. Remember it is Genesis, look for the steps you recognize, fit in the rest.

Beginning with Flamel and his work. There are several works by persons calling themselves Flamel. From studying this material I know they are different men. His work has been copied but the other explanations I have checked and dismissed. To me there is only one real Flamel and this is his work. It is not just this work though that solves alchemy, it is this understanding compared to other works. After you understand this you can compare, find things similar and see most is speaking the same story though written by a different person with a different way of explanation. I will show how to read this system of his, and compare it to others so that you can also compare. There are many series allegories that show the way of the stone. Some of them are not right, only a supposed understanding. Some of them are of other stones. Don't waste your time on things you can't see. Find what you can and slowly the understanding will lead you to many treasures. Before we are finished, I will cover enough that you will be able to read other alchemists if you try. Learn the steps, the times and usually within the allegory your looking at, part of it will show what and why it is as it is drawn. Usually a pictorial allegory shown is a part of a series. Look at that series, and see where the tablet is. Perhaps the one next to it is easier to understand, and that way, you do as I have done. Look to what I can understand. If you know what is next, then you at least have an idea of what the alchemists might be trying to show.

I will interject where I think it is important, or not easily understood. All alchemical information is similar to what is produced here. Never is straight talk given to you, always it is in 51 allegory. Always it is in a series, and each produced a series differently. What I will be showing is, that the series are copies of Genesis and there are ten steps to making the stone based on Genesis. Some showed this series in many steps. As you read all the material, you will find the ten steps of the stone are the same steps of Osiris! The times of the stone are those times of Osirs. The constellations used to purify Osiris are those same stars that give the effect we search for with the stone's process. There are very many facts to learn and consider. When known, it will become easy for you to see and understand. Read about Osiris, and then come back. It will give you a base. Remember the compost pile, and remember the life of a seed. All helps with understanding.

The Work of Flamel.

CHAPTER I - Of the Theological Interpretations which may be given to these Hieroglyphics according to the sense of me the Author

Authors Note. "According to the sense of me the Author" This is important, this is his interpretation of the process we must learn. Anyone that knew the process could figure this out and know Flamel as a brother so to speak. You probably can't figure it out if you don't know, or don't spend 30 years. Each alchemist did the same thing with an explanation, or did it his way! Would you accept an explanation by another that had already been given if you were a Master? Some of the works are easy to see, some very difficult. Some explain the process in a few steps, others use many. We are all different and we each have a different imagination and way of saying things. The alchemists were no different.

The work is as it is presented. Much of it speaks of Abraham's work. I will try to compare and make it easy to see and understand.

"I have given to this Churchyard, a Charnel-house, which is right over against this fourth Arch, in the middest of the Churchyard, and against one of the Pillars of this Charnel house, I have made be drawn with a coal, and grossly painted, a man all black, which looks straight upon these Hieroglyphics, about whom there is written in French: It voy merveile done moult Ie m'esbahi; that is, I see a marvel, where at I am much amazed: This, as also three plates of Iron and Copper gilt, on the East, West, and South of the Arch, where these Hieroglyphics are, in the middest of the Churchyard representing the holy Passion and Resurrection of the Son of God This ought not to be otherwise interpreted, than according to the common Theological sense, saving that this black man, may as well proclaim it a wonder of God in the transmutation of Metals, which is figured in these Hieroglyphics, which he so attentively looks upon, as to see buried so many bodies, which shall rise again out of their Tombs at the fearful day of judgement. On the other part I do not think it needful to interpret in a Theological sense that vessel of Earth on the right hand of these figures, within the which there is a Pen and Inkhorn, or rather vessel of Phylosophy, if thou take away the strings, and join the Pen to the Inkhorne: nor the other two like it, which are on the two sides of the figures of Saint Peter, and Saint Paul, within one of the which, there is an N. which signifieth Nicholas, and within the other an F. which signifieth Flammel. For these vessels signify nothing else, but that in the like of them, I have done the Maistery three times. Moreover, he that will also believe that I have put these vessels in form of Scutchions to represent this Pen and Inkhorn, and the capital letters of my name, let him believe it if he will, because both these interpretations are true. Neither must you interpret in a Theological sense that writing which followeth, in these terms, NICHOLAS FLAMEL ET PERRENELLE SA FEMME, that is, Nicholas Flammel, and Perrenelle his wife, in as much as that signifieth nothing, but that I and my wife have given that Arch. As to the third, fourth, and fifth Tables following, by the sides whereof is written, COMMENT LES INNOCENTS FVRENTOCCIS PAR LE COMMANDEMENT DV ROY HERODES, that is How the Innocents were killed by the commandment of King Herod. The theological sense is well enough understood by the writing, we must only speak of the rest, which is above. The two Dragons united together to one within the other, of colour black and blue, in a field sable, that is to say, black, whereof the one hath the wings gilded, and the other hath none at all, are the sins which naturally are enserchayned, for the one hath his original and birth from another: Of them some may be easily chased away, as they come easily, for they fly towards us every hour; and those which have no wings can never be chased away, such as is the sin against the holy Ghost. The Gold which is in the wings signifieth that the greatest part of sins commeth from the unholy hunger after gold; which makes so many people diligently to harken from whence they may have it: and the colour black and blue showeth that these are the desires that come out of the dark pits of hell, which we ought wholly to fly from. These two Dragons may also morely represent unto us the Legions of evil spirits which are always about us, and which will accuse us, before the just judge, at the fearful day of Judgement, which do ask nor seek nothing else but to sist us. The man and the woman which are next them, of an orange colour, upon a field azure and blue, signify that men and women ought not to have their hope in this World, for the orange colour intimates dispair, or the letting go of hope, as here; and the colour azure and blue, upon they are painted, shows us that we must think of heavenly things to come, and say as the roule of the man doth, HOMO VENIET ADIVICIVM DEI, that is, Man must come to the judgement of God may show mercy unto us.Next after this in a field of Syneple, that is green, are painted two men and one woman rising again, of the which one comes out of a Sepulchre, the other two out of the Earth, all three of colour exceeding white and pure, lifting their hands towards their eyes, and their eyes towards Heaven on high: Above these three bodies there are two Angels sounding musical Instruments; as if they had called these dead to the day of Judgement; for over these two Angels is the figure of our Lord Jesus Christ, holding the world in his hand, upon whose head an Angel setteth a Crown, assisted by two others, which say in their roules, O pater Omnipotens, o'jesu bone, that is, O Father Almighty, O'good Jesu. On the right side of this Saviour is painted St. Paul, clothed with white & yellow, with a Sword, at whose feet there is a man clothed in a gown of orange colour, in which there appeared pleats or folds of black and white, (which picture resembleth me to the life) and demandeth pardon of his sins, holding his hands joined together, from between which proceed these words written in a roule, DE LE MALA QVE FECI, that is to say, Blot out the evils that I have done. On the other side on the left hand, is Saint Peter with his Key, clothed in reddish yellow, holding his hand upon a woman clad in a gown of orange colour, which is on her knees, representing to the life Perrenelle, which holdeth her hands joined together, having a roule where is written, CHRISTE PRECOR ESTO PIVS, that is, Christ I beseech thee be pitiful: Behind whom there is an

Angel on his knees, with a roule, that saith, SALVE DOMINE ANGELORVM, that is, All hail thou Lord of Angels. There is also another Angel on his knees, behind my Image, on the same side that St. Paul is on, which likewise holdeth a roule, saying, O REX SEMPITERNE, that is, O King everlasting. All this is so clear, according to the explication of the Resurrection and future judgement, that it may easily be fitted thereto. So it seems this Arch was not painted for any other purpose, but to represent this. And therefore we need not stay any longer upon it, considering that the least and most ignorant, may well know how to give this interpretation.Next after the three that are rising again, come two Angels more of an Orange colour upon a blue field, saying in the roules,

SVRGITE MORTVIVENITE AD IVDICIVM DOMINI MEI, that is, Arise you dead, come to the Judgement of my Lord. This also serves to the interpretation of the Resurrection: As also the last Figures following, which are, A man red vermillion, upon a field of Violet colour, who holdeth the foot of a winged Lion, painted of red vermillion also, opening his throat, as it were to devour the man : For one may say that this is the Figure of an unhappy sinner, who sleeping in a Lethargy of his corruption and vices, dieth without repentance and confession; who without doubt in this terrible Day shall be delivered to the Devil, here painted in form of a red roaring Lion, which will swallow and devour him.

Authors Note. What you have just read is Flamels description of the fresco he has had created for all to see. What is said here might be what you could figure by looking at it, not realizing that hidden is an alchemical process that makes it possible for you to make the stone: This is something as he said put out for all to see. He could do this safely as the common man could never interpret it and know him as an alchemist. Another alchemist could with some time see and understand what is hidden within. What we will now be doing is going through each part, and trying to show the hidden information. It may seem obscure to you in many ways but I have a way of showing what is said and explained is true. Throughout the ages many alchemists have hidden the same process in different ways, after you have spent time and understood what is said in one way, you can pretty much go through any of the others described and understand what is there. Remember it is from an understanding of nature and what happens to life during the yearly cycle. A seed comes to life with the warmth of the sun and water in the springtime, it grows matures produces fruit lives on and lastly dies and is recycled. The stone of the philosophers uses the same forces to be made as a seed to live, and has much in common with life and death and what is found with the process of reproduction found in your garden. Now you have seen the One Line drawing of this fresco, to show the hidden oven "Like that of the Philosophers" that Flamel said was there hidden. The outline is that of the pyramid, and it is necessary to look and truly understand it. As we progress with Osiris, by design we find within this oven, the equal four arm cross. We find the scales of October, and by addition of a centerline, the Tau and Tet crosses. The four arms cross at the base becomes the river with four heads mentioned in Genesis. It is how the oven feeds the substance. Also, as you proceed with all the information covered in this book, you will find ties to the ancient past. Ties to Egypt, and to Osiris. Those crosses found in the oven are all tied to movement of the sun. Tied to ancient holidays, tied even today to things we hold dear. Now, you will know where they eventually came from, and what it was they first meant and why they were conceived and used. Lastly, if you will compare the colors Flamel describes in his drawing, they are the same as those colors of the stone. They come and go as I have shown them on my serpent! They are the colors of the stone; they signify the changes that must be found to produce them correctly in the correct order. Remember that that the color changes was the only way one could know he is working right! If you put into your matters a force, and get the wrong color, you can never take it away! You must start again. Though it is a natural process, each condition is as specific as H20. Each color is found correctly only by the correct condition. If you do not know the correct condition, and submit your substance to a wrong condition, your work will be lost and there is no way to fix! You cannot remove any force that is put into the matter. I lost many times, but each time I found something. Even if at times it only meant what not to do next time. Those problems were mine to solve, and with this work, each should never again see them.

The interpretations Philosophical, according to the Maistery of Hermes.

I desire with all my heart that he who searcheth the secrets of the Sages, having in his Spirit passed over these Ideas of the life and resurrection to come, should first make his profit of them : And in the second place, that he be more advised than before, that he sound and search the depth of my Figures, colours, and rowles; principally of my rowles, because that in this Art they speak not vulgarly".

Authors Note, I never felt I fully understood the rowles, and so I am not great with the understanding. I do think it necessary to consider here the Idea of Life and Resurrection To come. All of what we do is about life, death and resurrection of the matters. As we progress you will find that is exactly what the stone was about originally in ancient Egypt. As you consider ancient Egypt, the stone was first. From it astrology could be connected and constellations named plus the definitions given. A religion was then developed from this find. The stone and the matters of the stone are connected to our matters after we die. As the matters the ancients worked on could be resurrected perfect, it was believed they had found how God could resurrect ours. Thus, Flamel speaks of his fresco in this way.

"Afterward let him ask of himself why the Figure of Saint Paul is on the right where it Is the place where the custom is to paint S. Peter? And on the other side that of Saint Peter, in the place of the figure of Saint Paul?"

Authors Note. I figured first this is because of importance in the work. The church was built mostly to St. Peter as he was the Rock. Also it has to do with the process. St Paul and the colors are linked to the white (lesser) stone, St. Peter the Red or the greater stone. Also, it is a way of instruction. What St Peter did on earth would be recognized in heaven, and it is Flamels way of telling you that the work that you had been doing on earth or the lower part of the oven now had to be done in heaven or in the upper part of the oven. Alchemically this is where it was described as 'turning the wheel again' or repeating work that was done in a similar fashion.

"Why the Figure of Saint Paul is clothed in colours white and yellow, and that of St. Peter in yellow and red?"

Authors Note: The colors are linked to the two stones and the colors of them at that part of the process. The white stone is a yellowish white when finished. St Peter is yellow as this is the time for the yellow sun, and is red as with time and process it becomes a dark purple red color. It is his way of showing the sun and substance in the last step are joined. This also shows the colors that you should see if you do it right.

"Why also the man and the woman which are at the feet of these two Saints praying to God, as if it were at the Day of Judgement, are apparelled in divers colours and not naked, or else nothing but bones, like them that are rising again? Why in this Day of Judgement they have painted this man and this woman at the feet of the Saints? For they ought to have been more low on earth, and not in heaven."

Authors note: The location is another way of showing where the work is to be done in the oven, because of the times of the year. In the colder months the work was done in the upper part where it was warmer. Remember, in the past they had no easy way to keep their oven warm. This is also shown by the cloths. The diverse colors of Flamel, (Orange black and white) show the color of the substance from start to the mercury stage, (nine months later). The Orange color of Parenella show the color of the Salamander at that stage of the process. Also note that Flamel said, In Heaven. This is his way of saying the oven- pyramid, can be called heaven. Also, as to location within the oven, above is working in heaven, below is working on earth! We work in heaven during the colder months. Also we work above when less moisture is wanted.

"Why also the two Angels in Orange colour, which say in their rowles, SVRGITE MORTVI, VENITE AD IVDICIVM DOMINI MEI, that is Arise you dead, come unto the Judgement of my Lord, are clad in this colour, and out of their place, for they ought be on high in heaven, with the two other which play upon the Instruments? Why they have a field Violet and blue? But principally why their roule, which speaks to the dead, ends in the open throat of the red and flying Lion?"

Authors note: The two angles and the orange color is Flamels way of showing the Salamander of alchemy. The work was done in the lower section of the oven, and after that color (orange) is achieved it is raised to the upper section. The violet and Blue has to do with the next color violet, and the blue is water. The two angles also represent the two lights, sun and moon that had been doing the work in the below section for the salamander. There are two stones that can be made. One is always finished by only the moon. These colors are of the Red Stone, and his description now is about only the materials that is going to be of the Red Stone. To come to the judgement, remember we would now be moving toward the last step of the process where the work becomes a work of the sun. The roule ends in the throat of the red roaring lion to show what is started by the last step continues till the finish. It has to do with the three, two ratio I mention. This covers the last four months of the seven. You will understand the seven and the division of three and four as we go on. Also, when reading Osiris, when the substance is moved to heaven, the upper part of the oven, it is the same as Osiris going to heaven in process for the last four months. There he and the substance join with God, or that Good part of the light which is in the sun. Osiris becomes a God, the matters become the red stone. When Osiris is at this stage, he is said to be swallowing the Eye of Horus. In other words, he is directly now with the light, (sun only). The best way to show this understanding is too look at the eye of God over the pyramid on the back of a U. S. Dollar Bill. This is a very old symbol, and this is what that symbol is about. Osiris had to become three persons in one to become a God. He becomes male and female in the previous three months of work, and so now by uniting, he becomes male & female, God!

"I would then that after these, and many other questions which may justly be made, opening wide the eyes of his spirit , come to conclude, that all this not having been done without cause there must be represented under this bark, some great secrets, which he ought to pray God to discover unto him. Having then brought his belief by degrees to this pass wish also that he would further believe, that these figures and explications are not made for them that have never seen the Books of the Philosophers, and who not knowing the Metallic principles, cannot be named Children of this Science; for if they think to understand perfectly these figures, being ignorant of the first Agent, they will undoubtedly deceive themselves, and never be able to know any thing at all."

Authors note: Metallic Principles here has led many astray from the truth of alchemy. The sun is the seed for Gold. The moon is the seed for silver. These are the metallic principles he is pointing to. Note also he said the books of the philosophers. In another place he mentions the oven of the philosophers. Please consider he is not speaking of the ovens or books commonly used by the many looking for the stone. When Flamel mentions the First Agent, I believe he is pointing to first matter. First matter is the first matter ever made. That is the special combination of light, and vapor in the creation. That substance some alchemists called earth. That substance is the substance we must collect many times.

We can only collect it with this first Agent. The first Agent is the base we made, and this first matter we collect. They together make our first earth. Now the earth made in the creation one must consider, is less pure than the stone we are going to make. However, we made our stone exactly as it was believed God made the earth in the creation process.

"Let no man therefore blame me, if he do not easily understand me, for he will be more blame-worthy than I, inasmuch as not being initiated into these sacred and secret interpretations of the first Agent, (which is the key opening the gates of all Sciences) he would notwithstanding, comprehend the most subtle conceptions of the envious Philosophers, which are not written but for them who already know these principles, which are never found in any book, because they leave them unto God, who revealeth them to whom he please, or else causeth them to be taught by the living voice of a Maister, by Cabalistical tradition, which happeneth very seldom."

"Now then, my Son, let me so call thee, both because I am now come to a great age, and also for that, it may be, thou art otherwise a child of this knowledge, (God enable thee to learn, and after to work to his glory). Hearken unto me then attentively, but pass no further if thou be ignorant of the foresaid Principles."

Authors note: Again, the foresaid Principles It is so important to know he speaks of the sun and moon. It is more than just that, as we proceed and you learn more and more, it will become very plain they are the principles of which he speaks. If you do not know this one thing never will you find the stone. Also, the first agent. I use and egg. Flamel is colored in Orange, black and white. What is Orange? Whatever it is the first substance has to be of an orange color! The stone is made from a substance that is first orange in color. What is the color of the yolk of an egg? This is the only place in the alchemical texts where orange is mentioned, and I feel a way of Flamel to tell us something of the original substance.

"This Vessel of earth, in this form, is called by the Philosophers, their triple Vessel, for within it there is in the middest a Stage, or a floor, and upon that a dish or a platter full of lukewarm ashes, within which is set the Philosophical Egg, that is, a vial of glass full of confections of Art (as of the feumme of the red sea, and the fat of the mercurial wind) which thou see painted in form of a Penner and Inkehorn. Now this Vessel of earth is open above to put in the dish and the vial, under which by the open gate, is put in the Philosophical fire, as thou knowest. So thou hast three vessels; and the threefold vessel: The envious have called an Athanor, a fiue, dung, Balneum Marie, a Furnace, a Sphere, the greene Lion, a prison, a grave, a urinal, a phioll, and a Bolts-head : I myself in my Summary or Abridgement of Philosophy, which I composed four years and two months past, in the end thereof named it the house and habitation of the Poulet, and the ashes of the Platter, the chaffe of the Poulet."

Authors note: Many can argue about what is said here, but he uses the term ashes of the poulet. This is a chick! The vessel of earth alchemically is a vessel of water. The stager or floor is the lower section of the oven where we place the egg which is a vial full of confections. The section below the egg is a place to store your water for the never ending fountain! Note he said of Art. Which means a substance by art we will change. The pen and inkhorn is another way of saying pen equal sun, inkhorn equal the egg. I will show as we go on, any pointed object was always used to indicate sun! This comes from Obelisk and what is behind the understanding of it. When Flamel said "in the midst there is a stage" he means the upper section for work. The floor is the lower section for work, a play again with words. He also said that it "was open above" to put in the philosophical fire! Now, what kind of fire can one put in from the top of an oven? One cannot, except he uses the sun as the source of the fire! So, we have orange color, ashes of poulet, wings from mercury, and, vessel of Earth. The heaven and earth were created? The heaven is the vessel, the earth the moistures within the vessel, from Genesis.

"The common name is an Oven, which I should never have found, if Abraham the Jew had not painted it, together with the fire proportionable, wherein consists a great part of the secret."

Authors note: I show this with the side view of the mountain and the top view plates 2 and 4 of Abraham. Note the sun is at the side of the second plate, and is the time when it becomes a work of the sun. But, this is the second use of that plate when it is actually plate 9 of 10. This overlap we will discuss in other places.

"For it is as it were the belly, or the womb, containing the true natural heat to animate our young King If this fire be not measured Clibanically, saith Calid the Persian, son of Iasichus; If it be kindled with a sword, saith Pithagoras; If thou fire thy Vessel, saith Morien, and maketh it feel the heat of the fire, it will give thee a box on the care, and burn his flowers before they be risen from the depth of his Marrow, making them come out red, rather than white, and then thy work is spoiled ; as also if thou make too little fire, for then thou shalt never see the end, because of the coldness of the natures, which shall not have had motion sufficient to digest them together.The heat then of thy fire in this vessel, shall be (as saith Hermes and Rofinus) according to the Winter; or rather, as saith Diomedes, according to the heat of a Bird, which begins to fly so softly from the sign of Aries to that of Cancer : for know that the Infant at the beginning is full of cold phlegm and of milk, and that too vehement heat is an enemy of the cold and moisture of our Embrion, and that the two enemies, that is to say, our two elements of cold and heat will never perfectly embrace one another, but by little and little, having first long dwelt together, in the middest of the temperate heat of their bath, and being changed by long decoction, into Sulphur incombustible". Govern therefore sweetly with equality and proportion, thy proud and haughty natures, for fear lest if thou favour one more than another, they which naturally are enemies, do grow angry against thee through jealousy, and dry Choller, and make thee sigh for it a long time after. Besides this, thou must entertain them in this temperate heat perpetually, that is to say, night and day until the time that Winter, the time of the moisture of the matters, be passed; because they make their peace, and join hands in being heated together, whereas should these natures find themselves but one only half hour without fire, they would become for ever irreconcilable." See therefore the reason why it is said in the Book of the seventy precepts: Look that their heat continue indefatigably without ceasing, and that none of their days be forgotten. And Rafis, the haste, saith he, that brings with it too much fire, is always followed by the Diuell, and Error. When the golden Bird, saith Diomedes, shall become just to Cancer, and that from thence it shall run toward Libra, then thou mayst augment the fire a little. And in like manner, when this faire Bird, shall fly from Libra towards Capricorn, which is the desired Autumn, the time of harvest, and of the fruits that are now ripe."

Author's Note: First, Flamel mentions several parts of the process in these last couple of paragraphs. This is how they hide the work Never do the speak of the first step always with the first paragraph lets say. Yes in the first step we must keep the chick warm and remembering it is cold outside. Also it is out of the light. Not enough heat and it doesn't work, too much and you burn it! Like a birds nest is the best description, and you already have the length of time. You have to know the process. If you know the times as I have shown them, and know what is happening outside then you understand all these little comments he is making. Time, heat, constellations, substance all work together. Know the terms. Mercury is always used in many places, it is the substance, but it is not true mercury until it is Septembers Child finished by the drying of the androgyny in Virgo. Mercury also denotes and is connected to the moon. As above, when he mentions sulfurous he is linking it to the sun and so consider the time and what is happening. He mentions the time and that the chick must always be watched. If it gets cold, if it gets dry, too hot, all is lost! It is art, and it is a lot of work. I have lost so many times. Several just because I didn't consider the wind, and it blew my oven away!! It is made of glass, and doesn't have to fall very far to be smashed. I will tell you right now, the first step is the hardest. Just keep it warm and in the dark! I fail five out of six times. I still have yet to figure why. Note above the astrological sign he mentions, many are used and so they show the passing of the time. 16 months to the process as you will see as we proceed. The first tablet is the start in December, as it is also tablet 8, that shows the process is over a year long. Always compare to Genesis. Always compare to Nature, always compare to the life of a seed. The all which is outside is just that, outside. It is more than day or night, nice day or raining. It is everything taken into consideration as it happens throughout the year. It is like the compost pile, but it is taken further by art. Nature and man together can do more than nature can take it by herself. It is more than the man can do without nature.

Chapter III

The two Dragons of colour yellowish, blue, and black like the field.

Look well upon these two Dragons, for they are the true principles or beginnings of this Philosophy, which the Sages have not dared to show to their own Children. He which is undermost, without wings, he is the fixed, or the male; that which is uppermost, is the volatile, or the female, black and obscure, which goes about to get the domination for many months. The first is called Sulphur or heat and dryness and the latter Argent vive or cold and moisture. These are the Sun and Moon of the Mercurial source and sulphurous original which by continual fire are adorned with royal habiliments that being united and afterward changed into a quintessence, they may overcome every thing Metallic, how solid hard and strong, soever it be."

Authors Note: Please Note we have two dragons, one with wings, and the color blue. The color blue is water, the two dragons is the lights sun and moon as Flamel said. Note they are the source for mercury. Compare to Genesis, and to the tablets of Abraham. What we had in Genesis is earth and light created. In Abraham we had mercury with the two entwined serpents. That is understood as the two lights and water. He that goes about is fixed, but not at this step, he is called sulfur (the sun).

Female is tied to black (darkness or moon). We see the same mentioned battle, "to get dominance" and all it means is there is two stones that can be made, by either of the lights and depends on you the alchemist as to which succeeds. In nature neither gets dominant as they are always equal! In the process we will end with one or the other for which finish we choose. Note he said "colour yellowish, blue, and black like the field!" The field will become these colors when the first part is done right, and is the rainbow of alchemy. I show these colors in my pictures.

These are the Serpents and Dragons which the ancient Egyptians have painted in a circle. The head biting the tail to signify that they proceeded from one and the same thing and that it alone was sufficient, and that in the turning and circulation thereof, it made it self perfect.

Authors Note: By circulation it made itself perfect over time. "That it alone was sufficient." This is just as in the Emerald Tablet where it said, "it is a work of the sun." It is just a process of matter and nature repeated in a special way over long periods of time. Now he mentions the Egyptians painting these serpents in connection with the tomb. I have found and included that on the Tomb of Osiris the Ouroborous was painted, which is a serpent biting its tail. The serpent was there until Osiris was reborn as new birth baby in September. Now as I am showing the matters are recycled using the sun and moon, which are the two serpents, and as Flamel is pointing that out by saying the two represent this Ouroborous. That whatever they are, they were all that was needed to make itself perfect. Note also that he said it would overcome everything metallic! Or, this matter becomes the matter that can change a metal!

"These are the Dragons which the ancient Poets have fained did without sleeping keep & watch the golden Apples of the Gardens of the Virgins Hesperides. These are they upon whom Jason in his adventure for the Golden Fleece, powred the broth or liquor prepared by the fair Medea, of the discourse of whom the Books of the Philosophers are so full, that there is no philosopher that ever was, but he hath written of it, from the time of the truth-telling hermes Trismegistus, Orpheus, Morienus, and the other following, even unto myself."

"These are the two serpents, given and sent by Juno, (that is the nature metallic) the which the strong Hercules, that is to say, the sage and wise man must strangle in his cradle, that is, overcome and kill them, to make them putrify, corrupt and ingender at the beginning of his work. These are the two serpents, wrapped and twisted round about the caduceus or rod of mercury, with the which he exerciseth his great power, and transformeth himself as he lifteth. He, saith Haly, that shall kill the one, shall also kill the other, because the one cannot die, but with his brother."

Authors note: he mentions both the lights, and the two substances within the egg. First they must die and return to pure water and a base. Please note as we proceed how so much of the past mythology has been tied to alchemy. It is mans history, it is us you might say and mankind should know and understand this process to know our past and ourselves. The mythology was their way of expressing a truth in a hidden fashion. Here, in this first step we must kill and destroy the matters within the oven, so that we can remake them into something perfect. We turn them into a base matter that nature can remake into the perfect substance. All alchemists look for this base matter. Nature cannot work with a base matter made by man and so only a natural base matter will do. Whatever is made from the destroyed matter, it is a substance that nature can remake. Remember it has no seed after the destruction, and so whatever it is to become is only from the lights. The sun is the seed for gold? In time you will understand that is the seed we will put back into the matters as they are changed and recycled.

"These two then, (which Auicen calleth the Corassene bitch and the Armenian dog) these two I say, being put together in the vessel of the Sepulcher, do bite one another cruelly, and by their great poison, and furious rage, they never leave one another. from the moment that they have seized on one another (if the cold hinder them not) till both of them by their slavering venom and mortal hurts, all of a goare bloud, over all the parts of their bodies; and finally, killing one another, be stewed in their proper venom, which after their death, changeth them into living and permanent water; before which time, they loose in their corruption and putrifaction, their first natural forms, to take afterwards one only new, more noble, and better form. These are the two Spermes, masculine and feminine, described at the beginning of my Abridgment of Philosophy, which are engendred (say Rafis, Auicen, and Abraham the Jew) within the Reynes, and entrails, and of the operations of the four Elements."

Authors note: This now should be easily understood as the matters are put at the base of the oven and kept warm, also sealed. As it said in Genesis, the below waters are to be divided! That is exactly what it means, and so the oven is placed in darkness, divided from the light, and completely sealed so that no foreign substance can get into it. Notice how he mentions the first part, but also (loss of first natural forms to later take on a new form) two parts of the process that by time are many months apart (from death to life). Also, nature metallic, important to connect as they become of or of a metallic nature. This means they will effect or work with a metal. And last here, "operations of the four elements!" They are again, earth, air, fire and water. This points to how we work, and what we work with which is what is found outside.

"These are the radical moisture of metals, Sulphur and Argent Vive not vulgar, and such as are sold by the Merchants and Apothecaries, but those which give us those two fair and dear bodies which we love so much. These two spermes, saith Democritus, are not found upon the earth of the living: The same, saith Auicen, but he addeth, that they gather them from the dung, ordure, and rotteness of the Sun and Moon. O happy are they that know how to gather them; for of them they afterwards make a triacle, which hath power over all griefs, maladies, sorrows, infirmities, and weaknesses, and which fighteth puissantly against death, lengthening the life, according to the permission of God, even to the time determined, triumphing over the miseries of this world, and filling a man with the riches thereof."

Authors note: The Treacle is the below mixed with the above to produce the combination which is the third thing. Is this the medicine that will cure all ills? Not found among the earth of the living, or back to the rotting death process of matter. Also not found (not the vulgar kind) at any corner store, not found in a place where they could be bought.

"Of these two Dragons or Principles Metallic, I have said in my fore-alledged Summary, that the Enemy would by his heat inflame his enemy, and that then if they take not heed, they should see in the air a venomous fume and a stinking, work in flame, and in poison, than the envenomed head of a Serpent, and Babylonian Dragon. The cause why I have painted these two spermes in the form of Dragons, is because their stench is exceeding great, and like the stench of them, and the exhalations which arise within the glass, are dark, black, blue, and yellowish (like as these two Dragons are painted) the force of which, and of the bodies dissolved, is so venomous, that truly there is not in the world a ranker poison; for it is able by the force and stench thereof, to mortify and kill everything living. The Philosopher never feels this stench, if he break not his vessels, but only he judgeth it to be such, by the sight, and the changing of colours, proceeding from the rottenness of his confections."

Authors note: Finding black in nature is easy, always it is where there is no light and air! Below rotten bark of a fallen tree, below the compost pile, etc. Also where there is little oxygen. This in part is where the stench comes into play, not just the darkness but the rotting process and the warmth. In the past a man had no way of saying how rotten a thing was, and so he went by the smell! I will give a quote from Idaramled in this work that shows this. I still wonder how they sealed their ovens, but, it is not totally sealed as with mine. They have to leak the gas or the pressure buildup would blow the oven. This first step is really a terrible smell as bad or worse than anything anyone has smelled, and it goes on for several months. Flamel said he "knew it by the smell." How could he have if he had not been around it before? Answer, something about the smell, and if you do this process then you also will know as it is the smell you will never forget or find in another place. From the past, and Adiramled, "in the past a thing was known as to how rotten it was by the smell." As I said, the ways of the past need to be known. I leave the spelling as it was done by Flamel. Note also above he mentions principles metallic. And so again a reference that these two dragons, whatever they are, they provide what is needed for the metallic principles.

"These colours then signify the putrifaction and generation which is given us, by the biting and dissolution of our perfect bodies, which dissolution proceedeth from external heat adding, and from the Pontique fierieness, and admirable sharp vertue of the poison of our Mercury, which maketh and resolveth into a pure cloud, that is, into impalpable powder, all that which it finds to resist it. So the heat working upon and against the radical, metallic, viscous, or oily moisture, ingendereth upon the subject, blackness. For at the same time the Matter is dissolved, is corrupted, groweth black, and conceiveth to ingender; for all corruption is generation, and therefore ought blackness to be much disired; for that is the black sail with the which the Ship of Theseus came back victorious from Crete, which was the cause of the death of his Father; so must this father die, to the intent, that from the ashes of this Phoenix another may spring, and that the son may be King."

"Assuredly he that seeth not this blackness at the beginning of his operations, during the days of the Stone; what other colour soever he see, he shall altogether fail in the Maistery, and can do no more with that Chaos: for he works not well, if he putrify not; because if he do not putrify, he doeth not corrupt, nor ingender, and by consequence, the Stone cannot take vegetative life to increase and multiply."

Authors note: "The dissolution of four bodies," remember that part is the lights above which you separate. The waters below will be separated. Also note external heat that must be added by you. Now I will tell you this, it is easy enough to get the black of the yolk of the egg, but you must get a black that when the waters come back together you will find a rainbow. That is not easy to do and so it may just take you a time or two to get it right. If you do not find this rainbow, your work is no good! Throw it away, and start again. The rainbow is a series of colors of the bath, first it is a lime green for a day, then a sky blue for a day, finally a banana yellow for a day and then it clears up. This death is also the same death as that mentioned in the tablets of Abraham as the slaughter of the Innocence. More on that as we proceed. All I can tell you about this first step is that it is very hard to accomplish right. Everything has to be right. The warmth, the oven size, the egg size, if not all the proper ratio, it will produce a beautiful black egg, but not the rainbow.

"And in all truth, I tell thee again, that though thou work upon the true matter, if at the beginning, after thou hast put they Confections in the Philosophers Egg, that is to say, sometime after the fire have stirred them up, if then, I say, thou seest not this head of the Crow, the black of the blackest black, thou must begin again, for this fault is irreparable, and not to be amended; especially the Orange colour, or half red, is to be feared, for if at the beginning thou see that in thine Egg, without doubt, thou burnest, or hast burnt the verdure and jueliness of thy Stone. The colour which thou must have, ought to be intirely perfected in Blackness, like to that of these Dragons in the space of forty days: Let them therefore which shall not have these essential marks, retire themselves betimes from their operations, that they may redeem themselves from assured loss. Know also, and note it well, that in this Art it is but nothing to have this blackness, there is nothing more easy to come by: for from almost all things in the world, mixed with moisture, thou mayest have a blackness by the fire: but thou must have a blackness which comes from the perfect Metallic bodies, which lasts a long space of time, and is not destroyed in less than five months."

Authors Note: He mentions 40 days. This is just an allegory used in many places in the past and means nothing other than a time period. He is correct when he lastly say's five months, as if you count from the start to the May Day it is five months. I am still working on, "and not to be amended," as this would indicate that if your not entirely correct it is Ok as it can be worked out as you proceed. I have not as yet found this to be true. Each step is produced by those conditions you supply to the substance. As soon as you change the conditions, the process goes in another direction. If it is not correct when you change the conditions, it *cannot* go correctly to the next step. Never forget this. Each step has to be correct *exactly*!

What you put into the substance, can never be taken out!

"after the which followeth immediately the desired whiteness. If thou hast this, thou hast enough, but not all. As for the colour blueish and yellowish, that signifieth that Solution and Putrefaction is not yet finished, and that the colours of our Mercury are not as yet well mingled, and rotten with the rest. Then this blackness, and these colours, teach plainly, that in this beginning the matter, and compound begins to rot and dissolve into powder, less than the Atoms of the Sun, the which afterwards are changed into coator permanent. And this dissolution is by the envious Philosophers called Death, Destruction, and Perdition, because that the natures change their form, and from hence are proceeded so many Allegories of dead men, tombs and sepulchres. Others have called it Calcinatin, Denudation, Separation, Erituration, and Assation, because the Confections are changed and reduced into most small pieces and parts. Others have called it Reduction into the first matter, Mollification, Extraction, Commixtion, Liquefaction, Conversion of Elements, Subtiliation, Division, Humation, Impastation, and Distiliation, because that the Confections are melted, brought back into seed, softened, and circulated within the glass.

Others have called it Xir, or Iris, Putrefaction , Corruption, Cymmerian darkness, a gulf, Hell, Dragons, Generation, Ingression, Submersion, Completion, Conjunction, and Impregnation, because that the matter is black and waterish, and that the natures are prefectly mingled, and hold one of another. For when the heat of the Sun worketh upon them, they are changed, first into powder, or fat and glutinous water, which feeling the heat, flyeth on high to the poulets head, with the smoke, that is to say, with the wind and air; for thence this water melted, and drawn out of the confections, goeth down again, and in descending reduceth, and resolveth, as much as it can, the rest of the Aromatical confections, always doing so, until the whole be like a black broth somewhat fat. Now you see why they call this sublimation and volatization, because it flyeth on high, and Ascension and Descension, because it mounteth and descendeth within the glass. A while after, the water beginneth to thicken and coagulate somewhat more, growing very black, like unto pitch, and finally comes the body and earth, which the envious have called Terra Foetida, that is, stinking earth: for then because of the perfect putrefaction, which is as natural as any other can be, this earth stinks, and gives a smell like the odour of graves filled with rottenness, and with bodies as yet charged with their natural moisture. This earth was by Hermes called Terra foliata, or the Earth of leaves, yet his true and proper name is Leton, which must afterward be whitened. The Ancient Sages that were Cabalists, have described it in their Metamorphoses, under the History of the Serpent of Mars, which had devoured the companions of Cadmus, who slew him, piercing him with his lance against a hollow oak. Note this. oak.

Authors note: See how he talks of several steps in one step? He said "after the which followeth immediately the desired whiteness." This is not true as he said it, but as you read on "yet his true and proper name is Leton, which must afterward be whitened." Which takes three hot months, and then the drying of the androgynyn in moonlight. Then with Septembers Child we have the white mercury. The hallow Oak Is the shell. It is very light when finished and most moisture has been removed. See in Abraham where he said "consider the weight." with the third tablet. This had to do with the water they had and searched for. It can be found when you consider the weight of the egg as the water is removed from it. This is a good overview of the first steps of the process, it does stink as a grave, very bad.

He mentions the moisture, as nothing can rot if it is dried up and so they are needed. Leton is about the drying in moonlight only. That is how it is whitened. It stays a sort of greenish color all summer, and it will be a surprise to you when you dry in moonlight and it turns a beautiful white. It is so white in the shell which is bleached out perfectly white, it almost can't bee seen. Now Flamel said, "that if though has this you have enough, but not all." I can only say that what you have is a white substance, when dried is hard, and so it is ground up to a powder for the next steps! This is now the mercury of the philosophers. What I understand him to mean is this is a substance that they felt had the possibilities of all things. This I figured they believed because it is the only base for the stone, and they have the possibilities of make changes in metal and yourself medically. What this white substance has become remains to be seen by some chemists in the near future. You know what it was, and you know we worked on it for nine months. It is a pure substance now, a pure base matter. What it is and what it would do by itself I can't say. I know that what I produce within the oven, becomes a very pure matter.

From this point, I am more selective with the lights and light brought to it. The point is this matter is going to become a different substance made by light and vapor with the mercury? What is it? I can't say. I said that when I originally considered alchemy, I felt if there was any truth to it, then it had to be about something we as a society had missed, something we don't know about. Well, I can't read about what I am doing, and with what I do know, I don't know what really this substance is becoming. I understand it as far as an alchemical understanding, but what chemically remains to be seen. My red stone that I finish with the sun, will be like the sun, that is all I can say. The white that I finish with the moon, will be like the moon. The matters change from an organic rotten mess to a type of substance that grows from that matter with vapor and light. The ancients believed it was the light above, condensed below. I tend to agree with that statement, and I know not what it becomes. They said that it perfects what it touches, something...some change is there. I have looked everywhere, but nowhere can I read about a similar process.

CHAPTER IV

Of the man and the woman clothed in a gown of Orange colour upon a field azure and blue, and of their rowles.

"The man painted here doth expressly resemble myself to the natural, as the woman doth lively figure Perrenelle. The cause why we are painted to the life, is not particular to this purpose for it needed but to represent a male and a female, to the which our two particular resemblance was not necessarily required, but it pleased the Painter to put us there, just as he hath done higher in this Arch, at the feet of the Figure of Saint Paul and Saint Peter, according to that we were in our youth; as he hath likewise done in other places, as over the door of the Chapel of Saint James in the Bouchery near to my house (although that for this last there is a particular cause) as also over the door of Saincte Geneviesue des Ardans, where thou mayst see me. I made then to be painted here two bodies, one of a Male, and another of a Female, to teach thee that in this second operation, thou hast truely, but yet not perfectly, two natures conjoined and married together, the Masculine and the Feminine, or rather the four Elements; and that the four natural enemies, the hot and cold, dry and moist, begin to approach amiably one towards another, and by means of the Mediators and Peace-makers, lay down by little and little, the ancient enmity of the old Chaos."

60

Authors Note: This is the start and of the second step which is where we bring together the all. This is the start alchemically of the May-Day. Always by most alchemists it is about a sexes state, male and female. The above is male and female, sun and moon. The below is also male and female, the black substance and the water that is to circulate and mix with the above to carry it below. This step is shown by a deer and a unicorn in other series allegories, a lion and a female lion also has been used, a king and queen, two things showing male and female? These elements are married together, but not before spending three more months of work in these different conditions. Before we divided away everything and it was dark, now we set right out in the light with a vented oven. Still keep warm! This May-Day is to us spring, and the great force of nature seen as a bull coming to our matters within the oven to change them. We have here death! But we are taking it now toward Life!

"Thou knowest well enough who these Mediators and Peace-makers are, between the hot and the cold there is moisture, for he is kinsman and allied to them both; to hot by his heat, and to cold by his moisture: And this is the reason, why to begin to make this peace, thou hast already in the precedent operation, converted all the confections into water by dissolution. And afterward thou hast made to coagulate the water, which is turned into this Earth, black of the black most black, wholly to accomplish this peace; for the Earth, which is cold and dry, finding himself of kindred and alliance with the dry and moist, which are enemies, will wholly appease and accord them."

Authors Note: We separated the water from the egg, time and darkness, warmth and shape have changed the matters. We made a natural base by nature. We have returned the substance to what it was in the creation start. Now we bring it back to the black substance we made. It joins with the above by the circulation. When reading and considering Osiris, the black substance is Osiris in his tomb, taken apart and being reassembled with time.

"Doest thou not then consider a most perfect mixture of all the four Elements, having first turned them to water, and now into Earth? I will also teach thee hereafter the other conversions, into air when it shall be all white, and into fire, when it shall be of a most perfect purple. Then thou hast here two natures married together, whereof the one hath conceived by the other, and by this conception it is turned into the body of the Male, and the Male into that of the Female. That is to say, they are made one only body, which is the Androgyne or hermaphrodite of the Ancients, which they have also called otherwise the head of the Crow, or natures converted."

Authors Note: This is the First androgyny made! This is also in the mythology of Osiris and also, we will later make another crowned androgynyn. Turning the elements into earth is from the below absorbing the above. Consider Genesis. The head of the crow is from the black we made. We will again see black imparts called 'The return of the Crow.' Ill explain it when it is the right time. The natures aren't converted until the three months have passed. He said, "Conversions into Air." This is when we dry in moonlight at the upper work place of the oven and with further process, when we join to the above, substance and light. This also in allegory is seen as a toad suckling the breast of a woman.

The woman is the Isis moon, and the female constellation Virgo!

"In this fashion I paint them here, because thou hast two natures reconciled, which (if they be guided and governed wisely) can form an Embrion in the womb of the Vessel, and afterwards bring forth a most puissant King, invincible and incorruptible, because it will be an admirable quintessence. Thus thou seest the principal and most necessary reason of this representation: The second cause, which is also well to be noted, was because I must of necessity paint two bodies, because in this operation it behoveth that thou divide that which hath been coagulated, to give afterwards nourishment, which is milk of life, to the little Infant when it is born, which is endued, by the living God, with a vegetable soul.

This is a secret most admirable and secret, which for want of understanding, it hath made fools of all those that have sought it without finding it, and hath made every man wise that beholds it with the eyes of his body, or of his spirit."

Authors Note: To divide that which was coagulated is the water we collected now we must circulate. The Embrion in the womb of the vessel is so named I feel to reflect 'Septembers Child.' The alchemical term and the term connected to Osiris as new born babe, which becomes the dried white substance. Also, the womb of the vessel tells you the work is now again moved to the base of the oven, and not in air as the step just finished. This though will happen when finishing the Red Stone. Also, the white is finished above, consider like. Like means the below substances must become like the above, and it is done in air or in the above part of the oven. In Heaven is another description. For the most part, Flamel and other alchemists are always speaking of the red stone, few it seems worked for white!

"Thou must then make two parts and portions of this Coagulated body, the one of which shall serve for Azoth, to wash and cleanse the other, which is called Letch, which must be whitened: He which is washed is the Serpent Python, which, having taken his being from the corruption of the slime of the earth gathered together by the waters of the deluge, when all the confections were water, must be killed and overcome by the arrows of the God Apollo, by the yellow Sun, that is to say, by our fire, equal to that of the Sun."

Authors Note: The two parts again is the water divided into vapor, part always remaining below, part always raising again to absorb the above to take below. Here the below is still connected to the serpent. The arrows here is another way to show sun, as it is indicated by any pointed object in alchemy. As said by the alchemists. This concerns the red stone only. This would be starting October, and the start of the crowned androgynyn. Note at that time, October, we already made androgyny. Crowned Androgynyn is a step above plain androgyny. It is where Osiris become both male and female of the earth. Two of the three persons he needs to become so that he when further augmented by the sun, he is three in one, or as God!

"He which washeth, or rather the washings which must be continued with the other moity; these are the teeth of that Serpent, which the sage workman, the valiant Theseus, will sow in the same Earth, from whence there shall spring up armed Soldiers, which shall in the end discomfit themselves, suffering themselves by opposition to resolve into the same nature of the Earth, and the workman to bear away his deserved conquests."

Authors Note: This is about capturing the sunlight or see it as many sharp pointed objects streaming down into the oven. Here he is referring to the last part of the process, the last four months where sun and substance are joined.

"It is of this that the Philosophers have written so often, and so often repeated it. It dissolves itself, it congeals itself, it makes itself black, it makes itself white, it kills itself, and it quickens itself. I have made their field be painted azure and blue, to show that I do but now begin to get out from the most black blackness, for the azure and blue is one of the first colours, that the dark woman lets us see, that is to say, moisture giving place a little to heat and dryness: The man and woman are almost all orange-coloured, to show that our Bodies, or our body which the wise men here call Rebis, hath not as yet digestion enough and that the moisture from whence comes the black blue and azure, is but half vanquished by the dryness."

Authors Note: An overall of what your doing. The blue you can see as it is water within the oven, you can't see the matters as they are within the shell. It is supposed to be within always, and don't look and let the sun shine on them! You can and need to look at times and to clean very carefully. Here Flamel speaks of the process from several times and from several stages. You need to understand each step, to understand Flamel. Now the orange color is the color of the substance after it has started to absorb the above. This is with the start again in October or conjunction. Here it is known as salamander, and is because of the same color. It first goes black and white, this is the returned crows. it then turns an orange color. This is the Salamander of Alchemy in the fire. It is exactly orange, as an orange you eat. However, you wont see this orange unless you break up the substance, as it is a white color on the outside. I don't know why, only that it has to do with the light.

"For when dryness bears rule, all will be white, and when it fighteth with, or is equal to the moisture, all will be in part according to these present colours. The envious have also called these confections in this operation, Nummus, Ethelia, Arena, Boritis, Corfufle, Cambar, Albar aris, Duenech, Randeric, Kukul, Thabricis, Ebisemech, Ixir, &c which they have commanded to make white. The woman hath a white circle in form of a rowle round about her body, to show thee that Rebis will begin to become white in that very fashion, beginning first at the extremities, round about this white circle. Scala Phylosophoru, that is the Book entitled The Philosophers Ladder, saith thus: The figure of the first perfect whiteness is the manifestation of a certain little circle of hair, that is passing over the head, which will appear on the sides of the vessels round about the matter, in a kind of a cierine or yellowish colour."

Authors Note: When we dry it ends up the perfect white he is speaking of, but this is not till September under the constellation of Virgo. As it is done in moonlight only, it is hard to see and describe as how he is. It turns white! The citrine or yellowish is later with the forming of the white stone. This is not the white stone, but mercury that is formed in September. This is mixing different parts of the process to confuse those that don't know it. He does this in many places, and I think now I have pointed it out enough.

"There is written in their Rowles, Home veniet ad judicium Dei, that is, Man shall come to the judgement of God : Vere (saith the woman) illa dies terribilis erit, that is, Truly that will be a terrible day. These are not passages of holy Scripture, but only sayings which speak according to the Theological sense, of the judgement to come. I have put them there to serve myself of them towards him, that beholds only the gross outward and most natural Artifice, taking the interpretation thereof to concern only the Resurrection, and also it may serve for them that gathering together the Parables of the Science, take to them the eyes of Lynceus, to pierce deeper then the visible objects. There is then, Man shall come to the judgement of God: Certainly that day shall be terrible. That is as if I should have said; It behoves that this come to the colour of perfection, to be judged and cleansed from all his blackness and filth, and to be spiritualized and whitened. Surely that day will be terrible, yet certainly, as you shall find in the Allegory of Aristeau, Horror holds us in prison by the space of four-score days, in the darkness of the waters, in the extreme heat of the Summer, and in the troubles of the Sea. All which things ought first to pass before our King can become white, coming from death to life, to overcome afterwards all his enemies. To make thee understand yet somewhat better this Albification, which is harder and more difficult than all the rest, for till that time thou mayest err at every step, but afterwards thou canst not, except thou break thy vessels, I have also made for thee this Table following."

Authors note: Again here Flamel will skip around with discussion of several parts of the process. In the first picture here we saw the two dragons. We refer it to Genesis, or too the two serpents of Abraham above. The orange body is the water within the egg. In Flamels work he mentions why he used Parenella, and about her hair being all disheveled. This is the unicorn, and the stag. Paranella is the stag (consider horns). When you totally understand the process, and it's steps come back and read this and you will see many things. He finishes again above with an overview of the first 9 months of work, which, is not hard except that it has to be understood to know. All that matters is that you get the rainbow at first. It will not then fail if it is maintained. As to breaking your vessel. Your always working with an egg shell. It is very easy to break it, I know sadly from experience. You may read all the different mythology he mentions, but it won't help until you learn the steps. Or, as I did you can spend 30 years. That way, they will say things to you, not much before. Always the judgment, it is my opinion that this somehow was said and pointed to so that eventually you would find Osiris and what he was about. All of Osiris is about the judgment, death and resurrection.

CHAPTER V

"The figure of a man, like that of Saint Paul, clothed with a robe white and yellow, bordered with gold, holding a naked sword, having at his feet a man on his knees, clad in a robe of orange colour, black and white, holding a roule".

Authors Note: St. Paul is of course the color of the finished white stone. Now right here Flamel told you the color of the original substance. Black is the first alchemical color, and so, why orange before?

"Mark well this man in the form of Saint Paul, clothed in a robe entirely of a yellowish white. If thou consider him well, he turns his body in such a posture, as shows that he would take the naked Sword, either to cut off the head, or to do some other thing, to that man which is on his knees at his feet, clothed in a robe of orange colour, white and black, which saith in his roule, DE LE MALA QVAE FECI, that is, Blot out all the evil which I have done, as if he should say, TOLLE NIGREDINEM, Take away from me my   blackness; A term of Art: for Evil signifieth in the Allegory blackness, as it is often found in Turba Phylosophorum: Seeth it until it come to blackness, which will be thought Evil. But wouldest thou know what is meant by this man, that taketh the Sword? It signifies that thou must cut off the head of the Crow, that is to say, of the man clothed in divers Colours, which is on his knees."

Authors Note: We already spoke some of this tablet, but as here Flamel discusses it, we will go over it again as to how I have come to understand it. I said St. Paul was here used, as he was a lesser apostle. This is an overall description of the white substance that is a lesser base substance. Flamel is orange, black and white and represents the matters at those stages. To get white, the matters are placed in the upper section of the oven, and the top is taken off so that the moon can further purify the matters. We see this with Virgo, the Virgin and the drying in August to September. Set is overcome. Thus the colors of St. Paul, lined with gold to show that the light is a reflection of the sun. Yellow and white because the white stone is of a yellowish white color when finished. He mentions cutting off the head as it has to have the head, the cupel removed to do this. In another part of Flamel he will say, "the time for the Cupel is passed." Which means the time for the top of the shell is passed and now the work becomes directly with the lights. Not through the shell. Refer to the fourth day of Genesis and consider the third day. The waters now do not come together in one place, they are in the firmament and shine now directly on the earth. This white part is the white swan we see with the conjunction biting itself, or feeding itself with it's own blood. This is like again! The term used by the masters to show only lIKE materials may be used. The moon is now like the white substance, and so is the only light that may come to it for the next three months to finish that part of the work. Now that part of the work is if we choose to use some of the mercury to make the white stone. We may choose to use all of it for only the red! It is up to you. Flamel is orange! What is orange, and it is the first color. Now many say the first color to achieve is black. Here, Flamel does you a favor, he is telling you the color of the substance used, and to me it is an orange egg yolk.

"I have taken this portrait and figure out of Hermes Trismagistus, in his Book of the Secret Art, where he saith, Take away the head of this black man, cut off the head of the Crow, that is to say, Whiten our black. Lambspring, that noble German, hath also used it in the Commentary of his Hieroglyphics, saying, In this wood there is a Beast all covered with black, if any man cut off his head, he will loose his blackness and put on a most white colour. Will you understand what that is? The blackness is called the head of the Crow, the which being taken away, at the instant comes the white colour: Then that is to say, when the Cloud appears no more, this body is said to be without a head."

Authors Note: There are several allegories that show this one is of a 'White Man' all chopped up and his head is being held in the air. The allegory is referring to this part of the work. It is chopped up as we grind this white substance when dried to a powder; the head (top of shell) is chopped off as it is the method to proceed, with the process. These steps are shown in many ways, how to see them is to know the steps of the process. If you know your taking the head off and turning it white, and you see an allegory where a white man is chopped up, and you see he is holding the head? Can you compare to understand it? Consider what you see and remember the steps.

"These are his proper words. In the same sense the Sages have also said in other places, Take the Viper which is called De rexa, cut off his head, &c. that is to say, take away from him his blackness. They have also used this Periphrasis when to signify the multiplication of the Stone, they have fained a Serpent Hydra, whereof, if one cut off one head, there will spring in the place thereof ten; for the stone augments tenfold, every time that they cut off this head of the Crow, that they make it black, and afterwards white, that is to say, that they dissolve it anew, and afterward coagulate it again."

Authors Note: 'Bind and Loose,' an alchemical term is the same as "they dissolve it anew, and afterward coagulate it again." This has to do with the last steps of the process for multiplication. He is telling you the top is off there also. In the last step, we open and shut, bind and loose. This is open the oven, add water and close the oven, dry is bind, add water is loose. See how it is just water or water vapor and the substance, as here again he calls it serpent or connects it to serpent! At the end, by adjusting the water and substance to the proper ratio, it multiplies in the light. I am glad Flamel shows the many myth's that are tied to this work. Surly you can see the connection to the cycle of nature, and understand the black (death and dying stage) of the matters and how they are referred to. Also he here mentions how this substance multiplies after a certain period of time. Let me say it this way, I felt for many years that I was wrong in my work, as I was left with just a small amount of matter? How could this be the stone? However, when the matters reach a certain point, they start to multiply. The matters now become just vapor and light added to the substance, and it grows on a daily basis. It becomes the above condensed to the below. You can produce as much as you care to have. We will see this as we proceed, and when the multiplication is to happen.

"Mark how this naked Sword is wreathed about with a black girdle, and that the ends thereof are not so wreathed at all. This naked shining Sword is the stone for the white, or the white stone, so often by the Philosophers described under this form. To come then to this perfect and sparkling whiteness, thou must understand the wreathings of this black girdle, and follow that which they teach, which is the quantity of the imbibitions. The two ends which are not wreathed about at all, represent the beginning and the ending: for the beginning it teacheth that you must inbibe it at the first time gently and scarcely, giving it then a little milk, as to a little Child newborn, to the intent that Ifir, as the Authors say, be not drowned: The like must we do at the end, when we see that our King is full, and will have no more. The middle of these operations is painted by the five whole wreathes, or rounds of the black girdle, at what time, (because our Salamander lives of the fire, and in the middest of the fire, and indeed is a fire, and an Argent vive, or quicksilver, that runs in the middest of the fire fearing nothing), thou must give him abundantly in such sort that the Virgins Milk compass all the matter round about."

Authors Note: With the Salamander, for the first three months (the trident in conjunction), we will be adding much pure water again. This is turning the wheel again for further augmentation of the matters for only the red stone. You will understand this section better as you understand all the process. He speaks about several parts again here, compare the steps with each. The finish is different in the last seven months, I will show and teach this also as we proceed. Always the last is seven months, seven is everywhere and tied to those last months.

"I have made to be painted black all these wreaths or rounds of the girdle, because these are the imbibitions, and by consequence, blacknesses: for the fire with the moisture (as it hath been often said) causeth blackness. And as these five whole wreathes or rounds show that you must do this five times wholly, so likewise they let you know that you must do this in five whole months, a month to every imbibition: See here the reason why Haly Abenragel said, the Coction or boiling of the things is done in three times fifty days: It is true that if thou count these little imbibitions at the beginning and at the end, there are seven."

Authors Note: Now we discuss what is above to show how they confuse you. As I said, Flamel will bring in several steps to make it almost impossible to understand, unless you know the process. I already said it takes 5 months to get to the May-Day or to May. He then mentions the salamander, which is the first three of the second part of the work, and then above he said you have to understand the seven rounds, which I explained is the last of the seven months. See how he pointed to three times of the process? The fire and moisture is warmth and darkness in the start of the work to give you the black matters. You do that for the first five months. "It is true that if thou count these little imbibitions at the beginning and at the end, there are seven." Now count from January to August is seven months. Now at the end, second part of the process, are seven more! And so as he said, "it is true, there are seven at the start, and at the end. Always remember they want it to be almost impossible to understand. Lay it out on a piece of paper, then put in the times, and count, then it will be clear and easy to see. The first part is nine months. Take away the first day leaves eight. Take away the drying in moonlight and it leaves seven months of cooking in the fire. We then use seven more months to finish the stone, but again this is divided into three and four, for the two stones. How did I figure this out? Many years, many little pieces and slowly through understanding. Many trials believe me! In part it was and became a work of trial and error. If you fail, it teaches you something. I didn't figure each step sometimes the error taught me.

"Whereupon one of the most envious hath said, Our head of the Crow is leprous, and therefore he that would cleanse it, he must make it go down seven times into the River of regeneration of Jordan, as the Prophet commanded the leprous Naaman the Syrian. Comprehending herein the beginning, which is but of a few days, the middle, and the end, which is also very short. I have then given thee this table, to tell thee that thou must whiten my body, which is upon the knees, and demandeth no other thing: for Nature always tends to perfection, which thou shalt accomplish by the apposition of Virgins milk, and by the decoction of the matters which thou shalt make with this milk, which being dried upon this body, will colour it into this same white yellow, which he who takes the Sword, is clothed with all, in which colour thou must make they Corfufle to come."

Authors note: See, again he covers several steps. Also, and very important, "always tends to perfection, which thou shalt accomplish by the apposition of Virgins milk." "Of Virgins Milk."

Authors Note: This perfection does not come from the moon or the Virgins Milk, it comes from the sun, and so he said here. The perfection comes from the opposite of the moon, or from the sun. We finish then the red stone with the sun for the perfection, the lesser stone from the moon.

"The vestments of the figure of Saint Paul are bordered largely with a golden and red citrine colour. Oh my Son, praise God, if ever thou seest this, for now hast thou obtained mercy from Heaven; Imbibe it then, and teine it till such time as the little Infant be hardy ans strong, to combat against the water and the fire: In accomplishing the which, thou shalt do that which Demagoras, Senior, and Haly have called, The putting of the Mother into the Infants belly, which Infant the Mother had but lately brought forth; for they call the Mother the Mercury of Philosophers, wherewith they make their imbibitions and fermentations call the Body, to teine or colour the which this Mercury is gone out."

Authors Note: Again, two things. St Paul, and the red yellow color, he is now starting to speak of the finish of the red stone. And then he goes back, "putting the mother into the belly of the infant" to the white stone. The mother is the moon, Isis and remember like. This is shown with many allegories about toads and women breasts and such. The white is female, and always connected to women. The red is male and always connected to male and the sun. There is no mixing of the lights at certain stages. You have to know the color scheme and when you do, as soon as he mentions a color you know exactly where he is speaking of and what he means by what he is saying. Flamel will change from one step or part of the process with each sentence, and so read one at a time and understand it and connect it and then read the next. Note he said "baby, and mother" This is connected to by Flamel to Isis and Osiris, and Septembers child. When the toad is suckling the woman's breast, it is simply the substance not pure in the female, moonlight.

"Therefore I have given thee these two figures, to signify the Albifications, for in this place it is that thou hast need of great help, for here all the World is deceived. This operation is indeed a Labyrinth, for here there present themselves a thousand ways at the same instant, besides that, thou must go to the end of it, directly contrary to the beginning, in coagulating that which before thou dissolvedst, and in making earth that which before thou madest water. When thou hast made it white, then hast thou overcome the enchanted Bulls that cast fire and smoke out of their nostrils. Hercules hath cleansed the stable full of ordure, of rottenness, and of blackness. Jason hath powred the decoction or broth upon the Dragons of Colchos, and thou hast in thy power the horn of Amalthea which (although it be white) may fill thee all the rest of thy life with glory, honour, and riches. To have the which, it hath behoved thee to fight valiantly, and in manner of an Hercules, for this Achelous, this moist river, is indewed with a most mighty force, besides that he often transfigures himself from one form to another. Thus hast thou done all, because the rest is without difficulty."

Authors Note: In the last steps, the colors change quite a bit. For the red, it is white but goes to black and white. This is called in alchemy "The Crows returning to the nest." It then goes to an orange color, this is the salamander, and is orange about a month. It then goes to a lavender color, again for a month, it then turns to a red, but not the final purple red which is at the end. This is "he often transfigures himself from one form to another." The operation is a labyrinth as it is done below, and finishes above. Also, here is when the 3/2 ratio must be learned and used. I will keep this part my little secret for now.

"These transfigurations are particularly described in the Book of the Seven Egyptian Seals, where it is said (as also by all Authors) that the Stone, before it will wholly forsake his blackness, and become white in the fashion of a most shining marble, and of a naked flaming sword, will put on all the colours that thou canst possibly imagine, often will it melt, and often coagulate itself, and amidst these divers and contrary operations (which the vegetable soul which is in it makes it perform at one and the same time) it will grow citrine, green, red (but not of a true red) it will become yellow, blue, and orange colour, until that being wholly overcome by dryness and heat, all these infinite colours will end in this admirable citrine whiteness, of the colour of Saint Pauls garments, which in a short time will become like the colour of the naked sword; afterwards by the means of a more strong and long decoction it will take in the end a red Citrine colour, and afterward the perfect red of the vermillion, where it will repose itself forever."

Authors Note: I already explained the colors, I want to point out the seven egyptian seals.' Always Egypt, always seven.

"I will not forget, by the way, to advertise thee, that the milk of the Moon, is not as the Virgins milk of the Sun; think then that the inbibitions of whiteness, require a more white milk than those of a golden redness; for in this passage I had thought I should have missed, and so I had done indeed had it not been for Abraham the Jew; for this reason I have made to be painted for thee the Figure which taketh the naked sword, in the colour which is necessary for thee, for it is the Figure of that which whiteneth."

Authors Note: The second half, most is done above, but not all. The second half we build with light and vapor, the first half we dissolve and change .He said, "we make earth" and what this means is refer to Genesis, the waters now come together to produce earth, and that means the matters are changed so that light and vapor now build a new thing for you. All the colors I have shown them in my allegory of the serpent. In the last paragraph, he is telling you that the light of the sun and moon are different, and from Abraham I believe he is referring to the dried in moonlight Virgo sign. When understanding that, and like it become obvious as to how to proceed with each different stone. Besides that, he often transfigures himself from one form to another. Here he is actually speaking of the moon. but he used the term, he, which would again lead you astray.

CHAPTER VI

"I have so made to be painted for thee a field vert, because that in this decoction the confections become green, and keep this colour longer than any other after the black. This greenness shows particularlythat our Stone hath a vegetable soul, and that by the Industry of Art it is turned into a true and pure tree, to bud abundantly, and afterwards to bring forth infinite little sprigs and branches. O happy green (saith the Rosary) which doest produce all things, without thee nothing can increase, vegetate, nor multiply. The three folk rising again, clothed in sparkling white, represent the body, soul, and Spirit of our white Stone."

Authors Note: The color green. Hard to describe. I call it more a yellowish brown green. It is the rotten matter on it's way to being white. It never changes till it is dried in the moonlight and then , hard to believe, it does become so white it is hard to photo next to the white eggshell. The color green. This tablet is linked to the crowned king in the Abraham tablets. This color vert, green is the color of the field, and a place where you can find a crowned bull king! In other words, Flamels way of showing you the time of year as he wanted to show it for this part. The May-Day bull in ram. The three folks, bodies rising again. Two of male is the water from within the eggshell, and the sun. The female is the moon. Note that only the body can re-enter the grave and the other two cannot. This is proof of the shell of the egg. The waters must come together! The sun and moon cannot enter the grave! They must mix outside and the waters return, and they can shine through the walls of the shell or inner oven. This is the water circulating again and again. The lights are divided away from the substance at this first point or steps of the process as it said in Genesis. Here also he portrays the Savior Jesus Christ. In many of the pictorial allegories, as in the St. Thomas Shield a heart is shown, and is the pure heart of Jesus Christ. In older allegories or by those not christian a rose with seven petals would be used. Note also the color of the Robe of Jesus is a Pure citrine white, the same as the stone will be when finished, White Stone. Now we just finished in the prior work of Flamel, and overview that ended up with the finish of the work. Here now Flamel is back to the process during the summer, and production of the white mercury in September. Always he bounces around. All the alchemists do this and so it is why you have to learn the steps to figure what they are speaking of. Please note he shows above the cross of equal arms and the Tau Cross. This is related to when the Sun crosses the equator. All is seen as equal. Day light and day night, all equal. This is September, and is the birth of Septembers Child. In ancient Egypt, the Tau Cross and equal armed cross was raised. The Djed pillar also. More on the Djed later.

"The philosophers do ordinarily use these terms of Art to hide the secret from evil men. They call the Body that black earth, obscure and dark, which we make white: They call the Soul the other half divided from the Body, which by the will of God, and power of nature, gives to the body by his inbibitions and fermentations a vegetable soul, that is to say, power and vertue to bud, encrease, multiply, and to become white, as a naked shining sword: They call the Spirit, the tincture & dryness, which as a Spirit hath power to pierce all Metallic things. I should be too tedious, if I should show thee how good reason they had to say always and in all places. Our Stone hath resemblably to a man, a Body, Soul and Spirit. I would only that thou note well, that as a man indued with a Body, Soul and Spirit, is not withstanding but one, so likewise thou hast now but one only white confection, in the which nevertheless there are a Body, a Soul, and a Spirit,   which are inseparably united.

Authors Note: This is where we find our first androgynyn in alchemy. It is androgynous material as it was processed by both sun and moon, and so those aspect of male and female are now put into the material or substance. Note soul and Spirit. This is where these old terms originally come to us from. The spirit from the sun, soul from the moon. This material is what the earth was like created on the third day! This is the material alchemists believed all was created from!

"I could easily give very clear comparisons and expositions of this Body, Soul, and Spirit; but to explicate them, I must of necessity speak things which God reserves to reveal unto them that fear and love him, and consequently ought not to be written. I have then made to be painted here, a Body, a Soul, and a Spirit, all white, as if they were rising again, to show thee, that the Sun and Moon and Mercury are raised again in this operation, that is to say, are made Elements of air, and whitened: for we have heretofore called the blackness, Death; and so continuing the Metaphor, we may call

Whiteness, Life; which commeth not, but with, and by a Resurrection. The Body, to show this more plainly, I have made to be painted lifting up the stone of his tomb, wherein it was enclosed."

Authors Note: Look at Genesis where the waters had to come together "in one place." This shows the light had to shine through the inner oven, helping to show it had to be of an egg shell or material of that type which allowed light to pass through. This first resurrection is of Osiris where he is reborn a babe. Note he also said, "from death to life." Also that the body was enclosed, or covered always. This is On Osiris's tomb where we now have completed the circle of the Ouroborous. "From death to life." Now remember the body does not go into all the lights above, just into the moonlight. If it were put into both lights, it would be lost. He said that mercury, soul and spirit was raised! That is what was implanted into the substance, and so what it becomes by drying. Lifting the cover, in another place, Flamel said the "time of the cupel is passed." This means the time of the top being on is over. The substance is dried with the moonlight shining on it. Not through it as it had been doing. For the white stone, three more months of process with this substance and like. The like would be the light that is like the substance, or moonlight.

"The Soul, because it cannot be put into the earth, it comes not out of a tomb, but only I have made it be painted amongst the tombs, seeking its body, in form of a woman, having her hair disheveled."

Authors Note: Hair Disheveled. Please link this to the deer and unicorn. The unicorn represents the sun, (single point) the deer, (horns or disheveled hair) is the moon. Another way they used to show female by horns and horn for male. Now this fooled many, as a deer with horns is a male! When considering the unicorn, see the horn and compare to the obelisk of Egypt. Compare disheveled hair and horns of a deer.

"The Spirit which likewise cannot be put in a grave, I have made to be painted in fashion of a man coming out of the earth, not from a Tomb. They are all white; so the blackness, that is death, is vanquished, and they being whitened, are from henceforward incorruptible."

Authors Note: Note above that the spirit (sun) and soul (moon) cannot be put into the tomb. And so, how do they get there to join with it, the body. Also, note this. A man coming out of the earth is the same as water vapor coming out of a water earth source.

"Now lift up thine eyes on high, and see our King coming, crowned and raised again, which hath overcome Death, the darknesses, and moistures; behold him in the form wherein our Saviour shall come, who shall eternally unite unto him all pure and clean souls, and will drive away all impurity and uncleanness, as being unworthy to be united to his divine Body. So by comparison (but first asking leave of the Catholic, Apostolic, and Roman Church, to speak in this manner, and praying every debonaire soul to permit me to use this similitude) see here our white Exilir, which from henceforward will inseparably unite unto himself every pure metallic nature, changing it into his own most fine silvery nature, rejecting all that is impure, strange, and Heterogeneal, or of another kind."

Authors Note: This is whereIIKE comes into play, and also another very important point, "every pure metallic nature" This is a principle, A nature, which means not metals but the Light that represents that principle. The moon is for and is the seed for silver. The sun is the seed for and is gold. These are the metallic principles and must be used that way. They are what is mixed with the substance below. Consider the words of the philosophers about the earth and gold. The metals were formed over time from a remote matter. The remote matter is the earth formed during the creation, That is the substance you are now making, and so the metals can now be formed from that same matter. How? By further purification of the above trickling down into the below!

"Blessed be God, which of his goodness gives us grace to be able to consider this sparkling white, more perfect and shining than any compound nature, and more noble next after the immortal soul, than any substance having life, or not having life; for it is a quintessence, a most pure silver, that hath passed the Coppell, and is seven times refined, saith the royal Prophet David."

Authors Note: That it has passed the Coppell, which is the top, and is seven times refined. That it is most pure silver which is a most pure mercury. It is a most pure silver because it is finished by Virgo the Virgin. It has come from death to life. And in ancient Egypt, during September, there was a Set Holiday. The holiday was celebrated because of the same reason, death was overcome by the resurrection of Osiris. Set was overcome. Also above, he said "and shining more than any compound nature," which means in his way, to work with a single thing here which means it is dried in moonlight only. Now, we only have seven more months of work to go for the red stone!

"It is not needful to inperpret what the two Angels signify, that play on Instruments over the heads of them which are raised again: These are rather divine spirits, singing the mervails of God in this miraculous operation, than Angels that call to judgement. To make an express difference between these and them, I have given the one of them a Lute, the other a haultboy, but none of them trumpets, which yet are wont to be given to them that are to call us to Judgement. The like may be said of the three Angels, which are over the head of our Saviour, whereof the one crowneth him, and the other two assisting, say in their Rowles, O PATER OMNIPOTENS, O JESU BONE, that is, O Almighty Father, O good Jesus, in rendering unto him eternal thanks.

Authors Note: No comment necessary with this part.

CHAPTER VII

Upon a field violet and blue, two Angels of an
Orange colour, and their Rowles.

This violet and blue field showeth that being to pass from the white stone to the red, thou must inbibe it with a little virgins milk of the Sun, and that these colours come out of the Mercurial moisture which thou hast dried upon the Stone. In this operation of rubifying, although thou do imbibe, thou shalt not have much black, but of violets, blue and of the colour of the Peacocks tail.

Authors Note: First we are now working for the red stone. He says " must inbibe it with a little virgins milk of the sun," which means we now are concerned with sunlight, not moonlight. Although in the first three months of this part of the process both lights are used for further augmentation of the substances. As was said, "we must turn the wheel again." For this part of the work, we do again as we did in the May-Day, again we bring all the waters together. As this part of the process is started the substance will turn to an orange color. This is the Salamander as I have noted, and then will move to a lavender color on its way to red. Again the steps are blended together with the description of the work. The two angles are represented as we use two lights. The color blue is because we are using again a lot of pure water (blue).

"For our stone is so triumphant in dryness, that as soon as thy Mercury toucheth it, the nature thereof rejoicing in his like nature, it is joined unto it, and drinketh it greedily, and therefore the black that comes of moisture, can show itself but a little, and that under these colors violet and blue, because that dryness (as is said) doth by and by govern absolutely."

Authors Note: The first dryness is here again the dryness of Virgo and the drying that gave us the mercury! Again it is mentioned as we will work toward dryness with the finish of the stone when it will be of a dry ruby crystal substance. That is the last steps, these first are the three with water, the division of the seven of three and four. He again mixes up the steps somewhat. As he mentions "not much black!" The white goes to spotted black and white, where before it turned solid black.

"I have also made to be painted for thee, these two Angels with wings, to represent unto thee, that the two substances of thy confections, the Mercurial and the Sulphurous substance, the fixed as well as the volatile, being perfectly fixed together, do also fly together within thy vessel: for in this operation, the fixed body will gently mount to heaven, being all spiritual, and from thence it will descend unto the earth, and whethersoever thou wilt, following everywhere the Spirit, which is always moved upon the fire: Inasmuch as they are made one self same nature, and the compound is all spiritual, and the spiritual all corporall, so much hath it been subtilized upon our Marble, by the precedent operations. The natures then are here transmuted into Angels, that is to say, are made spiritual and most subtle, so are they now the true tinctures."

Authors Note: Consider now again the forth day of Genesis. The earth is finished. Here in the process it was the finish of the mercury and the lights flew within the firmament to shine upon the earth. Here the two angles are the lights doing that with our process. Remember the moon is the mercurious, the sun is sulfurous. The moon is soul and the sun spirit. They now fly within the vessel. The fixed body is the moisture that ascends, and descends within the vessel. This is making the second androgynous material, the crowned androgynyn. Also, this is as you read about Osiris, the tit and lion cloth pasted to the Djed Pillar. Osiris had to be all of the below, which was male and female before he could blend above to the God. There is more on the tit and lion cloth later to explain.

"Now remember thee to begin the rubifying, by the apposition of Mercury Citrine red, but thou must not pour on much, and only once or twice, according as thou shalt see occasion; for this operation ought to be done by a dry fire, and by a dry sublimation and calcination. And truely I tell thee here a secret which thou shalt very seldom find written, so far am I from being envious, that would to God every man knew how to make gold to his own will, that they might live, and lead forth to pasture their fair flocks, without Usury or going to Law, in imitation of the holy Patriarchs using only (as our first Fathers did) to exchange one thing for another; and yet to have that, they must labour as well as now. Howbeit for fear to offend God, and to be the instrument of such a change which prove evil, I must take heed to represent or write where it is that we hide the keys, which can open all the doors of the secrets of nature, or to open or cast up the earth in that place, contenting myself to show the things which will teach everyone to whom God shall give permission to know what property the sign of the Balance or Libra hath, when it is enlightened by the Sun and Mercury in the month of October."

Authors Note: The Balance in the month of October, remember I said Septembers Child referred to Set and Saturn, all this is now to tell you the time of year. This part starts in the end of September, tied to the constellation times. The astrological symbols cross the months. Septembers Child is finished in September. Virgo is finished in September. Virgo is the sign that starts in August. In his mention of the keys, this is shown in the next step and is part of the blending of the steps to confuse you. The balance was tied to the raising of the Djed Piller in Egypt, and to the Tat cross. The conjunction in alchemy is always about October, but you need to see how it is all tied together. Also, he said above, "Now remember thee to begin the rubifying, by the apposition of Mercury Citrine red." This is the last step again, and so another bounce to confuse you. The rubifying is the very end, and it is done only with sunlight. Now he said "where he hides the keys" This is the great secret. Look at the gold key, and count the Toes on the key. There are 3 and 2. The whole key to this last step has to do with understanding this 3/2 ratio. If you don't consider and find, you will fail. I will show this 3/2 ratio in other series allegories. Paracelsus wrote about it in his Aurora, chapter 13, an interesting and informative read.

"These Angels are painted of an orange colour, to let thee know that thy white confections have been a little more digested, or boiled, and that the black of the violet and blue hath been already chafed away by the fire: for this orange colour is compounded of the fair golden Citrine red (which thou hast so long waited for) and of the remainder of this violet and blue, which thou hast already in part banished and undone. Furthermore this orange colour showeth that the natures are digested, and by little and little perfected by the grace of God."

Authors note: As it is written, you would think that orange follows the lavender, but that is wrong. It is just how he is trying to confuse you but as you learn and know the process you will see and understand. The orange turns to lavender, and then to red. If you will find a pictorial allegory of the salamander, it will show it being tended by a man with a trident. Which means three months in the fire in this fashion, and the three is as I have said, a part of the last seven.

"As for their Rowle, which saith, SVRGITE MORTVI, VENITE AD IVDICIVM DOMINI MEI, that is, Arise you dead, and come unto the judgement of God my Lord; I have made it be put there, only for the Theological sense, rather than any other: It ends in the throat of a Lion which is all red, to teach that this operation must not be discontinued until they see the true red purple, wholly like unto the Poppy of the Hermitage, and the vermillion of the painted Lion saving for multiplying."

Authors note: Like all the steps of the stone, again water is used for all. If your substance dries for a day, the sun will burn it and it will be destroyed. Always there is moisture in the oven. As far as "arise you dead" this again now means the substance is moved to the upper section of the oven to help to keep it warm (remember October to December, this part and getting cold outside). For the white stone, it already was on the top of the oven and was worked there for three months to be perfected in the moonlight. It ends in the throat of the lion (red stone) as this is when moved, where the substance will stay till finished.   After then cupel is removed, (top off) you can see how we have made this second turning of the wheel stronger, or the lights are made stronger because they now do not have to go through the second oven to do their work.   Also consider Genesis as now the lights shine directly on the earth! Always we are moving toward the lights, as the substance has to get to the point it is dry, and can withstand the light, sun, and then it is like the sun. So, the first three months of the last seven, three of them white substance in upper section to produce the white stone. Only moonlight and substance with moisture. Red stone is done in base for three months, and then moved to upper section.   While in lower section it is flooded with water and open to lights above, both lights. When moved to top, it now will become a stone for the red, and so only the sun and ratio is used.

CHAPTER VIII

The figure of a man, like unto Saint Peter, clothed in a robe Citrine red, holding a key in his right hand, and laying his left hand upon a woman, in an orange coloured robe, which is on her knees at his feet, holding a rowle.

Authors Note: Here we have St. Peter because he was the most important apostle, and so he is connected with the most important stone, the red. The women, Paranella is here the stone, and is of an orange color. Again I remind you of the blending of the tablets. Remember, Flamel was orange, black and white, and was an overall of the first steps. Again here the orange is the color of the Salamander, and as it is time to move forward, after the first three months, as it is turning to lavender, and on to Red. As for the stone, it is time again to change the conditions. The conditions always have to do with the lights, and here as we work for the red stone, it has to do with the sun. We need somehow to increase the power of the sun! We need a more rich surrounding for the substance for it to become like the sun, and so somehow we need to increase the energy it receives from the sun. The colors of St. Peter, the red and yellow are the colors of the sun. Somehow St Peter, (the power of the sun) has to be augmented, and it is done by how you handle the moistures within the oven. He tells you that you are left with bind and loose. What does it mean, he also said, "open and shut." We have an oven, he mentions "within the vessels," we open and shut, we bind (remove water) and we loose (add the water). In many places, red is always used to indicate a work of the sun.

"Look upon this woman clothed in a robe of orange colour, which doth so naturally resemble Perrenelle as she was in her youth; She is painted in the fashion of a suppliant upon her knees, her hands joined together, at the feet of a man which hath a key in his right hand, which hears her graciously, and afterwards stretcheth out his left hand upon her. Wouldest thou know what this meaneth? This is the Stone, which in this operation demandeth two things, of the Mercury of the Sun, of the Philosophers (painted under the form of a man) that is to say Multiplication, and a more rich Accoustrement; which at this time it is needful for her to obtain, and therefore the man so laying his hand upon her shoulder accords and grants it unto her."

Authors Note: I have mentioned the 3/2 ratio. Look to the key of St. Peter, it has three toes on the one side, two on the other. You must learn what this three , two ratio is all about, and what needs to be added. From the St. Thomas shield, you see three fishes and Two of them were one way, the third another. I showed the woman pregnant, with three pointed logs and two round. There are many ways this three two is shown.

" But why have I made to be painted a woman? I could as well have made to be painted a man as a woman, or an Angel rather, (for the whole natures are now spiritual and corporal, masculine and feminine), but I have rather chosen to cause paint a woman, to the end that thou mayest judge that she demands rather this than any other thing, because these are the most natural and proper desires of a woman. To show further unto thee that she demandeth Multiplication, I have made paint the man, unto whom she addresseth her prayers in the form of Saint Peter, holding a key, having power to open and to shut, to bind and to loose, because the envious Philosophers have never spoken of Multiplication, but under the common terms of Art, APERI, CLAVDE, SOLVE, LIGA, that is, Open, shut, bind, loose, opening and loosing, they have called the making of the Body (which is always hard and fixt) soft fluid, and running like water: To shut and to bind, is with them afterwards by a more strong decoction to coagulate it, and to bring it back again into the form of a body."

Authors Note: If you will check the pictorial allegory of the Multiplication of Atalanta. We saw the pregnant women with the fire, the two fishes in the bucket, and the three pointed logs with the two round. That also is multiplication, and that tablet, remember the overlap? It would seem out of place. The three pointed Logs, what did I say about pointed objects? As you read on, Flamel mentions that you can loose your substance as the vessel containing it is very fragile. I did loose mine for this reason one time, as you bind and loose, your work is within an egg shell, it is very fragile and you must work very carefully.

"It behoved me then, in this place to represent a man with a key, to teach thee that thou must now open and shut, that is to say, Multiply the budding and encreasing natures: for look how often thou shalt dissolve and fix, so often will these natures multiply, in quantity, quality, and vertue, according to the multiplication of ten; coming from this number to an hundred, from an hundred to a thousand, from a thousand to ten thousand, from ten thousand to an hundred thousand, from an hundred thousand to a million, and from thence by the same operation to Infinity, as I have done three times, praised be God.

And when thy Elixir is so brought unto Infinity, one grain thereof falling upon a quantity of molten metal as deep and vast as the Ocean, it will teine it, and convert it into most perfect metal, that is to say, into silver or gold, according as it shall have been imbibed and fermented, expelling and drying out far from himself all the impure and strange matter, which was joined with the metal in the first coagulation: for this reason therefore have I made to be painted a Key in the hand of the man, which is in the form of Saint Peter, to signify that the stone desireth to be opened and shut for multiplication, and likewise to show thee with what Mercury thou oughtest to do this, & when; I have given the man a garment Citrine red, and the woman one of orange colour". Let this suffice, lest I transgress the silence of Pythagoras, to teach thee that the woman, that is, our stone, asketh to have the rich Accoustrements and colour of Saint Peter. She hath written in her Rowle, CHRISTE PRECOR ESTO PIVS, that is, Jesus Christ be pitiful unto me, as if she said, Lord be good unto me, and suffer not that he that shall become thus far, should spoil all with too much fire: It is true, that from henceforward I shall no more fear mine enemies, and that all fire shall be alike unto me, yet the vessel that contains me, is always brittle and easy to be broken: for if they exalt the fire overmuch, it will crack and flying a pieces, will carry me and sow me unfortunately amongst the ashes."

Authors Note: Please remember what Flamel is saying about the fire. Even here in this last step it needs to be governed. Yes, there can be too much and even now you can burn and destroy your substance. If you do there is no saving it. Whatever is put in *cannot* be taken out.

"Take heed therefore to thy fire in this place, and govern sweetly with patience, this admirable quintescence, for the fire must be augmented unto it, but not too much. And pray the soveraign Goodness, that it will not suffer the evil spirits which keep the Mines and Treasures, to destroy thy work, or to bewitch thy sight, when thou considereth these incomprehensible motions of this quintescence within thy vessel ."

Authors Note: The secret of making the stone is, if you have not already seen this, is to make it like the sun. How this is done, and your clue is simply this. In each step if you will review, the energy of the lights is slowly increased. In the end it is as in Genesis, between the substance and the light itself. It starts out in darkness, it is within the shell, it is flooded with water, but with each step, as I have here mentioned several, always the light is in a stronger position, always consider this as you do your work. It shines through the glass, through the shell, through the flood of water, and always something is removed or, perhaps there is less of something to make the conditions of the light stronger to the substance. If you will consider these only words, and follow the steps and times as I have outlined, it will become very easy to find the stone. You will become (as Flamel indicates) excited, awed, fearful, and you will either consider and make, or mess up and start again. Consider and control, and always try to understand those thoughts of the past ancient persons as they found and what it meant to them.

CHAPTER IX

Upon a dark violet field, a man red purple, holding the foot of a Lion red as vermillion, which hath wings, for it seems would ravish and carry away the man.

"This field violet and dark, tells us that the stone hath obtained by her full decoction, the fair Garments, that are wholly Citrine and red, which she demanded of Saint Peter, who was clothed therewith, and that her complete and perfect digestion (signified by the entire Citrinity) hath made her leave her old robe of orange colour. The vermilion red colour of this flying Lion, like the pure and clear scarlet in grain, which is of the true Granadored, demonstrates that it is now accomplished in all right and equality. And that she is now like a Lion, devouring every pure metallic nature, and changing it into her true substance, into true and pure gold, more fine than that of the best mines."

Authors Note: As with all of Flamels work like all of alchemy, we have here again an allegory. The red roaring lion is the stone. Flying because when you have it all the world is yours! You have health and wealth. I have seen the near end of the stone, It looks as though of crushed Rubies wet and glistening in the sunlight, truly a sight to behold. Consider though, this was after my search of many, many years. It is something I can't explain as to my feelings. I lost that stone, and I am in the process of working the stone again. At the time it really didn't bother me, the loss, as I had done it! I can always make it again. I am making it again. My loss as I have told you. Flamel told you, it is very fragile, and it is very easy to loose. I still have a few bugs to work out on the process, and I probable will for many years. How it works for me where I live, already I know it works much better and easier in the southern part of the U.S.. Naturally, more light! And so some of the things I learn here in the north of the U.S., are different in the south. There was an alchemist that said, "it is easier to do in the southern of France than the northern part." Hopefully, you now understand that statement. The colors Flamel mentions are of a yellowish and deep red. For some reason it seems as a 'chunk' it is the deep red, but as you grind it there is a yellowish tint to it. I don't know what this stone will do! I will someday if it is God's wish, know those things too. It is a long hard thing to do, and hopefully this work will help me finish all that needs to be finished. This has been a 'Lost Mystery' to all of us for so long. This is a Great part of our history, and much of what has made us who we are. I don't see it as they did in the past as perhaps you also will not. I doubt it will transmute a metal to gold, but I can see with my training that it may be a medicine. Hopefully it is and it will be of benefit to mankind. That is my greatest wish. It is as they said, "a work of the sun." All below is a work of the sun. I can see what I have made is an extremely pure substance that is made by the light and vapor. What is it? You consider, but to me it really is the above condensed to the below, and as I am a part of the above, I believe it will be like the best medicine you could ever take! It is "pure Light" and much more than just standing out in the sun for a while. It is about the matters being changed, and this is something not found naturally on this planet. Nature cannot make it, yet the work is really just Nature making it controlled by man!

"Also she now carrieth this man out of this vale of miseries, that is to say, out of the discommodities of poverty and infirmity, and with her wings gloriously lifts him up, out of the dead and standing waters of AEgypt, (which are the ordinary thoughts of mortal men) making him despise this life and the riches thereof, and causing him night and day to meditate on God, and his Saints, to swell in the Emperial heaven, and to drink the sweet springs of the Fountains of everlasting hope."

Authors Note: Again he points to Egypt!

"Praised be God eternally, which hath given us grace to see this most fair and all-perfect purple colour; this pleasant colour of the wild poppy of the Rock, this Tyrian, sparkling and flaming colour, which is incapable of Alternation or change, over which the heaven itself, nor his Zodiac can have no more domination nor power, whose bright shining rays, that dazzle the eyes, seem as though they did communicate unto a man some supercelestial thing, making him (when he beholds and knows it) to be astonished, to tremble, and to be afraid at the same time. Oh Lord, give us grace to use it well, to the augmentation of the Faith, to the profit of our Souls, and to the encrease of the glory of this noble Realm. Amen."

Authors last note on this part of the work Please note 'Zodiac.' I mentions the times of the year, and I point out the signs as we go trough the information. Many today with alchemy experience are not convinced of that. After considering all that I present, one can decide for himself, herself where the work is to be done. I have material here included that states, "because of the moment it happened." The ancients believed that time was important, and only because of the right time it happened! All nature somehow is tied to the time. This is a thing they learned and so they said so. I don't question what has been written.

Those Tablets of Abraham the Jew

Authors Note: The following tablets are those of Abraham the Jew. As you become more familiar with the work, compare what is here to other alchemical information and to other series allegories. Always try to see it compared to the yearly cycle (Genesis), to compost and to seeds going through a life of growth reproduction and death. Many things are pointed out that need to be seen and understood. Compare to Flamel.

In Abraham's work, most important is to see and understand that the tablets overlap! This is one of the ways the alchemists used to hide the process. The first three tablets (out of seven) of Abraham have a double meaning, and so are used twice to show the steps. So with Abraham, we actually have ten steps. Now, some of the alchemists didn't use this method, but showed the ten steps in many more, up to 150. Some of the alchemists did not show the whole process, but only showed the last seven months of work from September. To them Septembers Child was the base substance of the stone, and the making of the base was never taught. Now there are also tablets designed by false alchemists, they copied those of true alchemists but through misunderstanding left out important information. All this together makes it hard to read all the tablets, but by learning the steps and process I show, the others can be found out.

The First Tablet of Abraham the Jew.

Authors Note: What we see here is the God Mercury. Standing, holding a caduceus and another flying toward him with a scythe. Flamel said, "it seemed he would cut off the feet of the God Mercury."

"He seemed to my small judgment, to be the God Mercury of the Pagans: Against him there came running and flying with open wings, a great old man who upon his head had an hour-glass fastened, and in his hand a hook (or scythe) like Death, with the which in terrible and furious manner, he would have cut off the feet of Mercury."

Authors Note: By using what is here we can first say Mercury is one of the original or the oldest way of understanding. We find this is originally from the ancient Egyptian Gods of creation, and to me is linked to Thoth and to Hermes. He (Mercury-Hermes) was considered as a scribe to the gods and as such was considered as the inventor of all sciences and Arts known to the Egyptians. He was linked to earth, air, fire, and water. He became the God of the moon, and the measurer of time. Consider the moon going through its phases. Book of the Dead, pg. Cxviii. The old man in the cloud, originally I give this man the Name Set. Set is linked to the night, and we could say that the link is to the fight between light and dark, and that every day the darkness was overcome. In the first understanding of this tablet, look to the caduceus. We see two serpents entwined. This is sun and moon. The light and the dark forces. My understanding of the staff and serpents is this, there was created light, and that there is two lights or the two serpents. The lights always are trying to overcome and to get control eventually of the matters we work on.

Mercury is water in our process. Why, remember in the creation first all was water! As the creation progressed, this water and light combinations became earth. The first matter of the alchemists is of a mixture of light and water. In other words, the first matter created was from a combination of light and water mixed. It was a thick water. To link this with Genesis you will remember that on the first day, time was established. Earth was conceived. Light was produced, Heaven was produced. That earth was more than one type of water. Consider the contents of an egg and remember the myth of the Egyptians. We today never see day and night as some type of battle, but this was the understanding in the ancient past. And so, what does the above tablet mean in simple terms. Mercury I will describe as water. The staff he holds has to do with the two lights created. As messenger of the Gods, we can say that moisture attaches itself to both of the lights in our process. The light above combines with vapor, and produces something in the below. The old man, we can see as the second understanding of the tablet. There are seven tablets in the series of Abraham, but the process is overlaid. The first three tablets have the double meaning I mentioned so there is ten tablets, or ten steps to the process. He, the old man is giving us time twice. First by the scythe, and secondly by the timer filled with red sand on his head. The scythe we can link with the astrological sign for January (December 21), or the start of our process and also the start of the new year. This would be the time to start the process for the stone in the northern hemisphere. This tablet represents two parts of the process. The first is about mercury (water) and light combinations being produced, or being the substances of our stone. The second part, the old man has to do with the cutting off of the feet of mercury which alchemically is known as 'fixing.' This is done the second part of the process. The above is fixed to the below! In our process first we make substance by process and by combinations of light and matter. This matter is finished and becomes the base material for the stones. With this base matter we continue and fix the above lights to the below matter. The timer filled with red sand means it is time to convert the below substance by fixing to a red powder by using something from the above which is the sun. This will be explained as we move through the tablets, and you see the color changes and understand how the process is to go and how it works.

Mercury is the messenger of the Gods! He is a messenger because in the form of vapor he attaches to light, and carries it to the matter below as condensed moisture. What we are doing is changing a matter below by combinations of light and vapor which is added to the below substance. Over time the below substance become like the above, the sun or moon which was thought to hold a part of God (the Good) within it. As the below became like the above, it was considered perfect. Remember the God Thoth was connected with arts and science. This is both an art and a science.

The staff holds two serpents, this helps me to show that the light created on the first day was both of the lights above that we know, and not just one special light of creation. In another tablet this will be firmed up to further show the understanding. The ancients said, "All below was formed of earth, air, fire and water." Our society today never considered this to be a true statement. To make the stone, we must consider the ancients made it from these substances and from what I call matter. The compost pile when finished is full of matter, and we could call it unformed matter. It lies and wait for some seed to use it so that again it can be something here in the below. It is hard for me to find references to matter in those texts of ancient Egypt, but we will find the stone created the Osirian religion and so in consideration of Osiris, he is called "the soul that livith again," "the being that becometh a child again," "the firstborn son of "unformed matter," " the Lord of multitudes of aspects and forms." Also, "I am Shu (the God) of unformed matter," all from (Book of the Dead- lvii). By these references we can see that they considered matter as being unformed, and so the below became from this matter formed. In our process by the rotting that is first done, first step, we are returning matter to unformed as it was in the creation. This can only be done properly by nature controlled. One must consider that they, the ancients, worked somehow with matter to come to these conclusions and believed all those in the below as being from these few substances .

Considering the egg I work with. The shell of the egg is heaven, within are two waters. I start my process in December. The lights are above, it is cold here and so I keep my substances warm. What am I doing? I have something that is formed. It is to become something because it has seed within it. I must take all that away and return the substances within to unformed matter. In time, I will augment those substances unformed to the above and control it so that I can form that matter as I want. Consider the compost pile and what nature does naturally to formed useless matter. Consider also that those forces outside can only do so much as they are not controlled. The question is what can they do controlled, and what will the matter become?

As we proceed, you will understand and link all this together. Already you should be looking out your window. All that has come and gone is still right there in front of you. The water you drink today, consider all that has used it throughout the ages. Those trees and grasses, how many times has that matter been recycled throughout the ages? How many times has Osiris overcome Set, (light overcome darkness) and regeneration replaced what was here with what is here now? It is those conditions outside and a working process we know now as Genesis that makes all this work and be possible. Also, you know outside as our system that we live with. Consider these are forces understood as ordered to do as they do by God. Consider what can a man do with these forces as he learn to control them? What is impossible for those forces controlled to make? Consider also that Genesis is a system that works by conditions, and that man has gotten to the point where he is effecting those conditions, what is it man will unknowingly produce with those changes?

Mercury

1   Thoth of the Gods of the Egyptians – messenger of the Gods.
2   Combination of light and vapor.
3   Light is from either the sun or moon. Messenger is water (vapor) combinations.
4   Light has to mix with water vapor, and then condense and mix with the (base substance) earth
5   Adiramled said the earth was forming above the earth. This above formed earth is known alchemically as First Matter. Simply put, it was believed the First Matter formed in the Creation was light and vapor combination.
6   It can be moonlight or sunlight with vapor, or both. This combination will give us alchemically, androgynous material.
7   With the staff wrapped with two serpents.
8   Each serpent represents a type of light.
9   Staff connects to light, the messenger wrapped by two lights, two serpents, the sun and moon are indicated. Refer to the lights of Creation in Genesis.
10 Thoth, (Mercury) as messenger. The water can mix with sunlight and become sulfurous or have to do with the sun.
11 It can mix with the moonlight and become mercurious, having to do with the moon.
12 The residue is salt, the salt (earth) is what is gathered over time by the sun and moon and water interaction to the below.
13 Works with a base substance which we must first make, it can be mixed in two ways. It can only be collected by the base substance which will become earth.

The A. the Jew Tablets, ten steps or parts to the process.

1   They use the term mercury everywhere. When we have Septembers Child, (nine months of work) then you have the true mercury. This mercury is as the earth created in Genesis, the dry land called earth.
2   Flamel said "he touched his helmet," it has wings and I think he is kind of pointing out an egg as he mentions also the color orange and the ashes of a pullet. All have to do with a chicken's egg as you will see. The staff can be understood something like the obelisk, (more later).
3   The Old man, I link to father time with his scythe, and to the head or blade only to January, (December 21) and the astrological sign. As we go on you will see and understand a link to the ancient god of Egypt, Set. December 21 is used two times in our process or it goes on for 16 months. This I call the overlap, and is used to hide the process. It is connected to the position and travel of the sun.
4   The hour glass has to do with the second explanation for the tablet, and is connected to the last four   days (months of work), January to April and the finish.
5   The red powder (in the hour glass) has to do with fixing. Flamel say's you are left with binding and loosing, open and shutting. This second December is where we start to work for the red powder. We fix by opening and shutting, and with binding!
6   The start is just the waters and the egg, (the heaven and the earth).
7   The second understanding for this tablet is the old man and his scythe, or the eight of ten tablets.

The Second Tablet of Abraham the Jew

We saw in the first tablet Mercury holding a staff. This is the same as in Genesis, light was created on the first day. With misunderstanding many have considered that the light of creation was a special light, but it was not, it has been always understood (the creation) by those of the past as being about what is here. The forces used are the same, just that they somehow were controlled by God to do as he wished. In this second allegory, we see a mountain with two dragons on the front of it. The sun is to the side. On the top we see a Rose Bush being shaken by the north wind. First we remember that this second tablet is also the ninth tablet, and so two ways of understanding. The first is the mountain. Throughout alchemy texts, we are told of the mountain, and in many places, 'The Little Mountains.' What does this mean and how does it relate? The mountain above is the same as the pyramid design, and is the same as the design of the firmament. Remember in Genesis that the firmament called heaven was created on the second day. And so this mountain here is the same as the firmament, and in our process it is time that the oven or firmament comes into play. In my process I use an egg. In Genesis the waters were divided on the second day by being put into the firmament. In our process we insert the egg into the oven for the same reasons, and to remove from it what it was and to return it back into a base of unformed matter. Flamel in his discussion mentions that Abraham the Jew showed the oven in two places with his tablets, this is the first of the two. I also mentioned the 'Little Mountains.' You will see in the oven design that at the base of this oven, it is divided into four sections. This will be shown and discussed with that section on the oven. The little mountains are four small pyramid shaped divisions at the base, and as they are designed the same, they become the little mountains. The purpose of them is to return the waters below to the substance that will be placed between them, and I believe that this flow of water answers the question of the river with four heads mentioned in Genesis.

In the first tablet, we saw a part of the scythe to give time for December. Also we saw the hour glass to give a time for the red powder (second December). Here in this second tablet, if you will look at the two dragons, you will see they form a "WW" shape. This WW shape has to do with water, and also is the sign, astrological for February. One thing that needs to be mentioned, in tablet one we see a part of the scythe. In tablet two we see something that looks like a WW. Please remember this is hidden knowledge. The signs will not just jump out at you. Some are not there but are there because of metaphor. They are hidden in many ways. You may disagree with what I am showing with a certain sign, but when finished and you step back and look at all, you will then clearly see them and how they are hidden. First though, you must know this process. You have to have something to base your search on. The two dragons are also used to show the second part of the process, and are connected to what is termed in alchemy as The Crowned Androgynyn. I will show this in a more clear way with other allegories showing that part of the process. The sun is at the side of the tablet to show, in the second part, that it is now a work of the sun and has to do with the finish of the process which covers four month. There is 16 months to do this work. The second division of the work, the last seven months is divided because of the two stones made. The white is finished in January. The finish in April is for the red stone, and is linked to that red powder we saw in the first tablet. This will become clearer as we consider all, and understand the whole process. Other pictorial allegories will also show this part of the process. Flamel as you read his work, will tell you that he "transmuted to silver in January." As he goes on, he will also mention that he "transmuted to gold" in April. Those are not just dates when he made the stone, they are the dates used by all that did the work in the northern hemisphere. However all did not mention those dates as if they did, searchers would know that the dates were specific, and would link them to times of the year. Each alchemist said things, but always they were very careful not to say too much! To continue, the rose bush at the top of the mountain. It is shaken by the north wind as it is January and very cold outside. The oven has to be kept warm. This is shown again in the fresco of Flamel. He said it is "necessary to know why he is in heaven and not below on earth." When we discuss the oven and Flamels design, I will explain why and it is linked to time of year and the cold. It will be much easier to see and understand then. The rose bush itself. First I apologize as I can not see the drawing as well as I wish I could. The flowers or roses we see, I believe there is three on the one side, and then two on the top or other. If the painting was in color, I believe they would be colored red and white. There is a ratio to the work in the second half, and it is a 3/2 ratio. Here I will say that I will show this ration in several pictorial allegories to prove that it is there and needs to be understood and used. It will be found and easily understood by those other pictorial allegories I will show.

In our process, we have assembled the substances we need to do the work. We know we need the lights. We know we need to change matter here in the below so that we can make something new out of it. We know it has to be done as 'The Great Work' was done by God. We know only nature can make those changes, and with this part return our mater to a base material. To understand base matter. It is very important to realize that man *cannot* do this! I have read many works of practicing alchemists where they have returned matter to a base substance. For example, they used vinegar and reduced metal with it to what they feel is a proper base. All matter here in the below we have to realize is made by nature over long periods of time. We have to believe it is made of the four, earth, air, fire and water. To see this we have to think as the ancients did. We cannot remove the sunlight from a substance. We cannot make a substance as these four do. We also cannot make the proper base for this work in a lab or with chemicals. Only nature can make a proper compost pile, only nature and this oven can make the proper base. We seek perfection in our work and we do it with nature. Man cannot do this with all his labs and chemicals no matter how he tries. As the alchemists said, "There is one way, one substance, and one oven." If I am successful with my work and understanding, it is because I did as they said and I believed what they wrote. "Nature is our only teacher." I believe there is one oven, and one way, and one substance. As you read and understand all of this work, you will see that almost everything ever discussed of the past, religion, alchemy and nature comes together in some way. Coincidence, I don't think so. Lastly, the use of an egg and why? Not just because in ancient Egypt they believed all came from an egg, but just because it is organic matter, and the egg is just put together in such a way as to make the whole thing convenient. Probably, this substance can be brought forth by any organic matter we use. I don't know why it wouldn't work! I use in depth the book, "Art of Alchemy" by Adiramled. In the book, he said that "Organic, Inorganic, no difference." I believe he said this because he made the stone from an organic material, and it changed an inorganic material. If you understand, it shows all in the below is of one and the same material. We invented those words, they were unknown in the past.

1	First we see a side view of a Mountain.
2	This is significant because in many places having to do with the art,
3	mountains or little mountains are mentioned.
4	Why a mountain is the question.
5	The mountain is a referenced to the pyramid of Egypt,
6	and the perfect philosophical oven.
7	Flamel said, that Abraham the Jew had drawn it twice,
8	and that it is how he found the oven.
9	We have here a side view,
10	and in the forth tablet, we have a top view.
11	On the side of the oven we have two griffons flying or fighting.
12	This gives us the astrological sign 'WW,'
13	and is for fermentation, February.
14	This is a water sign.
15	On the top of the Mountain, we have a Rose or flower bush, bearing red and white flowers.
16	The red and white are drawn in many allegories found in alchemy.
17	They are drawn with a fountain with a red and white stream,
18	They are found with a mermaid bearing both milk and blood from her paps.
19	They are both connected with the sun and moon originally.
20	In this part of the process, and with this tablet two times are shown.
21	The red and white flowers are about the second January,
22	or over a year after the start, and indicate two things,
23	first the white flower indicates the white stone is finished,
24	and thus the work of the moon is now finished.
25	The red indicates it is now the time for the finish work of the red stone to begin.
26	This last work is accomplished by a joining of the sun (red) to the substance.
27	In other allegories this time period is also shown by the Crowned Androgynyn.
28	The meaning is the same.
29	Usually the Crowned Androgyn is shown with combinations of thirteen moons or suns,
30	Something at any rate which if counted will amount to thirteen.
31	The Crowned Androgyn indicates the same time as the red and white flowers.
32	At the foot of the mountain is 'blew.'
33	This indicated water,
34	and is also connected with the second interpretation of the tablet.
35	In the first part of the process the substance goes into the mountain. Warm and dark.
36	No water is involved except the water that in time will be removed from the egg,

37   and will collect in the base of the oven.
38   In the second part of the process the work being done with the sun also needs water,
39   and is the water indicated in the drawing.
40   Letting your substance set in the sun for only one day and being dry will destroy it.
41   I can never be without water if the sun is involved.

This drawing also shows clouds and wind blowing on the flowers.

1   The clouds are connected to the water and vapor that will be found in the oven at the second   stage.
2   The wind is a reference to the time of year,
3   and how it is cold outside and that it is necessary for the oven to be kept warm.
4   The freezing connected with January will also destroy the substance.

It should be remembered that Flamel stated that he transmuted to silver in January. It would be the   second January, or 13 months after he started.   Second understanding is connected with Crowned Androgyny. Tablet 2 is also tablet 9 in the steps.

The Third Tablet of Abraham the Jew

On this third tablet, it was said to be about a Beautiful Garden. A place where gold was found. It shows two men digging, but Flamel say's, "they couldn't find because they were blind, and they must consider the weight." They were looking for the source of the water. In the middle of the garden stood a hollow oak, and a rose bush. First, I said of the second tablet (the mountain) that it showed the side view of the oven. Flamel also said that he would have failed to find the oven had Abraham not showed it twice. Here we see the second design of the oven. If you will look, the design of this garden (an 'X' design) is of a top view of the oven. Like looking down on a pyramid. Flamel mentioned that the oven is the one used by the Philosophers, not a standard oven as used by those he found experimenting in their Labs. This shows twice the one oven used to make the stone. Flamel also said he hide the design of the oven in his fresco, and I have shown that with the one line drawing. His statement, "must consider the weight to find the source of the water" is about the process and also about Genesis. The firmament is there to cause the waters below to be divided. In this third tablet, that is what we are doing. The oven is in darkness, also as in Genesis, the egg within is rotting, returning to a base matter. The waters within the egg are being divided. The moisture from within the egg is removed, but forms as water within the oven. The oven is sealed and so none of the water escapes, so quite a collection of water appears. Consider the weight of the egg, it diminishes as the process works. The hollow oak, is a way of saying, the hollow egg Shell! The rose bush is a reference to the finish of the stone which is of a rose color. Again I apologize about the picture. I cannot count the number of the flowers, and so to guess I would say there are seven to signify the finish of the second half (seven months) of the work. In our process on the first day we organize our substances. On the second day the substances are kept warm and put into the oven. The second step continuing shown here is during this part of the process where the substance is slowly by nature being destroyed as to what it was, and is being taken back to a base and to an unformed matter. The blind men shown there are blind because of the absence of light which was divided away also in this step. This is the third tablet and is also the tenth tablet of the process. The darkness and water are about the first part, division of the below waters. The rose bush is a hollow tree or oak and are about the second part. The substance when finished is no longer mixed with water to work as it has been, and is a substance able alone to be with the sun above, or has become 'like' the sun. It would then be perfect, (Osiris has risen and is perfect). Osiris can ascend to the Gods above which he chose to do. If you will look to the middle of the allegory, you will see two fountains with a 'Y' design, where the water is coming from. This is the sign for April. Remember Flamel said he finished his work and transmuted to gold during April. Alchemically we have here the 'Ouroborous.' The serpent biting his tail. The matter within the shell is being recycled back to a base. All that it was is being removed, and it is becoming formless matter. In legend, this is Osiris in his envelope, he is slowly being destroyed. We actually do nothing in our process this first April. This tablet is inserted here to cause confusion for those looking for the stone, and is a way to hide the process. The first steps where we put the egg in the oven, it sets and wait's till May. Those working or trying to work Flamels process would naturally try to develop a part of it with this tablet, not knowing it is really about the finish, or a tablet with two understandings. Also, if you will look at the base of the tablet, you can count 16 squares. They represent the 16 months it takes to get to the beautiful garden. If you will look at the rows of trees, those of the left side are dark, those of the right side are in light. I believe this is a way to show the two parts. As we proceed with explanations of the allegories, you will see that everything put into an allegory means something.

1   A sweet Garden.
2   A Place where Gold was made.
3   Flamel transmuted to Gold in April.
4   This Tablet used twice in series allegory.
5   This tablet third and tenth in series.

Third Tablet Understanding

1   Process in dark.
2   Can't see where water comes from.
3   Must consider weight.
4   Weight of egg is decreasing.
5   Waters being divided.
6   Fountain is Oven.
7   Oven is Firmament.
8   Note Y design of twin streams.
9   Y Design denotes April Constellation.
10 April Aries the Ram.

Tenth Understanding

1   A Place where Gold is Made.
2   Count 16 black squares.
3   16 Squares is 16 months.
4   16 months to end of Process.
5   Stone is finished and linked to gold.
6   Gold is sun which is gold and seed of gold.
7   Finished in sunlight.
8   Rose Tree - In Ancient Egypt, rose stood for regeneration.
9   Rose-regeneration, A. E. Waite's book, Brotherhood of the Rosy Cross.
10 flowers- I believe 3 red flowers on left side of tree.
11 Two white lowers on right side of tree. Has to do with 3/2 ratio.

Please Note.

1   X design looking down of oven.
2   X Design is top view of oven.
3   X design shown in several pictorial allegories.
4   Flamel stated Abraham showed oven twice.
5   This is second place Abraham shows oven.
6   First place is side view of mountain, second tablet
7   Stone is finished, also time of resurrection of Osiris.
8   This second work is done (above work area) of the oven or in heaven. The substance is linked to the sun and with Osiris. He is linked to and joins with the god found within the sun. See Eye of Horus on american dollar bill!

Forth tablet of Abraham the Jew.

"On the last side of the fifth leaf there was a King, with a great Fauchion, who made to be killed in his presence by some Soldiers a great multitude of little Infants, whose Mothers wept at the feet of the unpitiful Soldiers the blood of which Infants was afterwards by other Soldiers gathered up, and put in a great vessel, wherein the Sun and the Moon came to bathe themselves."

Authors Note: This tablet uses metaphor instead of an astrological sign to give the time. The crowned king, "in a field Vert" (green) is how Flamel describes it. What do we see with a crown in a green field? A bull. The bull denotes the time of year, or May. This tablet is used to show the May-Day of alchemy. It is the third day of Genesis when the waters are to come together. Here soldiers are gathering blood! The blood is the water we separated from the egg by process. The water now will be fed back to the matters of the egg that have been changed into a base. The waters though first will circulate within the oven, again and again to unite the above and below. From Genesis, "let the Waters come Together." We see in the drawing, the sun and moon came to bath in these waters. This tablet has only the one meaning. We have killed the egg and contents, and destroyed all that it was or ever would be. We now will remake the substance. We do this by joining all of the creation to this substance within the oven, within the shell. Note, that it said in Genesis, "within one place." That one place is within the shell within the oven.

This tablet (The Crowned King) is a metaphor

1   The Crowned King is representative of a bull,
2   and or the sign for May.
3   In alchemy the time of year for this step is Called, 'The May-Day.'
4   Normally and in many a pictorial allegory it is shown with a bull charging a ram.
5   The crown of course are the horns of the bull.

6   In our process, the killing represented here is the destruction of the egg within our oven.

7   It has to be taken out, and taken apart.

8   The yolk of the egg if you have done things right, will be enclosed within the membrane found inside   the egg shell,

9   and will be a little black ball.

10   The color black indicates death,

11   that the egg has died so to speak, and the matter has returned to primordial matter. (Osiris in his Tomb)

12   The water of the egg, (the blood in the oven) has been removed,

13   and collected at the bottom of the oven.

14   This represents death, but it also has returned the substance to what the alchemists called primordial   matter. We now will move this matter forward.

15   It was thought that the world and all within it had been made with this matter through process.

16   A fresh shell has to be placed within the oven,

17   In the bottom half the black substance placed there and then filled with pure water.

18   The top of another shell will be placed over this collection,

19   and the process resumed.

20   In the first part of the process we worked in the dark,

21   now the oven has to set where all of nature can shine on it,

22   sun, moon, stars, fresh air, and still kept warm.

23   The alchemists tell you, a single substance,

24   a single oven,

25   and that no strange substance may be added.

26   Pure water is no stranger, and pure water will have to be added occasionally as it is lost. Never use dirty water of any kind.

27   Before the oven was sealed, now it is vented

28   and fresh air is allowed to enter.

29   As the water and substance mix, a beautiful thing occurs,

30   the Rainbow of alchemy appears.

31   Within 24 hrs the water will turn a beautiful lime green,

32   this will last for a day.

33   Then the waters will turn a beautiful sky blue,

34   again it will last a day and then finally the waters will turn a beautiful banana yellow,

35   which within a day will turn clear.

The oven sat in the dark for a period of four months to reach this stage.

1   During this time it has to be kept warm, (as a birds nest is the instructions).

2   It will now be processed outside, and always in light.

3   This next step goes on throughout the summer,

4   called the (three hottest months) by some alchemists and shown as three red stars.

5   If I was to say what the soldiers represented, I would say the small mountains.

6   They cause the water in the oven to be directed back to the center to the substance being processed.

7   There are many different pictorial allegories in alchemy connected with the so called May-Day

8   Not all are shown as this one,

9   but in each is represented a time for collecting water or dew.

10   In most of them if you will look, the light is represented in two streams coming down,

11   and represents collecting from two lights being sun and moon.

12   The above has to be collected by the below to be improved or augmented,

13   it can only work in one fashion,

14   and that is by the vapor within the oven.

15   First we have vapor and light.

16   The vapor absorbs the light during the day and night.

17   This vapor condenses and returns to the below to feed the earth within the vessel or shell.

18   This slowly makes a new earth.

19   The sun shining on the substance does nothing,

20   the moon shining on the substance does nothing, it must be a combination.

Now, I have shown that the sign is for the Bull Taurus and that it is for bringing the waters together. The word definition for the bull is **'congelation.'** Consider the third day of Genesis.

Fifth Tablet of Abraham

"always every seventh leaf was without any writing; but, instead thereof, upon the first seventh leaf, there was painted a Rod and Serpents swallowing it up."

Authors Note: The lower serpent of this tablet gives us the sign for Leo. The time is the end of Leo in August. What has happened is the waters have come together. That is what he is trying to show by the serpent, one, swallowing the other. Note we have here the two serpents that we had in the first tablet. We said they were sun and moon. Here they are lying on the ground, in other words the above and below are now joined. In alchemy this is the 'Androgyny Formed.' Male and female are now within the matters. Outside this is what you have done with your compost pile lying in the lights if you had one. This is what happens to all matters outside recycled with and by nature over time. The understanding is about all seed. Seed, be it male or female will unite with this material and grow. From Genesis, the waters have come together. In the third day of Genesis, there is an 'AND' word. That is yet to come, "and let the dry land appear." As I mentioned seed, the seed here was destroyed. It doesn't matter if from an egg, or from a plant, what needs to be understood is that what the matters were going to be is now all taken away. A new substance being androgynous is what we now have. It can be nothing by itself. That also is important to understand. You might ask, what can nature do with this material if it has no seed. Nature wants to do something with it? What if naturally nature made material that she could do nothing with? Can you imagine what we would now have lying around?

Nature has her way of using all material!

On this leaf, which is the fifth on the Abraham the Jew tablets, we see what is depicted.

1   One serpent swallowing another,
2   and a shaft lying upon the ground.
3   We have seen the last tablet was letting the waters come together
4   and I mentioned the and word.
5   Well, this tablet is telling you the waters have come together,
6   and we now have that mixture.
7   Note the staff and serpents were the lights above as we explained in the first tablet.
8   Now they lay on the ground, and one serpent is swallowing the other.
9   You might say this is Abraham's way of saying the waters above and below are mixed.
10   The lower serpent gives the time if you will compare it to August astrological symbol, Leo.
11   The three hottest months have passed.
12   The time period is actually now moving into Virgo,
13   and a time for drying.
14   For the dry land to appear is upon us.

As the waters come together.

1   We have made what is known in alchemy as androgynous material.
2   This is because we have used both lights to make the substance.
3   Sun being male, and Moon being female.
4   In nature, if you made a compost pile you would say it was androgynous material, why?
5   It was made outside using sun and moon and really, all of nature.
6   It is androgynous as it needs to mix with everything that comes to it.
7   If you made it with just sunlight or just moonlight, it wouldn't work right,
8   and you would wonder why and probably unless and alchemist, never know!

9   All things in nature that are taken apart end up becoming androgynous material,

10   it is the only way it can happen as all nature is involved with it.

11   And it is the way our planet continually reuses the material it has produced.

12   The word definition is digestion connected to Leo.

Sixth Tablet of Abraham the Jew.

In the second seventh, a cross where a serpent was crucified. This serpent we have above, first if you will compare to the sign of Virgo, you will find the right side of this serpent has the same outline as Virgo the Virgin. We have now moved to September. The serpent is now hung on a cross to dry! Our substance within the oven is raised to the upper work area, and is set in moonlight only (note one serpent), and is to be dried and ground to a powder at finish. This is the last part of the third day, "Let the dry land appear." and so the third day occupies three of the tablets, when to start, how long and when to finish. The serpent is hung on a cross, and I will show you how to find this cross within the oven. The oven has two places of work as I noted, and this upper section is used as it is warmer, and so used at the colder times of the year. It will be the warmest part of the oven. Now we are collecting only moonlight, it more easily is collected in the above of the oven. Remember this cross as we proceed if you will consider the scales of the sign for October. To this cross extend the arms, and hang the trays and you have that that sign. The substance now will become what is called mercury by the alchemists. Note we had mercury at the start of our process. That was the untreated mercury. This substance when dried is the purified mercury, and is now become the base of our stone we are trying to make. The substance is a pure now, virgin earth. Please note Virgo, and the virgin earth. If you will consider the astrological sign, you will see how the understanding of the sign coincides with the understanding of the substance and what we are doing with process. I believe this understanding is the original understanding and why they even came into existence. This is a very 'Old Science.'

Many have searched for the substance of the philosophers stone, and probably every substance found here in the below has been tried to make it, and here is the thing. The substance of the stone does not exist here on the earth, the base substance you have to first make to make the stone. Here the finish of the substance into dry earth, the change into mercury is that substance. As you look to September, consider the Osirian Mystery, and that Tat Cross raised in September. It was at the end of September 'when the scales came into play.' They are this same cross drawn in the oven and the small pyramids from the side view. The Cross with equal arms also was known at this time. All was in balance. The serpent is pinned to the cross with one spike! You might say at this part of the process, the dead serpent is the sun! It is not used here. Remember, we originally had two serpents and they were connected to the two lights.

1. If you will look at Virgo, the Virgin,
2. Note the curves on the right side of the serpent are the same as the curves on the right side of Virgo.
3. So time period, late August to late September. Virgo the Virgin is descriptive of the substance,
4. when it is dried!
5. A pure white substance made by nature,
6. but a substance nature could not make by herself.
7. The cross shows that the substance is to be dried in the top part of the oven, this has to do with
8. drying the substance only in moonlight and above the constellation Virgo the Virgin.
9. From mythology, two female energy sources, see Osiris and the Two Sisters.
10. We see the small mountains in the background,
11. they are indicative of the small mountains in the oven.
12. From the picture, you see the serpent is above them.
13. We also know now that the serpents represent the lights above,
14. and so one serpent here means one light.
15. In the last tablet, the two serpents
16. showed both were involved, and so here one.
17. Like is a word used by the alchemists,
18. and so we have reached a point with our substance where like is important.
19. When finished we will have a substance pure in nature,
20. it will be white and Pure.
21. Because it was dried in moonlight,
22. it is brought forth by the virgin (Virgo) in nature.
23. This is necessary as from this substance we will make either one or both stones.
24. The white stone deals only with the moon,
25. and so had to be finished by the moon.
26. The red eventually deals with the sun.
27. If we dried this substance with sun and moon,
28. we could not make the white stone from it as it would have male (sun) characteristics.
29. We had both male and female from our process up to the drying
30. and the substance was known as androgynyn,

31 By drying in only moonlight we produce Osiris and the virgin birth of nature..

32 We said that the substance turning into a black ball that it had returned to primordial matter   and this was seen as death.

33 We now have overcome death and the white substance is seen in that way.

34 It is seen as a substance that has the capabilities of being many or all things.

35 I might point out that in ancient Egypt they had a holiday celebrated during September

36 and they called it the Set. Holiday.

37 It was a holiday where death being overcome was celebrated.

38 I can't prove the connection, but I think it is an obvious one.

39 This substance when dried is hard and pure white,

40 it will need to be taken from the oven

41 and ground to a powder for the continuing operations.

42 Always being careful as to what light you allow to touch it.

1 The word definition is distillation."

2 If we distill something we are drying it, that is what needs to be done at this point.

3 Why the Virgin? We now have (when dried) the dry land called earth finished on the third day.

4 We also have what is called Septembers Child in alchemy.

5 Flamel said we have gone from death to life. In Egypt, a celebration of life over death.

6 Now for the explanation.

7 I have said we work for the time when the substance can withstand direct sunlight.

8 Why is that the lights are used to impart sex to the substance.

9 We can always add light, but never take it away!

10 This substance is the end of Ouroborous. We went from death to life, full circle!

This substance was said to be the base of all things by many Alchemists. This needs to be researched. Who knows what the possibilities of these substances will be? I know of no information of matters treated this way and over time. I do know that the pyramid was said to do wonderful things to matter within. Also to growing things treated within the pyramid. The pyramid focuses energy that I call Creation Energy as it is the energy all of the below works with. If all in the below is formed by those lights above over a 'Great Length of Time,' why would a short time purified matter not be of great benefit to us? The red stone as believed and as you will see and understand, is and becomes as the sun! This is the result of what we have always known as the 'Good Light.' If you have believed the light is good, can you see the ancients found a gift of that light, and they believed it was a gift of God!

The seventh tablet of Abraham the Jew

"And in the last seventh there were painted Deserts, or Wildernesses, in the midst whereof ran many fair fountains, from whence there issued out a number of Serpents, which ran up and down here and there."

Authors Note: On this seventh tablet, hard to consider exactly what it is about? We see mountains, and serpents and water flowing down. In alchemy this is called the Conjunction. The waters are coming together. Alchemists said, "we must turn the wheel again!" We have made and finished the material for making the stone, we have the virgin earth, the 'Dry Land.' We now start to repeat the process to actually make the stones of the philosophers. There are two stones to be made, one the white stone, one the more powerful red stone. One takes now three months to finish, (the white), the other or red stone, seven. The first part of the process takes nine months, the second part seven months This is the point where the one part mercury, is finished (nine months) and where we now begin the work for the stones, the second seven months. With the above pictorial allegory, remember what we are working with. A substance (earth), serpents which are lights, and water. They are now again coming together to further purify and augment the substance below. What we must learn and know here is that we are to make two stones with the material. Not shown in these tablets well enough to see. The white stone is just about the moonlight, and so never again will that part of the substance see the sun. For the red, we use both lights for now, but eventually it will be finished by only the sun. The material was dried in moonlight only as the lights have been given gender. The sun is masculine, the moon feminine. The white stone is of a feminine character, and is linked to the moon. Here you now can see why. If we dried the substance and used both lights, the masculine effect of the sun would be imparted to the material, and no white stone could be made from it! It would be ruined as far as to make the white stone. In alchemy this understanding is shown by a 'White Goose,' and sometimes a 'White Swan.' I will show this in another allegory, feeding herself by using her own blood for food. 'Like' is the word also for the same understanding. If here the lights are not Like the below, no stone will be made or finished correctly! The white stone moonlight, like only. When we work for the finish of the red stone, like or sunlight will be used only! This is how the term Like used by the alchemists is to be used and understood. There are other allegories where this is shown clearly and will be reproduced in this work to completely give you understanding. The white goose/swan is feeding on her own blood is like saying the white stone is now feeding only on the white light of the moon. For the red stone, it will become a stronger more powerful stone and so is further augmented by both lights. For the next three month time period, two things are going to be going on. This time period is from October until the end of December or the beginning of January however you want to say it. The white stone will then be finished, and is then the white flowers of the second tablet. The red stone will be finished with the two lights for the further augmentation, and at that point becomes a work of only the sun. So the red flowers or red powder of that tablet. Remember this is the seventh tablet here, the last tablet in this series, but the over lap now takes us back to that first tablet and the second understanding.

Tablet One, second understanding.

Mercury is the substance we are to use, the serpents we showed are the two lights. We had waters below and the two lights. The old man we know now as Saturn, or Set and we discussed that battle that must be fought by the matters. We see the old man with an hour glass on his head with red powder or sand within it. What does this mean? The second understanding from what I have said, is now the time to fix the material, and make the red stone. To fix we are left with open and shut, and bind and loose.

Tablet Two, Second understanding. We have the flowers on the top of the mountain. One is for the completion of the white stone, the white flowers. The red is saying we are now working for the red only. The sun is at the side of the tablet, and is saying it is now a work of the sun. At the foot of the mountain is 'blew.' This is water, we need as before to add water to the substance as it is how we 'fix' the light above and create a new earth! Always water is involved. Let your substance go dry for one day, and the sun will destroy your work and you will have to begin again. It is January and it is cold, the substance is at the top of the oven and will stay there till the finish. I said before that the tablets kind of blend together, that should be easier to see now. All cannot be said in one tablet, so it is necessary to see this blending of the matters and how to do it to understand.

The second understanding of the third tablet. We are back to the garden, "a place where Gold was found." Sixteen squares means the sixteen months have passed and now you have the red stone. It is the rose bush, which is like a metaphor for the red powder. It is a hollow oak as the stone is found within the hollow shell. The red powder has now become like the sun. The sun is perfect, the stone is also perfect. Osiris has risen and now can go to heaven to live with the Gods. Osiris is now three in One, androgynynous, (male female) and then linked to God (the sun).

In Genesis, we have moved to the fourth day where the lights are in the firmament, and can now shine onto the earth. The relationship has changed to the one we know today. The sun ruling the day, the moon the night. We now can know and use them as we want, and so by doing the 'Great Work,' that is exactly what we will do. The earth, stone, has augmented to the point it can stand now direct sunlight upon it. As we review other allegories and understand them, all this will be much easier to see. The fixing in tablet one, second time is the cutting off of the feet! The above is 'fixed' to the below. It just takes four more months to do that. It now becomes a work of just the sun, and why red is used. As we used Like, and moonlight with the white stone, we now consider like and sun with the red stone. What the substance has become I can't describe. It was organic matter.

It becomes a sort of crystal as the matters and light and vapor combine. It is something different! It is not something that nature can make, it is something nature made guided by you. Look out your window at all things that nature makes! She makes our world, and by Gods hand, has made us. Is it impossible for her to make anything?

This was for me for many years a hard tablet to get any meaning from. But it becomes easy when you consider a few things.

1   This step and tablet is about the Conjunction.
2   He mention deserts and wilderness,
3   and so remember we proceed on this step
4   with a dry white powder mercury from the last step.
5   What we are doing is again bringing the waters together for the red stone,
6   same for the white but selecting the waters to apply.
7   From the first tablet we found the serpents on the staff were the lights above,
8   and so here again the serpents are the lights.
9   The streams are the waters issuing from the small mountains,
10   or within the oven we are also adding water and the process continues.
11   We have the lights, circulation,
12   and the substance that needs to be augmented for the red stone.
13   What we will also be adding is heat to keep the oven warm as it is now again, winter.
14   The conjunction is shown as starting in October,
15   and is from the substance finished in September.
16   The substance is now the 'True Mercury' of the philosophers.
17   It is the only substance on the earth that can be made into 'The Philosophers Stone.'
18   The philosophers mention about every substance known to man
19   and tell you it does not produce the stone,
20   or is not used to produce the stone,
21   and one is left wondering what it could possible be made of ??
22   The answer is simple after you know,
23   the stone is made from a substance that you have to make.
24   It is not found on the earth naturally.

The Conjunction has to do with both stones.

25   For the red, we "turn the wheel again,"
26   the process continues.
27   It is basically a repeat of what we have done in the past.
28   All waters are used with the further augmentation of mercury.
29   The white stone, which is a lesser stone than the red,
30   can and is made from the mercury,
31   but the mercury is not first further augmented.
32   The white stone is made of like, is female and is from the moon.
33   We make it separately from the red,
34   we use only warmth, moonlight and vapor.
35   This next step takes three months and lasts until January where the white stone is finished,

36   and the final work of the red will begin.

37   What is important to realize here,

38   is we are making a substance not found on the earth.

39   Mercury is a special material.

40   It will form the white stone,

41   and the process is a reaction caused by moonlight and vapor in contact with the mercury within the oven

42   It literally is the above being captured or condensed to the below.

43   Please remember that the lights were 'Good.'

44   We don't really know what that means, but we will understand all this in the near future.

45   The red stone is finished in April. Osiris is resurrected to heaven. It is also Easter! All that we know of at that time are connected!

46

On how to understand and read the allegories of the Alchemists

When time could be said as covering the first few years of my studies, there were many times when I put my books aside because I just couldn't understand the messages. This continued for many years actually, and really it was probably 20 years before I had a fair understanding of what is shown with their drawings. I hate to say that, but it is true. In my discussions with others, many have said that the information should be just thrown away or discarded, as it was good for nothing. There was no understanding of it all. Many reasons were given but just misunderstanding of what alchemy is really about originally is the true reason why the material is misunderstood.

Today alchemy has become many things. Because we didn't understand the Great Secret of it all, many have come forward to say what it is their understanding based on their work. I would say their misunderstanding based on what they thought it may be about. There is a spiritual explanation, by Mr. Carl Jung. Alchemy is about man and how he is to improve himself spiritually. I would tend to agree that by the study man will improve himself, but originally alchemy was not about that. Alchemy was about the search for one true God, and if there was one, to know of him. After what was found and understood, it would lead to a spiritual uplifting of anyone who did the study, but originally this was not the quest. Another way of alchemy was Spagyrics. This was said to be from the great Paracelsus himself. The term to me just means lab alchemy, or working with chemicals and processes within a lab. Many today practice this type of alchemy. I am sure today that some of these lab alchemists have found ways to make gold with those chemicals and processes. However, I do not agree that this is what the originally alchemy was about. It is called the great work. Not because it leads one to a substance that can make gold, but because it leads one to and understanding of the workings of nature. Man must learn to use the forces in nature as God did! God created the earth and everything that is found here in the below. God is perfection, and God is the only perfection that there is. If man through his study of nature can or could find the perfection, then he found God! He proved to himself there was a God, that man could know of him, that man could do as God did. With a substance that man deemed perfect, he had understood and worked as God must have done. So, alchemy is the 'Great Work.'

Why is it then alchemy is still a secret? Why do we still search for the Philosophers Stone? Actually, there are many reasons. In the past alchemy was very cleverly hidden by all that found it. Probably because it was one way to stay alive. Because it was the work of God, it was believed the common man was not good enough to have such a precious gift. It was figured having it, the masses, would in some way destroy the world. It was believed by others that some powerful king would take over the world it he did have it. Many reason as I said, not many of them well thought out. For myself, as to why alchemy became so secretive, there are two reasons. The first was because in ancient Egypt, knowledge was for the few. It was power, and so it was contained in the temples of Egypt. Alchemy was a knowledge about God, and so not for the masses. The second reason we still see today. We say we now share our information, but it is not true. Secrets are secrets, and today we guard our secrets and they have always been carried on. Note that I said, "What we thought was a tradition," That may not be true. I have had a thing lets say with Moses. Believing in myself and what I have found, I often wondered why Moses had not fully explained alchemy to his followers? Did Moses keep secrets also? Recently on some tv programs, I listened to a flood story in Egypt. Actually, about 1500 BC, note I said about. The Nile river dried up and ceased to flow. All was lost. The workings of nature destroyed Egypt. Without the Nile, the society was lost, the temples were lost as to priest being there. Knowledge was lost (misunderstood). It was quite a catastrophe! They actually said children were eaten by the adults to stay alive. People were buried in mass graves, and society as we thought we knew it ceased to exist. From the program it was stated that a small Ice age had hit Europe, and was the cause of these weather changes in Africa and Egypt. This is a big story, but not for me to explain. It happened, and Egypt just ceased to exist as an organized society. Now Moses was several hundred years after this happened. Yes Egypt was being rebuilt, but the information was almost all lost about the past. Many have written that those living at that time in Egypt did not understand all the writing of the past, and so Moses, who was educated in those same temples, was not really versed with the in depth meaning of what they meant. For me it is reason enough to understand why Moses did not fully explain the meanings of some of those things he was taught in the temples of Egypt. Perhaps Moses did have a complete understanding. Perhaps he did teach some of his followers, I just haven't been able to find it (the explanation). In particular I am referring to Genesis and it's understanding as connected to the yearly cycle. For me, Moses may be given the credit of writing Genesis, but the information came from the temples of Egypt and was very ancient, long before Moses was found to be there. My opinion. As you read and understand all that is written in this work, it will be up to you to decide what you believe.

As noted, this chapter is to be about explaining how to understand the alchemical allegories. An allegory is a picture drawn to convey information. The information is hidden in the drawing. All of alchemy is in allegorical drawings, or in alchemical sayings. All of them are written in a way as to give information, but in a hidden way. I will show you how to understand much of what has been drawn, and how to link with the drawings what was said. I cannot show you how to understand all of the alchemical symbols. Why I have already explained to you. Others through not understanding have given a different explanation. Some have given spiritual explanations. Many Lab Persons have given Lab explanations. Some have copied series allegories and changed them to a Lab process. In all, alchemy is a mass of symbols and allegories that almost could never be linked together, or understood and explained. This work I feel will change much of that. I believe it is very important to mankind as this is our gift from the past. A true understanding of many of the things that were said and why they were believed. There are libraries of this material, and for the most part it lays around misunderstood and lost to mankind. I have said many times in the past, alchemy cannot be understood unless it is based on something, and that something is Genesis. The series allegories, and there are many, when written by a true alchemist are just that, An alchemists way of explaining Genesis as it pertains to the stone.

Genesis never ends, it simply changes where and how it works. As our world spins around the sun conditions are always changing. Genesis works with these conditions. The ancients recognized these conditions, and realized they worked in both parts of the world, six days in each. This is from theunderstanding of 'Two Earth' as described by the suns movement. All else we must know is really how they understood the days and what they were based on. All to them had to do with 'cycles.' As we go through the allegories, you will see they based it sometimes on the moon and her cycle, and sometimes on the sun but based on the same time period. A day is a month, based on the cycle of the moon. We quickly note the time with the period of the moon, but we don't with the sun. The alchemist though sometimes used the sun to point out time, and so again one sun was one month in time. Few would ever know that, that it was meant to be understood the same, but any alchemist would understand it. I understand it, and as we proceed so will you. Hidden information remember, and all you need know is the little tricks they used to hide it. Many ways were used to hide information, this is just one of those many.

There are two major divisions of time connected to the stone. The first is a time period of nine months, the second is for seven months for the 16 month total. I always say to count what is there on the fresco or allegory. It is necessary to know which time period is being shown by the allegory when counting. The first nine is the first turning of the wheel, the second seven is about the second turning of the wheel. The first is from Dec. to September, the Second is from Oct. to April. I will show and use many of the allegories to show these points. Now Seven is everywhere! Many of the allegories only cover this last seven days. I could say the last seven are really about the stone. Why? It is because the first nine are just making the right compost, the right 'base' to make the stone out of and many didn't show it! If I were an alchemist, and another showed the last seven, I would surly know he knew the first nine! Always look for seven, and when you see it know what it is about. There is more. In some of the series, April is shown connected with seven, why? It is the last of the seven months of the second part of the process. And so, seven is shown there. It is the 16 month of process, but it is the seventh month of making the Red Stone, the seventh month of the second half of the total process. These ways of counting will become familiar, and are necessary to understand what the pictorial allegory is showing.

Written Allegories

With the written allegories, much of the spelling will be as it was written in those old times. I don't think I need explain each of them as I have pointed out the process. It is important to be able to link what all these Masters have said down through the ages.

"Another emblem shows the mermaid-like Aphrodite (Venus), goddess of the sea, with a golden crown and twin tails. Of this favored symbol of the alchemists, the epigram in the .*Viridarium* states: I am a goddess exceeding fair, born from the depths of the sea, which in its course washes and surrounds all the dry land. Let my breasts pour forth to thee twin streams of blood and milk (*vac virginis*), which thou' canst well know. These two combined leave to be wrought upon by a gentle fire, then will the Moon, and Apollo (the .Sun) answer thy prayers."

Authors Note: With this pictorial allegory which I will include, if you will turn it over you will see the Ram's head. The Rams Head gives us the time of the May-Day. A time to bring the waters together. This is the start of the third Day in Genesis, and The fourth tablet of Abraham. The blood and Milk is the part of the sun and moon we are to collect with vapor.

"In the course of his remarks upon the foregoing operations, Mylius lays down four degrees of heat: ' the , first, slow and mild, as of the flesh or the embryo; the second, moderate and temperate; as of the sun in June ; the third, great and strong, as of a calcining fire; the fourth, burning and vehement, as of fusion. Each of these is twice as great as the preceding degree.' Stolcius' states that Phoebus [the sun] runs through the zodiac in a year, and recreates all seeds with his rays. Hence learn the four degrees of our toil. ..they are the Ram, the Crab, ,the Scales, and Capricorn (the signs of the four ,seasons, the two equinoxes and two solstices) "

Authors Note: Points Out a yearly cycle. also connections to the position of the sun.

"The celebrated Bath or Fountain of the Philosophcr is depicted in an illustration bearing a fundamental likeness to an earlier drawing given by Libavius *"Take our water, with ,which. no limbs are wet . (sophic mercury), , says Stolcius; make Sun and Moon bathe in it together. When thou hast accomplished this, let a Breath be combined with them; thereafter shall thine eyes behold two lilies. Hence what tree thou wilt shall arrange its own fruit on a tree and there from thou mayest pluck thee the fruits*

"The sole chosen Heroine, Miriam the Jewess is described in- the epigram as follows: "Of the race of Palestine, sister of Moses, behold Miriam equally rejoices and triumphs in the Chymic choir".

She knew the hidden secrets of the great stone. She has made us also learned, sage that she is, with her words. ."Smoke loves smoke, and is loved by it in return: but the white herb of the lofty mountain captivates both. The 'white herb, which'may"be Lunary, represents the white stage of the Great Work, white and red smokes signify mercury and sulphur of the philosophers."

Authors Note: Connections to Moses, Genesis and the pyramid. And so important for me to point out. Also, see oven by comments of mountain, and sun and moon vapor mixtures with smoke comments. The white herb, (Septembers Child) is pure white, and with Like, connected to the moon. It is formed at the top of the 'mountain.' The Two Lillies are the two stones that can be made from the mercury which at that time is white and in moonlight.

"The four Vases containing the crow, peacock, swan, and king symbolise various stages in the Great Work of preparing the.Philosopher's Stone. Stolcius' epigram runs thus With his skilled arrows the god of Delos (Apollo) lays stiff Python low, that he may lead his life in fire. But if anyone would know who tha't dragon is, the ancients say it is their sulphur. Yet, if you desire to know whence he of (Pelos gets his bow and arrows, the couchant lion will give thee knowledge.'

Authors Note: Arrows have to do with the sun. The four seasons or times of the stone are indicated. Python is or describes the matter we work on. Here he links sulfur to the substance we collect from the sun. Any pointed object is or does indicate the sun. Consider the obelisk

From *Atalanta Fugien: and M* Maier

"'To the~first"two engravings he assigns titles taken from the Emerald' Table of Hermes: The wind has carried him in, its, womb The earth is his nurse He continues with : "Go to the woman that washes clothes, and do thou likewise ". The epigram runs: Who- ever thou art, that .loves to examine hidden doctrine, do not idle" but take as thine example everything that can profit thee. seest thou not, how a woman is wont to wash clothes clean of stains by pouring hot water upon them? , ..Imitate her,; so shalt thou not be cheated of thine .art for the water ,'washes. the lees of the dark. Body."

Authors note: The Woman that washes clothes pictorial will be included. Washing is a metaphor for cleansing the matters below with warm water from the mixture with the moon. The moon is seen as female, and so when indicated to be used it is shown that way. In another pictorial allegory, it is shown by a toad sucking the breast of the woman. The woman is moon, the toad is the impure substance. So, we wash with sun and vapor, or we wash with moonlight and vapor while keeping warm.

"The production of colors in alchemical operations was always a source of wonder and admiration to the alchemists, who often likened transmutation to dyeing, or tingeing as we have already seen, In another place the artist depicts a talking vulture, which perches upon the peak of a .high mountain and cries without stint: "White am I and black ;and red am **I called and I lie not at all!"**

"Descending from the mountain-top to the great waters, Maier likens the Stone in a later epigram to coral"As coral grows under the waters and is made hard by the air, so the Stone " "A plant, flourishing moist beneath the waves of the Sicilian sea, has multiplied its <u>branches beneath the warm waters.</u> the name it goes by is CORAL. ..it becomes a stone." a ruddy color it has, This is befitting image for the stone of Physics."

Authors Note: First, the colors are correct as you will see. These are the main colors though with many others. Above, he is basically telling you the stone is formed below water, and is as I have shown with the process. Always water is involved or the substance is destroyed. The sunlight will destroy as quickly as it will build the substance. In fact, in only a few hours without vapor and the substance is ruined.

"The Stone is said to be of universal occurrence: .The STONE is said to be vile refuse, and to lie by chance. on the roads, that rich and poor may get it. In the high hills others declare it is among the breezes of the air, ,while others say it is nurtured by rivers. All these are true in their proper sense,but I ask thee to seek such great gifts in hilly places."

"O Beginning of the first Beginning, consider the end.
O End of the last End, see to the Beginning."

Authors Note, for The hilly places, refer to Abraham's work and the mountains, and within our oven and the small mountains. Also, 16 months this has to be watched and always taken care of.

"I reply to your minor premise: that the artist does not need 100 years for the perfection of his art, much less a thousand, since a few days, not amounting in all to so much as a whole year may be enough -for him , once his art is known and discovered .But for its discovery, unless one has learned it from another, many years are needed And in most cases even one's whole life has not been sufficient for it's perfection!

Authors Note: How True I know this statement to be! I have basically spent my life, but always I have learned and enjoyed. Part of the reason I discuss is I have spent, others don't have to but just learn from me.

"In this Book "The Golden Tripod."

Basilius has disseminated greater wealth than all the riches of the Indeas; he has endowed the fair fields of Germany with golden fruit" plucked in the Hesperian garden, and with" the golden fleece borne away from Colchis by mighty toil. ~ Here is something for you to admire and imitate', says Maier," adding cryptically, , Only seek it at the bottom of the vessel, or you will wander astray "

Authors Note: I guess you could say, "where the waters come together." alchemists point to many times, a part of the process. One must look at all the information to get all the understanding.

"You need not look for our metallic seed among the elements" If YOU do not understand this that you ought to understand,' adds Basilius, ' your not adopted for Philosophy, or God concealeth it from thee."

Authors Note: Now consider the elements! If that does not say the seed is from Nature, I am not sure what does."! But, the nature is the Light, the above condensed to the below.

"The First Key of Basilius"

"Let the diadem of the King be of pure gold, and let the Queen that is united to him in wedlock be chaste and immaculate., If you would operate by means of our bodies, take a fierce grey wolf, which, though on account of its name -it be subject to the sway of warlike Mars, is by birth the -offspring of ancient Saturn, and is found in the valleys and mountains of the world, where he roams about savage with hunger. Cast to him the body of the King and when he has devoured it, burn him entirely to ashes in a great fire, By this process the King will be liberated; and when it has been performed thrice the Lion has overcome the wolf who will find nothing more to devour in him. Thus our Body has been rendered fit for the first stages-0f our work

Authors note: The wolf here is again water! Overcome connects to Flamels and Abraham's Lion, before the drying in August-September time period. The three hottest months, are the three months pointed out. He also speaks of the Crowned androgyny, "offspring of Saturn," found in valleys and mountain's. "When he has devoured it" which means when he has absorbed that medicine from the sun only. Last step, "then dry to ashes in a Great Fire (sun) and have the stone that will change lead to gold!"

"when-ever the moon is full , remove the cover, and see how the work is -progressing," When the mixture turns solid or fixed, its colour should be red of a somewhat dark tinge, It ought to be treated in the manner suggested for forty weeks, beginning on the, 25th of 'March. By the end of this period the mixture Will have become so hard as to burst the vessel, When this happy event takes place, the whole house will be filled with a most wonderful sweet fragrance; then will be the day - of the nativity of this most blessed Preparation."

Authors Note: This must be read very carefully! You can't always remove the cover! And when you can you may not want moonlight! Now here he is speaking of the last third of the last four months. We are dealing with just the sun and the substance. See, he said to open and look in moonlight! He told you to destroy your work! You might do this if you do not know the process, and if you do, then to him you do not deserve the substance! A hard lesson to learn!

"In stating that the best shape is that which accords most closely with the pattern of nature. Norton is perhaps referring to the Philosophers Egg. Here he quotes a saying of Alburtus Magnus" If God had not given us a vessel, his other gifts would have been of no avail,. he adds, and that is Glass!"

 Authors Note: In many places the masters tell you, 'One Oven'! I find this to be true with my work.

Norton also invented a kind of oven, which he is more secretive,

"This is a new thing which shall not be
Set out in Pictures for all to see
Which suttill furnace I devised alone
Which has many a wonders more
Than is conveniet at this season to tell."

Authors Note: I have always called my Oven the Norton Oven as I found it when reading Norton!

It is hard to find in allegory, as it is seldom shown except in that way, 'hidden.'

Norton also gives most importance to heats,

"A Perfect Master you may call him true
That knows his heats high and lows!"

Authors Note: I should like to point out, the 'heats' high and low may be his way of pointing to the two areas of work within the oven, as we try to keep the heat even throughout the year.

"It is the Principle to work ,Metals,' writes Basil , of this spirit, .being made to a spiritual essence,"
Which. IS ,a meer air, and flyeth
To and fro without wings, and is moving wind which
After it's expulsion out of it's habitat by Vulcan (fire) is driven into it's chaos , into which it entreth again."

Authors note: and again and again and again - -

A popular alchemical aphorism.

"Nature pleases nature,
nature conquers nature,
 nature produces nature!"

"Son and Moone in Hermes vessell
Learne how the Collours shew
The nature of the Elements,
And how the Daisies grow."

"Greate Python how .Appollo slew,
Cadmus his hollow-Oake ., ,
:His new-rais'd army, and Jason how'
The Fiery Steeres did yoke."

"The operations taking place are linked in a very suggestive ways with the ancient fables of Cadmus and other mythological ideas."

"The conjoining of philosophic sulphur.and mercury teaches the operator the nature of how the various colours appear in due succession.

"Ben Jonson refers to. "The bulls, our furnace,.
Still breathing fire."

Authors Note: The Bull is the power of the sun, or so indicated especially in springtime, (Bull in Ram).

"In the words of the informative, Alphonso, King of Portugall " The form of the glass must be in the form of the Sphere, '.with a long neck and no thicker than can be grasped. with. a large hand, and the length of the neck Not above a span, and no wider than the Egyptian seal May cover it's mouth even as there be in a natural Egg three things, the shell, the white, the yellow, even so There be in the Philosophers Stone these three things, the vessell, the Glass For the egg shell, the white liquor for the white of the egg, and the yellow body for the yolk of the egg. there becomes a bird of the white and yellow of the Egg, by a little heate of the Mother, the egg shell still remaining whole until the Chicken doe come forth; even so by every manner of wise in the Philosophers Stone, is made of the yellow body, and white Liquor by mediation of a temperate heat of the mother the earthly substance Hermes bird, the vessell still remaining Whole, and never opened until his full perfection."

By Philalethes

"as' twenty-four full Florence glasses, neither more nor less '.
'let the height of the vessel's neck be about one palm, and let the glass be clear and thick. ..in order to prevent the vapours which arise from our embryo bursting the vessel '. As the vessel was' hermetically sealed' it was at times called the House of Glass, or Prison of the King.

The Little Mountains was another term applied to the Vase' and Its containing furnace; the' white herb growing on the little mountains."

Ashmole

A poem in his collection lays down that- ...
The Glasst' with the Medicine must stand in the fyre
Forty dayes till it be Blacke in sight;
Forty dayes in the Blacknesse to stand he will desire,
And then forty dayes more, till itt be White;
And thirty in the drying if thou list to doe right.

Alfred W. Sylvester Jr.

Another Poem by Ashmole.

'Though Daphne fly from, Phoebus bright,
yet shall they both be one, ,
And if you understand this right
You have our hidden stone
For Daphne she is faire and white:
But 'volatile is she
Phoebus a fixed God of might,
And red as blood is he.
Daphne is a water Nymph,
And hath of Moysture store,
Which Phoebus doth consume with heate,
And dryes her very sore.
Them being dryed into one,
or christall flood must drink
Till they be brought to a white Stone:
Which wash with Virgins milk
So longe untill they flow as wax

And no fume you can see
Then have you all you need to ask
Praise God and Thankful Be."

"The principal colours were said to develop in the order, black, white, citrine, and red. Thus, Paracelsus states: "Soon after your Lili (tincture) shall have become heated in the Philosophic Egg, it becomes, with wonderful appearances, blacker than the crow; afterwards, in succession of time, whiter than. the swan; and at last passing through a yellow colour, it turns out more red than any blood.""

"various -other colors followed black, , green followed white, and the rainbow colours of the peacock's tail also appeared during the process: "Betwixt Black and Whyte sartayne, The Pekokes fethers ,will appear plaine " wrote. Thomas Charnock in 1574.

Authors Note: The Rainbow comes with the start of the third day, or alchemically May Day! Between black and white as said!

Philalethes, writing in 1645, gave the sequence as black, the peacock's tail, white, orange, and red.

Basil Valentine and others denoted the black, white, rainbow, and red colours by symbolic representations of the crow (or raven), swan, peacock, and phoenix.

Authors Note: Here the peacock's tail is the rainbow!

"The supposed connection between the degree of heat
And the progress of the Great work was linked also with color changes.
Basil valentine in his ninth key wrote "The matter passes through several
varieties of colour and may be said to change in appearance as often as a
new gate is opened to the fire."

Authors Note: Perhaps I am wrong in not explaining each of these, but each is an overall of the
work. As you finish and understand exactly what I am doing throughout the year, come back and
reread these if you don't understand. When you do, then what is here will be clear to you. All
they say above is True. Many beautiful colors! Each come and go as we change the conditions.
All lead to the red, and finally to the perfect ruby red of the end. I have included my drawing of
the serpent, and those colors are right as they come and go with one exception, those within the
egg as it starts to turn black! That you never see and so, guess!

"The animation of the whole work by the breath of the four elements is perhaps allusive to the
Spirit of God moving upon the face of the waters in the creation of the world. For it has been
held that, " The first chapter of Genesis is the greatest page in Alchemy."

Authors note: Consider the words, " nature was our only teacher." Genesis is about what the
ancients found to be here, not about something they couldn't know or understand.

"The Philosophic Tree is shown with birds and an issuing Hermetic Spring; it's fruit is being
gathered by a man who has ascended a ladder with seven rungs."

Authors note: Please note seven rungs or steps!

"*Aureum .Vellus oder Guldin Schatz und Kunstka11zmer* (The Golden Fleece, or Golden Treasure
and Art-Chamber).Unaided Nature states the writer, does not 'produce things whereby imperfect
metals can in a moment be made perfect, but by the secrets of Our Art this can be done. .. although
the. ..Stone can only be brought to its Proper <u>form by Art, yet the form is from Nature.</u>"

"A Quote by the Alchemist senior -
Our fire is a water. If you can give a fire to a fire and mercury to mercury, then you know
enough."

Authors Note: All parts of the creation were waters. The sun then becomes a water! The substance
below when sulfurous and when is becoming like the sun is a fire. Mercury is from the moon,
and so when the substance is finished by the moon and is mercury, mercury (the moon) is then
being used to augment mercury the stone below.

"Flamel placed great Importance to the sequence of colors in the operations of the Great Work,
he set them in his fresco   " a procession in which is represented by order all the colors of the
stone as they come and go" with this writing."

"Much pleaseth Gods procession. If' it be done in devotion. "

Authors Note. The allegory of the serpent drawn by the author represents these colors as they appear during the times of the year as I have seen them. They are the same as those of Flamel. Please note that 'Gods Procession' is the cycle of the year. What else could it be?

"Then the first-time that I- made projection, was upon , Mercurie, whereof I turned halfe a pound" or thereabouts, Into pure Silver, better than that of the Mine, as I my selfe assayed, and made others asssay many times. This was upon a Munday, the 17. Of January' about noone, in my ~ house, Perrenelle onely being present; in ,the yeere of the restoring of mankind, 1382. And afterwards, following alwayes my Booke, from word to word,. I made projection of the Red stone upon the like quantity of Mercurie, in the -presence likewise of Perrenelle only, in the same house, , the five and twentieth day of Aprlll followlng:, the same, .-- yeere, about five a clocke In the EvenIng; which I trans-muted truely into almost as much pure Gold, better assuredly than common golde, more soft, and more ply- able. 1 may speake It with truth, I have made It three times, with the helpe of Perrenelle, who understood it as well as I, because she helped mee in my operations, and without doubt, if shee would have enterprised to have done it alone, shee had attained to the end and perfection thereof. I had indeed enough when I had;once done it, but I found exceeding great pleasure and delight, in seeing , and contemplating the Admirable workes of Nature within The vessels."

Authors Note: Note January and April the same year, and the admirable works of nature, not a chemical lab type of process, and "within the vessels," or more than one. Also, "contemplating the works," or, he could not be doing a process he knew, he was doing something he was trying to understand, much different. This is very important to note.

From Pernety.

"The first aim. of the true philosophers Is to find a remedy for the Ills which afflict human nature ; the second is to discover a ferment, which, when mixed with imperfect metals, is able to show that they contain gold, which, before the projection, was enclosed in them, In company with heterogeneous particles. ...The ferment does no more than hasten a purification for which Nature requires ages, and which in some instances Nature could not effect at all in the absence. of an active purifying Agent."

Authors Note: The active purifying agent is the combination of the stone with the heterogeneous particles! Some of the material was considered to already be gold, all that needs to be done is to cure or purify the rest. It was thought that below the earth, the above seeped into the ground, since the time of the creation, and slowly the substance was being turned to gold. So, all metals found in a mine lets say, that weren't gold, were on their way to becoming gold! However, nature works slowly, the stone caused a sudden change.

"According to another scale, the Sun In Aries, Leo, and Sagittarius indicated the first, second, and third grades of the Fire."

Authors Note: This is true, Aries is connected to May-Day. Leo is the end of summer and the start of drying in Virgo for the base white (Septembers Child) substance. Sagittarius is the end of the (wheel turning) to Make Crowned Androgynyn leading to the last step. Again the constellations to tell time, again the year passing by is indicated.

"Nothing " he state maie let more your desires, Than ignorance of Heates of your Fiers ; and he, goes on to say that many of. Gebars. Cookes ' were deceived in this matter, despite their great knowledge of' books. The fire, once .kindled, was maintained without interruption until the consummation of the Work."

Authors Note: If one did not know that the heat was from the sun, one would never find. Yes, at times of the year additional heat was needed, but the main working heat to change the substance was the sun or moon, and their combinations.

"Paracelsus," reduced the number of processes to seven. It was even held, by singularly Optimistic adepts that the stone could be prepared from a single material, in a single Vase, at a single operation.

Authors Note: Seven is tied to the last seven months of work! This took a base substance to perfection.

From Glauber,   in summarizing the preparation of the stone, "we may fitly subjoin this Poesie making for our present Purpose, and expressing the same in a few words, Dissolve the fixt, and make the fixt fly, The Flying fix, and then live Happily"

Authors Note: Need I say dissolve the water, make it fly and mix with the lights, condense and feed the below until perfect?

"According , to a statement dated 1526, occurring in *Gloria Mundis* the Stone. is familiar to all men, both young and old, is found in the country, in the village, in the town, in all things created by God; yet it is despised by all. Rich and poor handle it every day. It is cast into the street by servant maids. Children play with it. Yet no one prizes it; though, next to the human soul, it is the most beautiful and the most precious thing upon earth, and has power to pull down kings' and princes. Nevertheless, it is 'esteemed the vilest and meanest of earthly things."

Authors Note: This to me is matter that is recycling! Who enjoys being around it? None of us for sure. Paracelsus at one time, by request held a meeting where he was asked to explain alchemy and some of the stone. He brought in a pile of Dog dodo!! Of course he never explained as the audience laughed and walked out on him! Something to think about! I refer to the compost pile, but actually it is to all matter recycling. Some of it is very nasty, and is though found everywhere.

"Philalethes states in .*A Brief Guide* to *the Celestial Ruby* that the Philosopher's Stone. is called a stone, not because it is like a stone, but only because, by virtue of its fixed nature, it resists the action of fire as successfully as any. stone. In species it is gold, more pure than the purest.

If ,we say that its nature is spiritual, it would be no more than the truth; if we describe it as corporeal, the expression would be equally correct."

Authors Note: "If we describe it as corporeal." Or, from a lowly substance and so consider the dog dodo. Now note fixed, and it is in the first tablet of Flamel and the Abraham Tablets where it is fixed! But, remember I showed that tablet as also the eight tablet in the series. That it then would be fixed to the sun or gold! It resists the action of the fire when it is like the fire, or when finished as a stone. It only then will resist the fire! It has to be recycled before we can augment it in any way.

"Ripley regarded the Stone as a triune microcosm Basil Valentine depicted it as composed out of one, two, three, four, and five, these numbers indicating respectively, the primordial matter the two fold mercurial substance, the three principles *(tri prima)* the four elements, and the quintessence."

Authors Note: Just another way to describe the process."

From Ben Jonson to sum up in the following words.

Your *Lapis _Philosophieus* 'Tis a Stone, and not A stone, a spirit, a soul, and a body: Which if you ,dissolve, it is dissolved; If you coagulate, it is coagulated; If you make it to fly, it flieth"

Authors Note: Consider that it is both substance and water until finished.

"As a tender babe is first fed with snow white milk, so the stone must be nutured with pure milk! In discussing this emblem, 'Waite , suggests that Melchior was. invented' by Maier as a peg upon which to hang the cloak of certain Christian mysteries. Maier describes Mechior as a Christian priest who has graduated in the hidden mysteries the hidden science . In the emblem he wears elaborate sacerdotal vestments, and is engaged in celebrating mass. In the person of this exponent of, the debate, writes Waite, .Maier represents their-mass as a work of the hidden science and the sanctuary of its mysteries, are those of the Philosopher's Stone. It is said also (1) that in the Sacrament of the Altar are Concealed most profound. secrets of spiritual Alchemy; (2) the perfection of the Great Work is the birth of the philosopher's Stone in the Sacred Nativity; (3) that its sublimation is the Divine Life and Passion."

(4), that the black state represents the death on Calvary; :and (5) that the perfection of the red state corresponds to the resurrection of Easter and the Divine Life thereafter .' Maier adds that. these earthly things are a picture. of those -which are heavenly '

Authors Note: This is to be considered when we see a pictorial allegory where a heart is used where a rose would be normally by a non-christian. Also, as you learn the connections to Osirs, reread and consider. The stone was connected to Christianity in many ways, and that is basically shown here. All of the stone is from the very first true religion based on death, and resurrection.

Much of our religion of today is based on this lost past religion. Here another is saying, and I understand and agree.

"Some" alchemists depicted the existence of a universal primitive matter, known as the Bird of Hermes, which was supposed to emulate the eye of its poetic creator by roving continuously from heaven to earth, and earth to heaven. Further, the imaginary Adamic earth, "red earth " or virgin earth " was said-like the Stone itself-to be of universal occurrence; so that the secret of its identity had to be preserved by the esoteric brotherhood. When " we have once obtained this,' wrote Isaac of Holland, the preparation of the" Stone is only a labour fit for" women, or child's play.' Even this pronouncement, however, was possibly a play "upon words. " "Women's ,work was sometimes held to be allusive to the feminine principle of the Great Work ; but. Trismosin likens philosophical sublimation to Woman's work, work which consists in cooking and roasting until done!"

Authors Note: I have explained this, we simply wash the material with the lights until it is totally cleansed. It then is purified by the lights, and so is the reason why the light above is Good!

Authors Note: 'Eye of it's Creator.' That Eye is linked to the sun in the ancient religion of Egypt! The 'Eye of Horus.' I must apologize to you, my readers as to the origin of this material. It is scattered throughout alchemical books. I know I should have before you the reference material, but I don't! I had collected the sayings as important over the years, but never minded where it is from in many cases. However, it can be found in any collection of alchemy books. To me this was and is the proof of what alchemy is about, those little things they said. You must be able to bring it together somehow to understand it or forget it. My work ties into all this as it is said and then gives a clear understanding. I will always be collecting more, you would be surprised how sometimes it is hard to know where and what is being pointed out.

"In ancient Egypt the Ouroboros Serpent was thought to stand for eternity. It is found at least as far back as the sixteenth century, BC. It is also found with Greek manuscripts of the Alexandrian Period. Being connected to Cleopatra, The Chrysopoeid (having to do with gold making) The enclosed words "All is One" refers to the unity of matter. The Serpent biting it's tail has been linked to the circulation in the oven, and to the changing of the matters. An inscription associated with Cleopatra runs, "One is all, and by it all, and to it all, and if one does not contain all, all is nought."

Authors Note: Note the connections to the tomb of Osiris I have pointed out. Who can say how old this really is? It is connected with Osiris as his matters being recycled, destroyed, which is the time period before the May-Day. The 'all' is actually everything outside, sun, moon, constellations, all has to be brought together." The serpent was on the tomb, and was there until he again was reborn a new child in September, It is about matters recycled from death to a rebirth.

"From George Ripley, in his work, "The Compound of Alchemie." _ - Containing Twelve Gates, O Unity in the substance and Trinity in the Godhead, As thou didst make all things out of one chaos, so let me be skilled to evolve our microcosm out of one substance in it's three aspects of magnesia, sulfur, and mercury."

Authors Note: Matter, sun and moon. (Three aspects). 12 gates = one year!

"From a fourteenth century Statue (a copy) at Notre-Dame In the design the dragon is shown climbing out of the athanor (furnace) with the bishops crozier thrust down it's throat - This is to be understood as meaning a shaft of celestial light is necessary for kindling the fire of the athanor for the work of the stone

Authors Note: The shaft is light, again consider the Obelisk.

"The most familiar form of the talismanic serpent is the caduceus this was usually, but not always, associated with Hermes, or "Mercury The normal form is a winged wand entwined.. by two serpents, but sometimes the wings are absent. It has been stated that the original form, attributed to Thoth, was across, symbolising the four elements ..proceeding from a common centre. The central stem of the al-chemical caduceus was sometimes held to consist of' gold of the Philosophers' and the two serpents were said to represent either the male and female or the fixed : and volatile principles.

There is little doubt that alchemy inherited the symbol of the serpent from the early mythological systems disposed, around the cult of serpent-worship. This cult, in turn, was closely bound up with sun-worship and phallism. Serpent-worship, which was very widespread in the ancient world, possibly arose in Babylonia.

Authors Note: I include because most that never knew, have said things like this.

"The serpent; or dragon, in mythology as also in alchemy, was susceptible of numerous interpretations. "More subtil than any beast of the field, " it was symbolical of divine wisdom; also of power and creative energy; of time and eternity; of life, immortality and regeneration. Moreover, the serpent was used as a solar emblem, a phallic emblem, and an emblem of the earth sometimes also it symbolised the hermaphroditic principle In the earlier cosmogonies, as the symbol of activity, it was sometimes associated with the egg.symbol of passivity. Further, it is of interest that: the Sun-god and Moon-goddess, or Great Father and Great Mother were figured not only as lion and lioness, bull and Cow, etc., but also as male and female serpent. In -alchemy, the dragon, or serpent, is often used as a genera-tive or sexual symbol. Sometimes male and female ser-pents or dragons are pictured as devouring or destroy-ing each other, thereby giving rise to a glorified dragon, typifying the Philosopher's Stone, or transmutation; The same symbol may also denote putrefaction Winged and wingless serpents or dragons symbolis the volatile and fixed principles (merculry and Sulphur respectively; three serpents, the three principles, mercury sulphur, salt; and a serpent nailed to a cross, the fixation of the volatile."

Authors Note: The ancients saw the serpent as a renewal of matters. As the serpent lost its skin, and looked reborn! It represented the process and what happened to the matters within. The original understanding was lost, and you can see how the loss causes the changing of ideas as to the original meaning. This has happened many times with understanding of the past.

Hermes Vase, or the Hermetic Vase. Figuratively, the egg was regarded by the alchemists, as by the ancient civilisations, as a symbol of creation; the Greeks ap- proached still nearer to the alchemical point of view by envisaging it as a container of the four elements. A delineation of the".Philosopher's Egg, pub-ished in Atalanta Fugiens. of 1618, carries an elusive reference To the Philosophers Stone "There is a Bird in the world, higher than all, the egg whereof to look for, be thy only care." -:A yellowish white surrounds it'soft yolk aim at this carefully, as is the custom, with the fiery sword; let Mars (iron) lend his aid to Vulcan (fire), and thence the chick arising will be conqureror of iron and fire."

Authors Note: The bird is the pyramid is the firmament! I will show you the two nests when we discuss the oven. The firmament flies in the air as it was believed in the past.

"Ben J Orison makes play with. the same kind of thinking in The Alchemist:

"Surly. That you should hatch gold in a furnace; sir,
As they do eggs in Egypt!
Subtle. Why I think that the greater miricle
No eggs but differ from a chlcken: more
Than metals in themselves.

Surly, That cannot be.
The egg's ordained by nature to that end;
And is a chicken in potentil.
Subtle. The same we say of lead, and other metals,
Which would be gold, if they had time.
Mammon. ' And that, Our art doth further.

Subtle. Aye, for 'twere absurd .
To think that. nature in the earth bred gold.
Perfect In the Instant. -Something went before.
There must be remote matter..

Authors Note: The remote matter is how to understand the matters in the shell when destroyed to a base.

"BenJonson gives a clear picture of Sulphur and mercury as male and female principles:

Of that airy
And oily water mercury is engendered
Sulphur ,0 the fat and earthy part.
(which is the last) supplying the place of male
The other of female In all metals
Some do believe hermaphrodeity_
That both do act and suffer. But these two
.Make the rest ductile.. malleable, extensive,
And even in gold they are for we do find .
Seeds of them by our fire, and: gold in them;

And can produce the species of each metal
More perfect thence. than nature doth in earth."

Authors note: Please read carefully and compare to the process where you can.
For example, "Supplying the place of male which is last." Remember the sun and finish with the substance. Note gold is referred to but is never said that gold is used. Note, principles. Words are really a funny thing. The masters really couldn't hide the material if you understood what it is they are speaking of! You cannot secretly describe a thing you know of if you are speaking of it in any fashion, if you speak the truth!

To Understand the Pictorial Allegories.

There are many pictorial allegories connected to alchemy. Many (singular) that you see are from a series of pictures. That series shows the different steps of the stone. Now briefly about the overlap. Some series do not use the overlap. Some use only or show the last seven months of work of the process. Some alchemists used a few pictures, some used many. Remember, it was up to those that drew to show the same process in a different manner, and to do so in a hidden fashion. always another Master of alchemy could be able to read what you have drawn. Myself, I always start by looking for those steps which were easily understood! In some of the series none of it is easy. What I have done now in the next few pages is to show selected steps that do have easily seen (with explanation) information. Some of the pictorial allegories, each thing in the picture is there for a reason. Some of them are very spread out (one step covers several pictures allegorical). Find the steps you can see, then fill in. If you know what should follow, you should be able to see what it was about. Remember they are seldom in order, or in a proper sequence. The overlap can cause much of a problem with understanding, especially with a series with many pictorial allegories. Sadly, there is also series here from false alchemists! If you learn the steps, and how they are basically shown, this will not be a problem with a little work. Today our society makes books of puzzles to occupy our time. Here is the 'Greatest Puzzle!' let it do the same.

Allegory Explanation - 1 How to read the allegory.

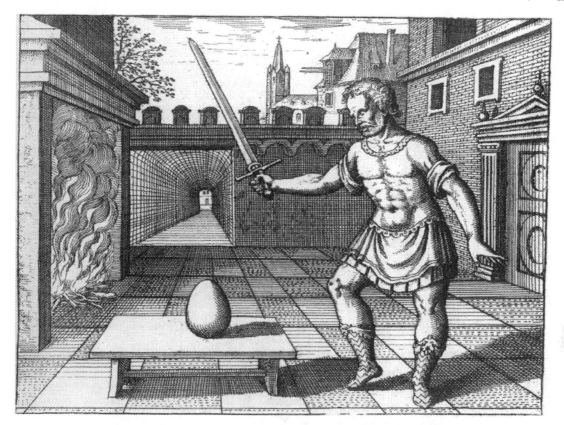

The Eight emblem of Atalanta Figurines.
"To Pierce the Egg with a Flaming sword"

As with many of the allegories, in one there is many things said or pointed out. Remember that each part of the drawing is there for a reason, and perhaps all of the drawing means something to be understood. First with this allegory, which part of the process is he trying to show if that can be determined. With this one it can. The process has two main parts, the first takes nine months, the second we said takes seven months. Here if you will count the ramparts on the castle wall beyond the gentleman, you will see seven of them. The sword is between the third and forth of the ramparts. This time is after the third month of the second seven time period, and before the forth month. This is the time we work for the red stone and as I have said it is now a work of the sun. The pointed sword, all pointed objects indicates the sun, and comes from the understanding of the Obelisk. So what he is telling you here is to pierce the egg with now the sun, and when to do this. If you will look at the shadows you can tell the sword is pointed at the sun above. If you will look just above the egg, at the square shape in the wall, you will see a tunnel or doorway. If you will look closer, you will see the outline of the oven. When we discussed the second meaning of the Flammel tablets of Abraham, I said they blend together. On the first we had the hourglass and the red sand within. I said it works with the second tablet, and means it is now time to work for the red stone and the finish of the work. This was January the second year, and this work would go on for four months until April. Here we see the same mountain in the wall, and we see the time but shown differently, and that it is time to work with the sun only! The stone is becoming 'like' the sun. The fire is there to remind you to keep your substance warm as it is January and cold outside. Also, before we move on, this is the eight tablet in a series of fifty. How do we explain it is about the finish if it is found near the start of the fifty? It is due to the overlap, and here we see it again as a way to hide the actual process. Not all series have the overlap, but Atalanta does and is like Abraham's tablets. Now if you will consider Osiris, and what is said in this work, this is after Osiris has become the Crowned Androgynyn. This is where the body of Osiris disappears. The body is moved from the (earth position below) to the heaven position above in the oven. From the mythology we find Osiris has become of the earth, both male and female. With the ascension, he is to united with the eye of god (sun) and so to become three persons in One. Actually he unites with the 'Eye of Horus.' Male, female, god, he would then be perfect. In April that process is finished, in April the stone is finished. Osiris would be perfect, the stone is perfect. Osiris ascends to heaven to live with the gods forever.

Compare this division of the ramparts to other similar pictorial allegories I am showing.

Lambsprinck, eight and ninth tablet in order.

You see first here the two white swans. This is the substance and the moon or that part of the process. From mythology, this is Osiris and Isis during the time of Virgo the Virgin. Perhaps it could be seen as the 'Two Sisters' from the same mythology. This is the time when Osiris is reborn as a child, and is known alchemically as Septembers Child. Remember it is a Pure white substance as the moon! Now look to the next tablet, please note there are seven steps to reach the King. These two tablets again show the place in the process between September, the white substance completed, and then here seven months to go (the steps). With most, not all of the series you can go to them and find tablets that you can understand, then remember the process, the overlap with some and go on. This second tablet, if you will look at the structure that the king is setting in, it has four posts and the base has that half circular shape that you will see in many of the allegories. It is all a way of showing the oven was known by the alchemist that drew the allegory. The thing that makes the allegories hard to understand is each set was drawn differently than others had done so. And so each set has to do with the imagination of the alchemist doing the drawings. Each had to show the same process, but he had to do it differently, and so the many different series allegories. Some used a few words and a few drawings, some used many! Here, it takes seven steps to reach the king. The king is the sun or god from the mythology of Osiris. The cross and globe in his hand connects to the cross with four equal arms used to indicate that time of year, September, by the ancients. This part of the allegory is very similar to that part of Flamel where he shows Jesus coming and holding the globe with a cross within and one above. This simply shows the same time. Those crosses are from ancient Egypt, and I have come to believe the Tau Cross is from the design of the southern crux! It was noted in the sky at the coming of Osiris at this time of year, read the mythology, actually read the whole book!

The eighteenth tablet of Johann Mylius

This is called the "Green Lion of the wise."

Please note this is the 18th. tablet of 20. There is no overlap with this series. I have selected this as a tablet to explain because it is of the same time period as the tablet of piercing the egg with the flaming sword. There we Had the sword and ramparts to tell us the time. Here we have the seven stars, and the water level. Please note that it cuts between the third and forth star as did the sword with the ramparts. Note in the water we have both the sun and moon as is used in that first part of the series of the second seven months For the red stone. Note here in the top, we have the lion eating or attempting to eat the sun. This is the red stone and the finish with those four months. The green Lion being the substance and the sun binding together. I believe green lion is just a reference to the power of nature and these forces, when combined to the substances of the stone. In other allegories of this same time, or others that are about this same time, look for the pool. Sometimes it is shown as a swimming pool, with sun and moon in it and it will have three walls around it meaning for three months. Sometimes the pool is shown with fancy corners and they are designed around three in one corner. Again the three corners will mean for a time period of three months. Usually this time is shown somehow with three and water. At the start of the three, it is the 'Conjunction of Alchemy' and I will show some of these. You will see a trident, meaning for three months and water in a jug. Again, three and water. If you will recognize which part of the process, the first nine or the second seven, and count if there is something to count, you will know exactly what they are trying to show. I will go over many of them. Lastly here, can you see the oven design at the base and left side of the drawing by slant as in the oven. You could say this left side base shows left small mountain in oven!

The Crowned Androgygyn. Tablets 17 & 18 of Johann Mylius

The androgynous material mean alchemical that it has both male and female attributes. These of course would be from the sun and moon. To count here we have twelve moons and one sun, or thirteen. I will show this again. This is the Crowned Androgynyn because it is the second time for this to happen. In the first part of the work on the start of the May- Day, we used both the sun and moon to do the work. We made androgynous material. This second part count moons, there are twelve. From the start to the conjunction to January it has been 12 Moons or months plus one for the sun. The white stone is finished. Now it is time, the 13ᵗʰ month to start the work of the sun. Thus the sun on the top here. The androgyny is standing on the moon, and so this part is a work of the moon is finished. The material has gone from the black stage to the white stone shown by the three serpents. Also it shows that three months of work, first part three of the seven, have been accomplished. Note also, as I said with the green lion, look to the below and left. This is the same as it shows the base of the oven where we were doing this part of the work. It will now be moved to the upper part of the oven. This is Osiris as androgynous, and so now mounts to heaven to join with the god. We will continue with the other allegory of the work of the sun. See the 'Eye of Horus.' Note three serpents, two looking a different way?

To continue with the thirteen. Here we have thirteen suns and means this part is the work of or with thirteen suns. Holding the lion means it is now going to be a work for the sun or red stone (lion is connected to sun). He is on a little mound to show the work is in the top of the oven. It is again the Crowned Androgynyn. This is tablet 17 of Johann Mylius. I showed you prior to this the tablet of the lion where the water divided the seven. Remember that I said the tablets blend together to understand. Here tablet 17 and 18 are about that same part of the process. We are going from working on two substances to one. The white is finished and the red is continued. Three days of the seven have elapsed, and four months to go. It is the following January. With Flamel and Abraham, it is about the second part of Abraham's first tablet. This is where the red sand hour glass comes into the picture. Also, this is Flamels tablet where he has Paranella, and the key of 3/2 ratio. Here, if you will look at the black thing on the ground, see how it is three, but two look the other way? It is the 3/2 ratio needed to know. Again, knowing the process and steps and times of the year, the allegories become easy to read. We go on. Know the times and what happens at those times. Then start to learn how to read these allegories.

Emblem 12, Michael Maier

We have here one of my favorites, and one that shows very secretive information. First time is shown by the fishes in the barrel half. We are at that same time again, The start of the work for the red. There is no concern here for the white stone that is finished. The fire and cooking is to show to keep warm as we have discussed. The cat is said to be about the secret fire, and so I would say, a cat is like a lion is about the sun is the secret fire. Note the windows are open, consider the forth day of Genesis where it said the lights now can shine on the earth They are in the firmament! It almost looks like the river is flowing into the window, and it was drawn to do exactly that. The upper closed windows by their cracks show the design of the oven base where the four division is found. Here is another place where I will show you the 3/2 ratio that needs to be known and understood. Please note the three pointed logs, and the two square ones. This is no accident in the drawing, they mean something and it has to be know. In many of the series this ratio is shown. One place by three fishes which I will show tied to the St. Thomas Shield. In Flamel, by a key that has three toes on one side, two on the other. All the 3/2 ratio that needs to be know and understood. Hopefully with this work I will it will become familiar and easily seen. Showing the woman here is also to refer it to the allegories about it being a work of women as far as multiplication is concerned. Flamel said that is why he used Paranella, as it was a normal thing for a woman. Here we see the same thing tied to the end of the process, multiplication. When you understand the 3/2 you will see how tied to it. We will go over the 'woman that washes

Cloths.' One might think it is connected to female but it is not, just backwards. It is a work of male, and joining to the sun. What is meant is the material is washed clean to perfection by what your doing these last few months. Can you think of a better way to hide a masculine work than to show as a work of women? This is the second January. Please note the design of the base here as is the base of the oven. This design of the base with the half circle cut out is used in many places to indicate the oven. The one oven to use that is!

The fifth Tablet of Michael Maier

As I have been telling you to count, here we have seven flowers. This is about April, and the finish of the stone, and the second (seventh month of the process) counting from October. This tablet is the same as the garden of Abraham's tablets, (counted as 16 though). And so to compare and see. Abraham counted from 0 to 16, here the count is from 9 to 16, or just the last seven. Many alchemists drew pictorial allegories that only counted and showed the last seven of the work. You have the crowned lion which represents the finished stone, it is below and now Like the sun. The blindfold, the dark object all are reminiscent of the substance of the first part of the work Being in darkness. It is April, and the work does still need extra warmth to work when considering the first part (The Abraham Tablets). The heart, some of the Christian alchemists used the heart instead of the rose as a symbol. Usually the heart is found inside of the cross with four arms which we will discuss with the oven. So to understand this allegory, two parts of the process needs to be known. Also, as this is the fifth tablet of twelve tablets, with this series the overlap is used again. As Flammel said, "Some of the tablets have a double meaning." The overlap is used in many of the series allegories. If you counted the seven and wondered what they represented, can you see again how you would be led astray if you didn't know of the overlap. Can you see how you would never work the process right? The overlap comes from Osiris, and his process originally. The heart comes from connections some of the masters wanted to make between the stone and the Sacred Heart of Jesus Christ. Cupid is mentioned in the Osirian mythology I have presented. If you consider all and how worked, it all gets to generation in nature over time. That is what man found of God.

From Atalanta Fugiens, Michael Maier

We have here the Hermaphroditus drying in the moonlight. As considering the Tablets of Abraham, this is the same as the hanged serpent. The matter is dried in moonlight on the top part of the oven. It is kept warm to help drive off the moisture. This substance is both male and female if you will remember. We with process have just finished three months of work using both lights above. The sun, male, the moon female, and these aspects of the light have been put into the matter. The cot here is the same as the upper work area of the oven. This matter when dried and ground to a powder will become the base matter of the two stones (Septembers Child), and Goose/Swan for white stone. It will be a perfect white powder. The matter is so white that within the eggshell it is hard to capture with a camera. It has come from black to white, from death to life.

It is though just the base matter of the stone. Nine months have passed us by but still there is seven months to go for the finish. This is the first androgyny produced by the process and is not the Crowned Androgynyn. Crowned comes by turning again! Crowned is matter raised above what is natural.

131

The Cabinet of Minerals by de Goude Son

This is the first two tablets of this series. Please look at the first and compare to Abraham's. We had mercury and the caduceus Here we have a shepherd and a staff with a grapevine, can you see them as the same? With Abraham we had the mountain on the second tablet, with this second tablet, can you see the pyramid shaped oven looking down from the top? A spiders web is used in several allegories to represent the oven shape (linear perspective). This is a different way to show the same steps by another alchemist, the same but drawn differently!

Lambsprinck third Tablet of the series.

This stag, and the unicorn , the two that are found in the forest. What is shown in a hidden fashion is really the sun and the moon. The unicorn by his single horn represents the sun. The stag by the multiple points represents the Moon and the many ways that light is seen. The unicorn's horn is like the Obelisk! As we go through Flamel, at this point with his allegory he mention's his wife's hair being all 'disheveled.' The disheveled hair is the same as the stags horns! And so Flamel and his wife at that point are representing the two lights above now coming into play with the work. A really good imagination is needed to read the allegories, but mostly what is needed is to understand the process, and what is happening in order and at what time. Then when you see an allegory like this one, note its place, what should be happening at that time, and try too understand how that alchemist showed that part of the process. Many modern day alchemists have considered the unicorn to be female. The horn shows what and how it is to be understood. As Flamel said with this tablet, "it was necessary to show a male and a female." Here also is shown by the horns, a male and a female!

From Basil Valentine's 12 keys illustrated by Maier.

As I mentioned the conjunction, and the start of the seven (end September), I want to show this in several places. There are many things to discuss with this allegory, and shows how much can be combined in one. First look to the left to the swan in the background (from Septembers Child). This is the start of the work for the white stone. In many places she is shown biting herself to produce blood. From the mythology, this was originally a dove! (See Massey's book). This is about Like as I have explained. Below the swan, we have the janus head over fire. This head is used in the old calendars to indicate January, looking back at the past year and also looking ahead. What it means here is time, the work goes on until the next January. How long is the time? If you will look at the trident, it goes on for three months. As it is a pointed object, it actually means three months of work by the sun. As the conjunction is in October, please note from the mythology the 'scales' that were erected at this time of year. The scales mean October. January is three months hence. Note that water is being collected in the jug, as is in your oven 'again.' We are turning the wheel, 'again,' for the red stone. We will be finishing the work for the white with the three months process (white from goose). You are the bishop, and you are again marrying the two natures of the sun and moon with the one red stone. It is October, and there must be heat added to the oven to keep it warm. There is a rainbow behind, and that is because of the beautiful colors to come to the substances within the oven. The white stone none, but for the red, first is orange, and we will discuss and show with allegories of the salamander, then to a lavender or purple color, and then to a red color and finally, ruby red as like wet rubies in the sunlight. I have included a drawing with the colors as they come and go. Note the staff of the bishop has the cross on it (Tau Cross), another indicator of the time (September) from mythology. The red stone at this point is Osiris and what is needed is for him to gain both male and female principles from the earth before he can unite above with the gods! That is why the wedding. The matters of both lights are again joined with process.

Seventh Key of Basil Valentine

Note scales for October or start of Conjunction. Note oven design within the circles. Note sword indicating a work now of the sun.

Emblem 3 - Valentine *Azoth*

Emblem 5 of Atalanta Fugiens

The above allegory shows the toad of alchemy suckling the breast of a woman! All this means is the toad, (substance) is being worked by the moonlight. For example, the androgyny drying in the moonlight would satisfy this allegory. The white stone later being joined to 'like' and moonlight only also. This would be true until the step was finished. The moon is also indicated when they speak of 'The Woman that washes Cloths,' what they are pointing to is the female moonlight washing the matters and perfecting. Sometimes it only means a washing type of work and could be by the sun.

Emblem 21 of Atalanta Fugiens

This emblem shows the process of the stone, and here how to make the true oven.

Mathematically, if we 'square a circle' we have what we know of as PHI. PHI is the ratio we use to make a true pyramid. This works out to be 1.618 times ½ the base for the height. With a 6" base pyramid, the height to be a true pyramid would be 3 X 1,618 or approx. 4.9. This allegory said , "From a man and a woman make a circle, a square a triangle and lastly a circle again." So, from the sun and moon make the circle and square which gives the triangle or true pyramid, and lastly circle again which is circulation, and so you will have the stone.

From Basil Valentino.

It is the sign for October. All is in balance as the sun crosses the equator. In the oven it also means all is to come together again! The wheel is turned again for the next three months for the red. So we see it for October in the process. In Ancient Egypt with a meaning tied to the position of the sun. As you read from Mr. Massey, the balance. This was raised in September, (near the end) in ancient Egypt. See Mr. Massey's book, you should see the link. An ancient religion by becoming hidden, became alchemy, also hidden! The balance is used here to show fire (sun) and water (moon) and earth is to unite again.

Mariah the Jewess

We see here Mariah the Jewess, prior to this we see a monk, perhaps Valentine himself. Prior, by the sign of the balance we knew it was October astrologically. The first of the seven months of work to go. Here we see May. How do we see May, by counting the five flowers. Also, we see oven design, (mountain or hill shape) and also by the vapor design. The idea that the above and below waters need to come together. In Genesis this would be the third day. Mariah was linked to and was said to be the 'Sister of Moses.'

St. Thomas Shield

The shield of St. Thomas is a favorite allegory of mine. All of the process is with one picture and so much easier to see and understand. First an overview of the shield. The color red has to do always with the sun. Blue always has to do with water. White has to do with the moon and the white substance produced by the moon. Here we also have the color brown, and I would say it represents the earth. The first thing we see is the cross with four equal arms. This is from the oven design on the base, and will be shown further with the oven explanation. Also as you understand the mythology, the cross with equal arms originates from the time period when the sun crossed the equator. The equal arms simply means all is in balance. If now you will consider the two top sections of the allegory, please note the pyramid/oven design. Remember I said the process takes us 16 months.

In the first quadrant we see eight columns. They are blue and so have to do with water. We are either removing it, or adding it always. In this quadrant we also see three red stars. If we will remember the dates of the process, the first is Dec. 21, the start. The next important date is the May-Day, then August. It is eight months from December to August and so why eight columns. The three red stars represent the three hottest months of this time, and so denote the May-Day until August. The three hottest months are sometimes mentioned in alchemy, however I have lost that reference.

The second thing I look at is the top arm of the cross. I count nine water drops, and a green stem with seven leaves. This is the division of the process as I explained, sixteen months, the first part nine, the second seven. The nine drops of water also denote the drying from August to September (Virgo).

In other words, we remove the water from the substance in September, the drops are white to show this is done with moonlight only. Above we see the vase with the small black object. I think reminiscent of what we started with, and the first color, black. The green wreath or crown represents the power of Natural forces. Especially at this time of the year.

In the second quadrant we see the brown earth, and three arrows. We also see in the third quadrant three white serpents, and on the cross three blue balls of water. All the three's work together. Remember, I said at this point we start to make two stones. The three arrows represent that stone that we will make with the sun and moon first part for three months. The three white serpents represent the three months we work also for the white stone with moonlight only. The three blue balls of water tell us that for these three months water is involved. Consider if you will the allegory, green lion, and the shining sword and ramparts. All showed three, and in those and others they showed the three months connected to water. They also show in their way, sun and moon as is here by serpents and arrows.

In the third quadrant, we see the three white serpents. Please note two are looking one way, the third is looking another. This has again, to do with the 3/2 ratio I mentioned before. It is white as of goose, (alchemy) but originally, white as of dove (mythology of Osiris).

In the last quadrant, we see four stalks of grain on the earth. We are growing something! They are red as they are here connected with the sun. Also the four is the time period of this part of the process. If you will count the times, we have eight in the first quadrant. Nine is pointed out in the top of the cross.

Then comes the three, and finally for sixteen, the last four. Note the division between the last seven, three and four. Note again the red and connections to (the three red stars) and sun in this last quadrant.

The shield when understood makes it very easy to see the whole process. The heart in the middle, This 'St. Thomas Shield' was drawn by a Christian, and so where we can usually find a Rose, sometimes the heart symbol connected to Jesus Christ was used. I am not sure why five drops are within it unless it somehow means to show the connection to the May Day. I tell you to count, and five is in many places connected to that time period of the process. Note the pyramid shape with the two top quadrants!

From Egypt

The next few pages are copied from Mr. Peter Tompkins Book, 'Magic of Obelisk.' The work is copied from the walls of ancient Egyptian temples. The few should be looked at together, with time and process considered. 'Set in the Net' is the overcoming of Set by Horus and so September when Osiris is reborn a Child. The 'Division of the Cycle by six.' Refers to the yearly cycle. The division of the birds above the net by four and three, I have explained. This division is shown in many places of alchemy. The nets indicate the 'Scales of October', and is when this time starts. Now the abstraction of the division by six and to curved to linear measure has to somehow be related to the cycle of the planet with its rotation around the sun. Or perhaps it would be better to say they relate it to the 'movement of the spheres somehow.' All this is tied to what they found and considered tied to death and rebirth and finally, resurrection of the body to heaven! It is about matter as compared to our own matter after death, and time with the 'all.' It convinced them (the results) of what they looked for and gave them this belief that all men if they lived their life well and was good, would result in a new birth and everlasting life with God! Consider this again after reading the information discussed from Mr. G. Massey's book.

"This relief appears on the west side of the south wall of the hypostyle hall in Kamak, part of a scene called .'Hunting Birds." In an adjoining relief, the figures of Thoth and Sechat were sculpted in relief by Seti I then intaglioed under Ramses II. In the hunting scene a net is filled with birds in a thicket of papyrus reeds surmounted by seven birds in light separated in groups of three and four by a phoenix, or bennu bird. The horizontal rope is pulled by Horus with his falcon head, watched by the young pharaoh, while in the next panel, the homed Khnoum looks toward Thoth, master of numbers and measure, with his arms out- stretched, indicating a fathom of 6 feet or 4 cubits. His proportion, said de Lubicz, indicates the essential numbers for a hexagon, the division of a cycle by six, and the means of translating curved into linear measure. This is no banal hunting scene, de Lubicz observed, but a symbolic one, tied to mythology. This is the location where Set was caught in a net by Horus. Se- chat, standing by Toth. is described as the one who will conceive and raise the royal child, who, as Ra, will mount the throne of Horus. Here, said Schwaller. is a cabalistic scene which indicates the capture of an abstraction. He then proceeded to analyze the meaning of each single symbolic thread in the net.

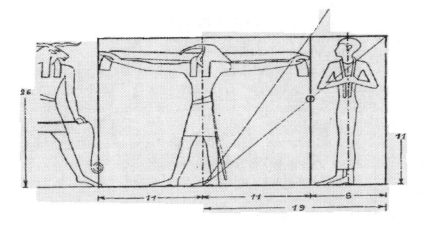

"The advantage of the system of symbols over the phonetic, says de Lubicz, is that the meaning of symbols lasts indefinitely, from lifetime to lifetime; and the fundamental purpose of the initiatory texts is to convey the truth of resurrection and reincarnation. To anyone unconvinced of this truth, the glyphs, says he, will remain a dead letter. And not only did the glyphs have a cosmic meaning, they were further amplified by the sound attributed to them, which, when reverberated, could magically key in the past. The technique was rediscovered by L. Ron Hubbard in Dianetics, where the mere repetition of a key word can bring into focus in full three-dimensional color and sound a whole scene from the past, no matter how remote. The whole of history, the whole of the "akashik record,'. is available to man merely by tuning his consciousness, perhaps by reciting a mantra."

Authors Note: There is little information that I am finding that links the alchemical process with the ancient religion so dramatically. I have shown the division of seven by three and four now in many places. Here we see Set, captured. This is the September I point to when he is overcome. Osiris is reborn. Here, for the young pharaoh, evidently there is seven months and the same process for him to go through. The division of the cycle by six to me is pointing to the division of the year by six, as the sun is in each hemisphere. This is I believe just one of the steps from the ancients that tie directly to alchemy.

The Djed was raised in September, a lion cloth and a tit was tied to it! They represent the three months of work by sun and moon for advancement to Crowned Androgynyn.

Here the Alchemical process must be considered to understand. The time is end of September, the matter is again placed in the 'lights' for further purification. Lion cloth is sun, Tit is female moon. The connection to the alchemical process was not known by Budge, by Massey, or even today by our scholars. The process is the base for the religion and for astrology .The matter became the model for the man. As the matter was resurrected pure, so could the dead matters of the man by God. From Mr. Massey, "Tet is the name of a very ancient God tied to Osiris." The Djed, Tat or Tet pillar was also the emblem of stability represented by Ptah, the fourfold support of the universe. From a Mr. Clark, tied with this, he had a problem with the symbolism of the tit and lion cloth. "This union of male and female had some meaning, but it is impossible to connect it with the rest of the symbolism."

"This annunciation scene found on the walls of the Temple of Luxor, shows Thoth, the Divine Word or logos, hailing the Virgin queen. Announcing she is to give birth to the coming son or sun. In the next scene the god Kneph with Hathor gives life to the queen. Knaph is as the Holy Ghost, or Spirit that causes conception. Impregnation is apparent from the Virgins fuller form. Next, the mother is seated on the midwifes stool, the child in the hands of a nurse. In the scene of adoration the child is enthroned, receiving homage from the gods and gifts from Three Wise Men. The child announced, incarnate, born and worshipped says Mr. Massey, was the representative of the Aten- sun, the child-Christ of the Aten cult, the miraculous conception of the ever -Virgin mother in the sky!"

"The raising of *DIEd*, or its awakening has been called the Mysteries of Mysteries, or the Secret of resurrection. The human body is described is an illusory solid perishable, but what caused it was a real solid: the original djed, or word of Amon-Ra-Ptah. This djed word or pillar of Osiris, is described as the base of relative stability and principle of whatsoever is durable in the fluctuating Osirian world of becoming and return.

Mans job is to make his own djed or inborn word, secure against destruction. When awakened, mans djed becomes his incorruptible body. It is said to remain a prisoner of earth and Osiris unless Ra comes to deliver it by untying the rope or undoing the knots. The two principles of Ra-osiris are seen as the life givers of the human djed, symbolized by the two souls of Ra and Osiris shut up in the djed, or pillar. As such they are the two currents of universal life whose source is one, though they are two in nature.This duality is the cause of terrestrial continuity and the endless metamorphosis of the Osirian way To escape from such slavery the soul of Ptah-Ra must absorb the Osirian: The universal must vanquish the particular." Mr. Massey!

As the process continues, the matters are taken above what could be produced on the earth. They become divine. This is a direct connection to the above good light and why! The material is refashioned as the earth created, and then raised above that level to eventually be as 'God,' or to be able to be 'with God!'

On understanding the Djed, Tat, or Tet Pillar, and the Legend of Isis and Horus.

Long ago, when I decided that I would spend some time with alchemy, it was because I felt that it had to be based on something. It was easy enough to consider that the search for the stone was there just because of greed, as it turned metals to gold. However, after thinking about it and our society, I felt long ago alchemy would have been dismissed. There must be something there to base it on, something overlooked by our scientists. In my search and throughout this book, I have expressed that something. Form, shape, time, yearly cycles, all things we know of but do not use or study as to their scientific possibilities connected to matter. Now, there is more. More than just the tangible things we can learn to use, it is the beliefs and the philosophical aspects of a past society that we today need to understand. More, it also is necessary to know the mythological and how they are connected to us. The ancients saw all as one, and we also to understand need to see things in that way. Surprisingly to me, our religious beliefs today, are based on what the Egyptians found and believed many thousands of years ago. Our beliefs though have been brought to us as 'original.' In reality, I have come to find they are just a rearrangement of the past and what was found there. I refer to the mythology of ancient Egypt, in particular to that of the creation, and to the becoming of the original gods of that society. Osiris, Isis, Horus, and Set. When is it that coincidence becomes fact, mythology becomes real? The commandments are found in the prayers of ancient Egypt. Genesis when understood is the same as their considerations of the creation. Osiris, was said to be made of the same substance as the original god, thus becoming the 'Son of that God.' Osiris lived, died, was resurrected and went later to heaven. Is it just a coincidence that his (Osiris) times are the same as those we know of today linked to another? His matters were brought back together in September. He was resurrected in December, and finally, he went to heaven in April. These are the same times. I mention, and I think have proved that are the times of the stone we have searched for, so long. In reading many books, it seems that mythology and history are linked in a society. Today reading the mythology of Isis, one would simply say it is a myth. Just a made up story and shows the simplicity of the thinking mind of the past. But is it? Was it based on more, and in actuality, based on how early man came to be able to control matter? Eventually by that means came to believe they had found how God could resurrect man after death? The way is a process we called Genesis. Genesis by our society has long been misunderstood. It is the way of the yearly cycle. It is about conditions here on our earth, and how all things evolve based on the conditions that matter is subject to. Genesis is about our yearly cycle found and believed by those of the past, started and designed by God. A cycle always in continuation for the stability of the creation. Always to maintain the earth created. A place for the man to live, but not the stable place the early man thought. A natural cycle yes, but evidently also a cycle that man can effect as he is presently, and a warning, one that man should realize that he is not God, and the cycle can get out of control and will. It could be the demise of the man that changed it.

The ancients found this cycle, learned how to control matter by understanding it. They found that man was special because of it, and hid what they knew in their beliefs. All we need to know is what it is inked to, how linked, what are the steps of the matters, and how are they linked to the times of the year, or to Genesis. The mythology, the physical, the religious, the mystical and the superstitious, principles of nature, all come together as one. They through understanding again give us the ability to control matter. To say it another way, art, (alchemy) is those forces found in nature controlled by the man in such a way as to be able to remake the matters and to make them perfect. It is about energy, the sun, and an active expression of the mixture of light and water. Anciently, in Egypt, Al or El meant God, and cham meant the sun. From Adiramled, his book by him called "Art of Alchemy." The word means "The power of the Divine solar influence expressed in nature." From Genesis we note, "The Light is Good," all of which means the ancients did not believe as the sun being God, they believed God had put something of himself into the light. To capture it was the way of perfection.

There are many books written on the capabilities of the ancients, Egypt in particular. Their temples are designed after nature, and principles found there. Books can be written by what is found on one wall within many of the temples. However, always a piece of the puzzle was missing. What was the mythology of Isis all about? Was it based on anything? Was there any fact or natural process, any history or substance linked with what they so strongly believed? Until now, there was only the understanding that it was linked to the generative principle found during the yearly cycle, mostly tied to plants or to agriculture. It was about the generative principle, but a principle to be used with matter. We as a society just did not know that.

Our scholars cannot be faulted by not finding or understanding what it all was based on. It was hidden knowledge. It also to our society was taboo to speak about let alone to write about. To know and understand also had the ability to change our world if understood, and if the science is true. My point in all this is, if the ancients found a truth, is it not a truth today? If it is a truth can we not as a society know of it and understand it and live with It? Truth does not hurt, it makes us a better society one capable of allowing us to move forward. This truth gave us a way of life we still live today. As a society though we are unaware of it. I believe though the names have been changed, much we hold dear comes from what the ancients found and left for us to also find again. I don't believe then that it was a hidden truth, but our societies have through misunderstanding made it so. As always, each must learn and consider what it is that they will accept, and how they will live their lives. Information and understanding is just that, to be known and accepted or rejected has always been the privilege of mankind within the different societies.

In consideration of the Egyptian religion one may postulate that somewhere in the distant past there was an event, or series of events, something learned or found that gave stability to mankind at that time. A thing quickly found, or a thing that may have taken many years, perhaps lifetimes to know and understand. Consider the 25,000 year cycle of the equinox. We call it a procession, a movement of the stars above our head and a slow circle traced in the sky by an imaginary pole attached to the earth. How long by observation alone, if that is how they did it, would it take to find? The Cheops pyramid is built according to PHI! We today may only know of that because of teachings that they gave to us. The movement of our sun and moon became paramount to them, and they lived a life based on a religion created to include these movements. But there was more to it than just the movement of the stars, or the sun and moon. It was about those cycles created by these movements, and how they effected matter. It was also about how man was effected by these movements, how he was created and lived within this system of bodies. Also if there was a god or series of gods connected to it all that he could know. It became a knowledge of man, a belief that what happened to matter found around him, also could be what would happen to his own matters at death. As man found and learned the regular occurrence of this system, he found and knew of its stability. He concluded that he was special, because he was able to find. That those things that could be known he could revere in his own way. Perhaps to understand and use in some method to know even more of what might be allowed. The Djed, Tat and Tet then became markers of these movements, of the stability, and even more, they represented movement of those objects close to the earth, (the sun and moon). Also throughout the year, those lights far away, the stars and their constellations also were considered. This was important because matter, of which man is also formed could be worked by these lights and believed purified. As man is of the same matter, could it be that the worked purified matters meant their own matters could be resurrected and purified by God?

In other places of this book, I have explained how matter is slowly purified by these lights within a pyramid shaped oven. Always the work within the oven is based on the times of the year. We don't start our garden in December, but in spring. There is a time for everything someone has said, and with these markers and with this process, that is of the uppermost importance to understand. As it is tied to the myth of Isis, Osiris and Horus, with Horus finally overcoming the evil Set, (matter is purified), those markers must also connect. First was the process. You cannot develop a religion, and then find it in nature. However, we, I didn't know that. Understanding this mythology tied to the alchemical process will explain completely the Djed and other markers of time and place. Those markers linked to both what happens at times of the year, to the matters changed because of the forces at those times of the year. It is hard to explain mythology and what it is based on. The right way of understanding is to say the process was found, and then by man the story, (mythology) was made up. To them though remember it was a created religion. It is the base for most religions today. I accept this.

The Djed, never known or truly understood by us, has been described as "The Mysteries of Mysteries," or the "Secret of Resurrection." It is based on, connected to, the 'Word' of Amon Ra, Ptah, and what would become known as the 'Stability of Osiris.' We see that these times of Osiris, of these pillars are the same times as those I have pointed out connected to the stone. The matter at that time of the year indicated was believed regenerated to a point of being close to near perfection. Now this is December 21, any year for example. It is the time when the sun has moved to its point furthest south, and now begins its movement north. For reasons of understanding, the battle between Set and Horus has been going on for a year since the last Dec. 21. Osiris has been born, but he also lived, died, reborn and is in the process of being resurrected. He is near perfect, (following December) but not perfect. There is an overlap (same overlap as in the alchemical process) of the process from one year to the next. Originally this is where the overlap of the alchemical process (that I show) must have came from. There is for him (Osiris) more to go, or come, as we will understand by connecting the times of Osiris to the alchemical process. There is no other way for it to be understood. No other material to base it on.

Now Set, the evil one in the mythology is overcome in September. The sun crosses the equator. This is shown in two ways, a sign of we describe as a cross with four equal arms, and the erection of the Djed Piller. The cross with equal arms meant to them everything of the all, was in balance. In September it also is a sign of death being overcome, and was celebrated by the ancients in that aspect. Whos death? That of Osiris in the mythology. The place was on the Nile Delta, at Busiris known as the city of the 'Djed Column.' A great feast was said to be given when the waters of the Nile fell off, near the end of September. It was about Osiris, but here the rebirth of Osiris, ending with the raising of the column. However, please note that Osiris is not resurrected perfect until spring. This is just a time of rebirth for Osiris, (September) and he is seen as a child newborn. In the alchemical process, I consider this part (finished in September) just a base matter made by the substance we destroyed and regenerated. We alchemically call it 'Septembers Child.' Please note the similarity of the terms. Osiris here needs to be somewhat understood in the same way. In September, the matter we turned white by the use of the moon, and by the use of the Virgin Virgo (constellation) is the same matter as was believed as Osiris at that time of year. However, the physical (practical in alchemy) is understood in a mythological religious way. The alchemical process takes us 16 months. The life and times of Osiris, 'mythological,' must be seen in the same way, from death to perfection. This also connects it to their holidays as they celebrated them over the same time period. We need connect a religious, a mythological, a practical and a physical understanding.

The process starts in December, when the sun is moving north. It was a sign for the death of Osiris which is the same as the death of the matters we work on. It is the same as the second day of Genesis, when the matters are divided. We never saw that as a death of the matters, but it must be understood in that fashion. This stability also is that the process repeats exactly every year. It took 16 months for Osiris (mythological) to live, die and then to be reborn, and then more time to become perfect. This is as the process to make the stone, it is accomplished exactly with the same time periods! With ancient Egypt, this process was always going on. The start of one was also the finish, that was going on from the prior. To them it was a daily, and a yearly battle. The erection of the crosses and pillars showed which holiday they were celebrating, and for which aspect of the process it was tied to. The Tat cross, as compare to the cross with four equal arms, was a cross as of the Christian type, with an elongated stem. This cross was erected at the time when the day was shortest, Dec. 21, at the winter solstice. This is when Set, darkness was thought to be overcoming. The days up to this point always were getting shorter. Dark was overcoming light. The light compared to Osiris was the shortest, and the night compared to Set, was the longest. The design of the cross I believe came from the position and movement of the sun. The stem is started from the base, being linked to the equator. As the sun moved south to the solstice, the shaft was formed. The horizontal part represented the east west travel of the sun. Here though, it represents it's furthest travel to the south. The hope of the cross, or tied to the cross had to do with stability, and the fact that from that point the days became longer. The mentioned forces of nature being positive were again returning. The Tat Cross with erection would then be understood as a cross of hope!

This understanding (the Tat Cross) comes from what has been called a 'daily battle' between Osiris and Set. Here at this time of year, the days were the shortest. Growth of vegetation was inert, nothing was growing! Death, Set seemed to overcome. The erection of this cross then was said to represented hope. Today we have the same understanding tied to that shape. The sun at it lowest point, was starting to come back. Set would again be overcome, the regenerative power would again sustain all living things. This was known as 'Osiris Tat.' You will also note, in alchemy, we move at this point to the last steps of the purification of the stone, December 21. With Osiris (the stone), he was purified by male and female (sun and moon), from October until December. Consider when you read the "tit and lion cloth." Now the final purification by spirit (sun only begins). Osiris was to join with the 'Eye of God' (Horus). The stone is tied to this same part of the process, and is accomplished in the same manner by being purified by the sun (Horus). The physical Osiris is now linked to the 'God of the Light.' He has become like him, and to be able to be with him (God). The stone also has to become like the matters above, the sun or perfect. Both are to become spirit, both comes from being tied to the sun in the last step. This time (Dec. 21) was linked to the resurrection of the matters. Physically it means the matters were raised to the upper part of the oven. This is where Osiris's body disappears, (in mythology) as he has gone from the tomb on earth to heaven. Consider Flamel where he said he and Paranella was in heaven. This is done within the oven, and the understanding I have shown as places to work. Below on earth, above in heaven!   Osiris, and all around them, the ancients would again see the days lengthen, as the sun came back to repeat the cycle. Osiris was slowly purified and in their religious belief, becomes three Persons in One. He was male, female, from the preceding operation and with the final joining, he becomes God also. This made him equal to and able to be with the Gods above.

Consider again the Crowned Androgyny of alchemy. The Crowned Androgyny is a term connected to this part, and is explained as we form the stones. Work from September unto December gives this name and aspect. Osiris had to become all that earth could offer him, or to become both male and female so that he could go on. In our process this is exactly what we do with the matters that are to become the red stone. We turn the wheel again, we bring all forces back to the matters again for further augmentation. Now to go back, and to say more about Djed is necessary, and more of a proof of that explanation. The column was raised in September, death was overcome. All celebrated with a joyous holiday. The Djed was erected, Osiris was reborn. His process continues toward pure spirit, as Osiris, and our matters likewise also will by eventually joining to the sun. Now, when the Djed was stood up in September, a 'lion cloth' was attached, also a 'tit' (a knot of cloth). The lion cloth is a connection to the sun, the tit to Isis, which is female. It was said that this item was a feminine garment, and was a garment of shame or impurity! There was a misunderstanding of this statement, 'shame and impurity.' We connected it to Isis, we connected it to Virgo, and I said Osiris needs to be further perfected. He is impure at this point, there is no shame. I see some misunderstanding of those statements, but how could one understand without knowing the steps of purification tied to the physical. In the past, none knew of this parallel with matter and the stone. They in actuality (tit and Lion cloth) tie the matters of Osiris, to the above lights, sun and moon. Alchemically, 'to turn the wheel again.' To move the matters of Osiris and the stone further near perfection so that both can join at the proper time with the next and final step. This was to be removed (tit) when the male and female Spirit was made one (December 21). Now with the alchemical process, this is the time when the substance is to be united with just the sun. another way of saying that here is why the 'tit' was removed. Both aspects of sex are joined, soul and Spirit are one matter. It was not shame, it was need! Here though, In the mythology we see that Osiris still needed further augmentation to become like the sun (god). When like the sun, (in April) then he would be the sun, or as the sun, and then the lion cloth could be removed. This is again as the process of the stone. April the stone is finished and a pure substance. April Osiris is resurrected pure and as a God. The stone is Like the sun! The stone is now like god (ancient belief)! Need I say more!

This was a time (from September to April) connected to and then called The Seven Khnemmu, or was know by that name. I ask, 'what is seven?' We see seven in so many places of alchemy, so many places of religious text! Seven is connected always to the seven months of needed work of Osiris to become pure. It also is tied to all of us with this belief! Why is because the ancients shows that all that die go through this seven steps and months of purification to be able to unite with god! There is no other way to go to heaven. The ancients connected the process of the stone, to both matter of soul and spirit, and lastly to spirit alone. The perfection finally came from the last four of the seven days, when he was linked with pure spirit (sunlight) which here on earth was that link to god alone that he had to have.

Osiris, had to become both male and female to then link with the god. He then would be (three persons in one) male, female, god! It in their way was a blending of the matter to the divine.

According to the Mystery of Tattu, this was a way of two to become one, to produce a soul that would live forever. To the ancients this was a blending that produced a matter beyond that of the human, the two halves, male and female were blended forever. The division of three and four months, is found in many religious connections, and the seven is also tied to many things. All have to be from this last seven months of process and how it is linked with the religious understanding.

From available information, I read that equality was to be considered at this time between all things. The birth of Septembers Child, is also connected in alchemy to the conjunction. We see the cross with equal arms erected. On high places, on hills and on mounds a pair of scales was also to be erected (near the end of September), or, time of astrological scales and 'Conjunction.' Please note it is stated "on hills and on mounds a pair of scales was also erected." Was to be is the connection, September is followed by October. The scales is the astrological sign for October. This is also the place of work within the oven. The scales are found in the side view design of the oven. We can work below between the four small pyramids, or on what was called the 'draw bridge which is above' and sets on the four small pyramids. The substances must be further processed. The scales is the sign of this time, and all things are to come to the matter in a balanced fashion. This simply means both lights above are matched or used equally. Osiris is blended. This is again the same as in the steps of the alchemical process. October follows September. The scales (astrological sign) follows the Virgin Virgo! This I point out as what happened in the past religion is the same as I have found in the alchemical process. Those scales the ancients raised on high places is the same as the substance being worked on within the oven. First came the alchemical process, then came the astrological, then the religion.

For clarity's purpose. In the books that you can find to read, it will say that Osiris is resurrected in September. This is true, but you need remember he is (resurrected) reborn as a child. We need also to mention here, that the below is always linked to the above. The alchemists say, "as above, so below." The ancients expressed this in a slightly different way, or, what was happening above, was happening in the below. This is important here with the birth of Osiris, or his rebirth. He is reborn during the month of September, but this is under the sign of the Virgin, Virgo. In other words, his birth is linked to the above constellation, Virgo, and seen in that way. It is both a physical and a spiritual happening, and always linked to the cosmos. Please see the shown allegory included from the 'Temple of Luxor.' The virgin birth was to be understood as mythical, not as an actual physical fact. You will note that through the many steps of the stone, and the links to Osiris, all is done in that way. He (Osiris) is shown in the springtime with the horns of a ram. Why, is because of that time of year is shown astrologically as the ram. The bull, 'Apis Bull' was next, and was connected to that constellation and to the overpowering strength of the sun at that time of year. Leo later is the sign, and it is shown by two lions. This also with the sun crossing the equator is linked to the 'two horizons' (known as) and two Obelisks that were raised to celebrate equality. This equality, two earths, two horizons, all need be considered when understanding Genesis as covering both earths, or yearly repeated in both hemispheres. Six days in each, or the twelve days making up one year. All of the above constellations in their own way are linked. If you will compare the definitions connected to the astrological signs tied to the stone, (Osiris) you will find they are tied to what is happening to the stone (Osiris) physically here in the below with the process. Where the definitions concern the overlapping months, remember the differences in the process at those different times of the stone. All that I have discussed concerning Osiris never happened in the physical, my opinion. But was to be understood as mythology to us, religious beliefs by them. It is to also be understood from their viewpoint where they lived in such a way as all was tied together, the below and the above. They found how to develop this matter, and changed it into a belief system. Also, this material (history of Osiris) comes from a very ancient time, perhaps up to 10,000 years in our past. There is written records that Sir W.Budge (Book of the Dead) refers to as being ancient in 4500 BC. I would like to say, that they at that time were using the astrological signs tied to their beliefs. To see and find an arc in the sky, how long would one have to observe to be able to show the arc? My own opinion would be that ¼ of the arc need be seen to know that a circle would eventually be produced. That alone could connect to 10,000BC. Also, I saw a program of Egypt where J. A. West showed that the sphinx could have been located as it was to point out the Leo constellation, 10,000 BC. It would have been just below the horizon, or positioned as the sphinx was. I agree with his findings. There is no connecting material as far as saying "we did this to matter, and so believe it happens to our matter at death." But, I believe that is exactly how they understood it, and that understanding gave us what we have today as far as religious beliefs! If they could make matter perfect, god could make our matters perfect! If man found this way, then man was special. If man could perfect matter, then the special man would also be perfected by God at death by this process. And even then though, it would depend on how the man lived his life! Many things were tied to it. There was no forgiveness of a bad life! One reaped what one sowed, I also agree with that.

So, the erection of the pillars, in conjunction with the movement of the sun and how matter was controlled and believed could be perfected here in the below. Considering the beliefs of the Isis mythology, it was more than stability connected to the yearly cycle of matter, dead and growing. It became a belief system, one in places continuing today (different cults to Isis). It is the final explanation (could be) of the understanding of the symbols and natural understanding of principles of the ancients. Those principles are tied to the forces around us, and when controlled they can (their understanding) perfect matter. This still remains to be seen. What was found and believed in the past we will not accept today as a belief, just another way of understanding the workings of nature. The ancients in trying to find out what man was, looked for knowledge in their surroundings, and found by this process God and stability in all that they studied. Knowing man was just another form of matter, they compared that matter to all matter, and as all matter organic could be perfected, they felt they had found not just god, but principles. When connected to the man, meant to them that he (god) could again raise up the man. Thus he, the man, by this understanding could live forever. It is more though than just these pillars, and placement coinciding with the movement of the sun. All Egypt must be considered. The Obelisk was though a ray of the sun. The shape of the pyramid was a place where God could come, and in fact the shape of the pyramid was thought to be the original shape of the original God. Soul, and spirit were believed from the lights, and a part of one body in man. The creation of all from an egg was believed similar to be the way god created the earth. The renewal of matter was compared to principles found in nature. They used a serpent, a dogs head, and ibis, and so on because that was to them the only known way to express those principles they found. All of this was based on some happening, and a series of events! That series of events originally must have been that of matter and how nature treats it in the ever renewing cycle of the year.

I want to show, the mythology is only a part of what needs to be understood. It is the facts of the mythology that are needed to be tied in. The problem is that the facts are scattered throughout the book, 'Book of the Dead,' and in some of the remaining temples. It seems to me a collection of what I can find is necessary to firm up the times of the stone, and how it all coincides with Isis and Osiris. First, what is the Book of the Dead? The Title has been translated as 'The Coming Forth by Day.' My understanding of this alone is to say it was a series of works that instructed the dead how to resurrect and to be able to come back to the 'Day.' What this means is an escape from the night or the dark, or the tomb, and to again be able to walk with the living. That they could come back as male or female, man or beast. Consider the androgynous material. As you consider that, also the Sphinx, consider it again when you see the Sphinx as half man, half animal! It seems to me to be only a marker for a graveyard. Tied to the understanding that man could come back, as male or female, man or beast. Others have said that the Egyptian life was lived as a preparation for dying so that they could live in the other world with the gods forever. It would seem it also was a way the could come back and walk again the good earth, in any fashion he should choose.

The only question really is, what was it about matter that they found that caused them to believe and live as they did? The answer is of course, the stone we call Philosophers! Something of the matters perfected caused them to believe they had accomplished what they set out to do, and that was to find IMO, God! As there are so many similarities in the alchemical material, as connected to Osiris, one can hardly dispute that the one is tied to the other. Time now will tell us exactly what the material is and what it will do. When we know what it will do, many of us will set back and try to reason out what it means today!

1. A passage in the (chapter CLIV) Theban Recension, The name of Temu is coupled with Osiris as gods whose flesh never saw corruption. This again is linked to them being of the same matters.

2. The Ka was believed to be the special active force that gave a man life. The ka is what we now understand to be the Spirit. Sprit is the active force we received from the sun during creation. Soul would be that force we received from the moon. Somehow Osiris was believed created from spirit as the original god was pure spirit, and Osiris was of the same material. All others I would say were understood to be created with both lights, (as the original gods are connected to these lights) and so a different material. A better way to try to understand is related to our process. In the first steps of regeneration, from May until August, the two lights are used for the matters. With my understanding of Genesis, the below, man included, was created as androgynous material. A step or so below what Osiris is to become. What one must also remember about Genesis and the creation, the steps are there but they are done in six months or six days of creation. That is how it was understood that god could and did it, man cannot do this, but by art, man could copy the process to resurrect matter (Osiris). Presently I can only say Osiris was created above what man was created, and somehow this was understood so that he could be resurrected again! Perhaps man conceived this was necessary so that Osiris in (religious aspect) as a 'Son of God' gave him the ability to be resurrected by process. Something in their way of understanding allowed the matters of Osiris to be regenerated so that he could reunite with god. For the rest of us, we have to go through a similar but different process. The perfection of the matters showed them that matter could be resurrected by god. Man only found the way it was done, but with the matters of a man, it had to be the same and so could be done by god! The process proves that to them.

3. From Herodotus, "Mysteries existed in ancient Egypt, especially those in connection with the annual suffering and death of Osiris". It would seem, some believed, they were from a prehistoric culture, and probably the remains of a neolithic cult. For the most part, they are tied to agriculture. Always was the question, why were they considered mysteries? Even Herodotus would not talk about these mysteries and say what they were connected to except in a general way.

4. Osiris, the meaning of the name. The oldest and simplest form of the name was As-ar. It was thought by the earlier Egyptians that the name meant 'the strength of the eye.' this to me makes sense, as it means that Osiris again was of the same matter, and so the same as the eye (the sun) which was how they saw the original god. The name also though (in later times) was connected to Ra, however, Ra was the sun, and connected to the day, where Osiris was connected on a level base with Ra, but of the underworld or the night.

5. The myth of Osiris is or has been connected to the daily treck of the sun. Many writers have favored this connection to the daily verses the yearly course. I believe with this work, those interested will see it is the yearly course that defines both the workings of nature, and those workings being the same as the trials of Osiris, showing the correct understanding. The Osirian mythology has never been understood, perhaps now that will change.

6. Mistakes in the understanding of Osiris being connected to the moon, rather than the sun. It was though by some of the near Egyptians that because the moon is connected to humidity, moisture and growth that it was closely connected with the understanding of Osiris. Also, Osiris (in mythology) ruled to the age of 28, which is one period (days in cycle) of the moon. Typhon, in the destruction of the body of Osiris, found it at the full moon, thus the cutting of the body into 14 pieces is the same as the 14 days of the waning moon. All of this, though connected to the moon, cannot be understood without knowing the steps of the philosophers stone and the times. Why is that the process, the regeneration of Osiris is closely linked to the moon. In fact as I have stated, Osiris is brought back to a base substance in September by the moon only, (female principles) and also connected to Virgo. In other words, Isis, the moon, female, is placed in the grave or tomb with Osiris to produce this effect. We know it as Isis, being Virgo the Virgin. Virgo is the virgin which produces the virgin soil so to speak that we with further process produce Osiris perfect. But even that is more connections with both lights, eyes, sun and moon. Osiris could never rule equally with Ra if he was produced by the moon, a lesser light. The two lights work together throughout the year. Both are connected to growth and vegetation. To the compost pile or the recycling of matter naturally which shouldn't be forgotten. Not only is the matter growing, always some of it is being reduced into a base substance so that next cycle it will again become some plant, or a part of the plant. The cycle is overlapping always, that is the way it works. Both lights are needed, but with the mythology we need to know what and why each played a part and how. The one will explain the other.

7. Always in parts of my work I ask, what is seven? I have shown, and use several allegories that seven is the last seven months of the purification process of the matters, or Osiris in part. It is from October, the scales, until the final at April, the finish of the stone and of Osiris's passage back to being pure again. I never really related it just to the moon, as, from what I have found the last four months of the seven are of the matter and the sun. Now if I back up a little there is seven months of work by the moon. When the waters come together in May until the following January is seven months. This would be a completion of the white stone which is finished by the moon, but also is a finish of the matters which are to be the Osiris but only to a point (the following Dec. end). I mention this because in the mythology of Isis, we find she was imprisoned by Set in a summer dwelling, and she is preceded by seven scorpions. This is related to the start of summer, and the winter months.

In our process we can see this as from May to December. It is also (time wise) September to the following April. I believe that all the seven is related to or from September to April. I just have the problem of the moon not being used during the last four months of a part of the mythology saying, 'seven.' I just wanted to point this out. Probably this seven is connected to in alchemy what we call the white stone. There is little matter that I can find that does describe this lesser stone. However, we must always remember, not much information of the mythology is around to compare to, or to see completely. Isis, the moon is seen by several different societies in this fashion, and described in similar ways. I believe there is more information to find with this understanding, but as of yet I have not been able to do so.

8. Both Isis and Osiris are seen in or connected to swamps and marshes. I believe this is so because of the rotting vegetation usually found there, and the lush green growth. It is a place where the waters are coming together, and new life is being formed. In the one drawing included, it shows Set captured in a net! It also is from a place near a swamp, as bulrushes is within the picture. I am sure there is something I am missing with connections to the swamp. It may be the 'dead matter' that is found there. At the base of any swamp, there is much rotted matter depending on how old the swamp is. Somehow this may have been a source to them for matters they may have worked with. It has been a consideration of mine as of late. I usually use the compost pile as a reference to matters being recycled. In the climate they had, and type of plant life? I don't know if they ever had a type of compost pile. The swamp dead matter would be and is the same type of material.

9. Isis, the 'lady of Sept.' was a springtime astronomical symbol, and a name given to her. This is also linked to the star Sothis (Sirius). I note it because of the name itself, Sept. Though I have found no connection, this needs further research. Septembers Child, as being produced by Isis, Virgo, that constellation. Remember the sun crosses the equator twice, one in September, one in spring where this name is connected. This also links to the time just mentioned when Set imprisons her. In the one Set is a battle to be fought, in the other, a battle won. Depending on which way the sun is moving. Also, the mythology was misunderstood by the near Egyptians, it is possible that even they no longer knew the correct way of understanding. This shows how ancient the mythology had become even to them! There is though enough for us to retrieve all and understand. Best, there is enough to find the stone and to understand where all this came from originally. Egypt is an old country. Those laws and principles they found and used were I am sure changed as the man grew and learned more as is done in any society. Not all was changed, not the basic principles, but perhaps some of the understanding.

10. Horus. The son of Osiris and Isis, the one who overcame the evil Set. Horus had no fewer than seven forms. The forms are not important, again, seven is important. Set was overcome in September, with seven months of process to follow. He was overcome in September by Horus. I feel the seven forms were connected somehow originally to the seven months. Also we find with Horus that he had helpers in the Taut that helped care for the deceased, "four of which had special importance." I can't prove it but I believe these four were connected with the last four months of the seven months of process. Always we find this division of the seven by three and four! The special importance had to do with the or tied to the work of the sun the last four months.

11. From the Theban Recension, there were seven halls or mansions that needed to be passed through by the soul before it could be received by the Gods.

12. From the Bible, and I believe connected with the past. Revelations 1:4, "grace to you and peace from him who is and who was and who is to come, and from the seven spirits that are before his throne".

13. Revelations 4:5 And before the throne burn seven torches of fire, which are the seven Spirits of God.

14. Revelations 5:6 and between the throne and the four living creatures and among the elders, I saw a Lamb standing as though it had been slain, with seven horns and with seven eyes, which are the seven Spirits of God, sent out into all the earth.

It would seem whatever one wants to believe, one must approach God through seven of something. As to the seven horns, Osiris is usually, sometimes connected to a Ram. This has to do with spring and the time of the greatest effect of the sun. The seven eyes I believe came from the understanding of the original god being connected to the 'eye of the sun.' To the 'Eye of Horus.'

I am a man with a hobby. I couldn't even guess the time I have spent trying to understand and then to put it to paper. The whole thing is as a hobby, I have been able to spend the time, my adult life trying to figure out the basis of fact that is involved with all this. I believe it would be almost impossible for a man to do that needed and as we all do, to work a job. Even if that job had to do with ancient Egypt. There are so many things that need to be brought together to see it in a way that can bring to us an understanding. The other problem, is that it is all hidden knowledge or based on some mythology. Things we don't base credibility on. I will, to make things somewhat clearer, draw a times of the year map, so to speak, and with it I will place the times of the stone, the months of the year, the different crosses used, and place Osiris where he is transformed in the different stages. Always remember, as with the stone, the system overlaps. The transformation of Osiris overlaps, as in nature, a seed produced needs the next year to become a plant, and to again reproduce. If you will consider the life and death of a plant, and it's seed is about the same as that of Osiris. I am sure that this information should be and will be drawn out to a many page explanation, but not by me. My work is a series of facts so to speak, and should be read in that fashion. Always consider outside, the workings of nature, what is happening to matter or seeds, and consider why the ancients saw things as they did. I see them as a people wanting in many ways. Most importantly wanting as we all do, to know if man is special, and if there is 'One True God,' and how to know of him. Nature as they said, was their only teacher. All we try to see we must see in that way, and the sun and moon causes all that happens here in the below. To link those lights to god or a part of god would seem to me to be only natural. I believe our past, and the ancient past is our heritage, and that we should know and understand it. Perhaps by better knowing our past we can better move forward. It still remains to be seen if there is a philosophers stone, and if it will be of benefit to mankind. I believe it will. It is a slow way to control matter, and if I was to describe it, I would say a way to make it perfect.

Only nature knows how to do this, and the ancients I believed found this way by imitating nature. I am sure when we completely understand what they did, it will benefit us. How we hold it to ourselves remains to be seen. Also, I was lucky, but I think those that experiment will understand. Much of what I found I found by accident as you do when experimenting.

A timeline of events according to Osiris, and the stone.

December 21. Jan. 21.   Feb. March. April May June July August September October Nov. December 21 is the start of our process. Is the time to start the life of Osiris. Is the time of the Tat Cross. Is the time to remove the tit from the Djed Pillar (must be remembered from overlap) as several things happen with this ongoing process. The sun was coming back from it's shortest day. In the alchemical process it is a time to set aside an egg to be kept warm. With Genesis it is the first day for the northern hemisphere. Those things mentioned were created, the original god and the matters for Osiris, and light. It, with Osiris is also the time when he is tied to pure sunlight, or to pure god or spirit, however you want to see it for his final purification to perfection. Just remember some of these things are one year apart. With the alchemical process, the matters are tied to now, the sun for the red stone. The white stone is now finished. Three of those seven months have passed.

Jan. 21. This is the time Osiris goes into the coffin (his envelope) and was destroyed. In alchemy the egg goes into the created firmament. It is the start of the second day of Genesis. It is also the first month of Osiris being tied to the sun for complete purification (with the passage of one year). In alchemy this is the auroborous start.

February. Ongoing process with Osiris, and the matters within the egg.

March 21 Ongoing process with Osiris, also with matters of the egg. This is also when the sun moving north crosses the equator. All things are equal. The ancient Egyptian sign is a cross with four equal arms. This is when Isis is known as Sept., and near when she is thrown into a prison by the evil Set. This is also the start of spring. Osiris is known by the sign of a ram which is tied to April, the next month. This is the third day of Genesis when the waters come together, again, spring. All is in balance because of the position of the sun. This understanding I believe is why on the third day, the waters could come together.

April. See how one day separates two ideas about nature? The start of spring, Osiris this month will complete four months of further purification, and then can ascend to god in heaven. The philosophers stone is finished, and would be 16 months old. From the start of the first step, Osiris lies in his tomb. With Genesis the matters of the egg are being destroyed. Osiris is dead. What the egg was needs to be destroyed so that the matters of the egg can be remade. Matter that was is returning to a base that nature can reshape or remake with process.

May. Known as the May-Day in alchemy. Osiris is ongoing process in one aspect, in the other he has risen and is now in heaven. The egg has gone through it's destruction process, known as the (alchemically) ouroborous. However ouroborous is understood to be there until Osiris is resurrected in September. It has, the matters been reduced naturally to a base. This is the same base as understood of the waters in the creation epic. This same type of thing is happening to the body of Osiris. This has taken the egg four month, the same four months of destruction, as is the four of purification for Osiris. Two things are going on, in the one we subjected Osiris to pure sunlight, (for perfection), in the other, to total darkness (for destruction). One moving closer to god, the other moving away from god, (moving from the light) described as the only hell!

June. The sun reaches it furthers point north. Summer solstice. The first of the three hottest months are passed. This is known as a hot bad time to the ancients living in Egypt. It is also a time when the god Set is starting to wan, as are the length of the days as the sun now starts to move in a southerly direction. June is also the sixth day in Genesis. Remember there are two hemispheres in the earth, the north and the south, and each must be created over again and in the same fashion. The god we know may have rested on the seventh day of our creation, but the ongoing process of Genesis did not stop. It goes on forever. From the May-Day, the matters of the egg are exposed to the sun and the moon. The androgyny is to be made from the Ouroborous. This is during these three hottest months of summer.

July. Ongoing

August. Ongoing

September. Many things again in September. The matters of the egg are purified in moonlight only, and become now a pure white substance (Septembers Child is created). The matters of Osiris is the same, and he is rising from the crypt, but is not pure by any means, not pure enough to go to heaven and be with god. For him, and the stone, seven more months of purification need to be done. Alchemically we know this time as Septembers Child, produced by Virgo. The death of Osiris has been overcome. Set is at this time overcome by the son Horus. He, Osiris, is raised but not in spirit. The stone is likewise only a base material now ready to be purified. Osiris is now ready to start the process of purification. This is the start, with October, sign scales astrologically, the Tat cross also of the seven months. This is also the summer solstice, the sun again crosses the equator, moving south. 'Horus was erecting the Tat in Sekhem' with the raising of Osiris from the sepulcher. This at that time was celebrated with a love feast. The triumph of the soul regenerated in Tattu. A blending of the sexes in a union linked to the soul of Osiris that would live forever. The Djed Column was raised with tit and lion cloth.

October. The raising of the Tat Cross. In alchemy both lights are again brought into the process, we "turn the wheel again" as the alchemists said to do. The white substance (soul) of the egg is divided into two parts, one for limited purification to the white or moon stone. The other for the red or sun stone. The one three months, the other seven more months of work. One must here realize that the end of one astrological is sometimes seen as the same as the next astrological time. The Djed was raised in the end of September, as was the cross with equal arms. In alchemy we use October as the time of the scales? This overlap can only be explained in this way. The scales were erected. Scales are for October, and so how to explain? To them it indicated an ongoing process, and as the below is linked to the above, this was the next step in that progression.

November, Ongoing duel process.

December. 21, The finish of the white stone, the start of the completion of work for the red stone to be joined to the sun, spirit. The work of the Djed Piller, the winter solstice. Here the tit would be removed, this is linked to the work just done where both lights were used. Further purification was needed and accomplished. This is explained as now the joining would be just with the sun (Lion cloth). This explains the so called mystery of Tattu. The souls were blended back into a single being, the first three months. Alchemically we see this as the Crowned androgyny. What this means is the further purification from October to December was done by both lights. Also what this means is Osiris had moved to a substance beyond that which was similar to the earth in the creation. The earth was considered pure, but was of an androgynous form, being both male and female. He, Osiris was soul and spirit, but a second time of augmentation by this process was needed. We show this in alchemy, first androgynous material is made, then Crowned Androgyn is made. He needed to become pure spirit as of yet. This would be accomplished now by direct contact with the god through the light of the sun.

The second January. Ongoing process with Osiris. Ongoing until April for his final restoration and then resurrection. Ongoing with the matters of the stone to become pure spirit (like the sun).

Because of my limited ability to collect ancient works of Egypt, and because of the scarcity of the material, I use material from where I find it. The following material is from a lecture series by a Dr. Marie-Louise von Franz at the Jung Institute Zurich, in 1959. The ancient works and sayings are the material I use rather than the comments of Dr von Franz. Where the work is from actually I will note when possible.

" Oh my son, when you desired to go away to fight the treacherous Typhon (Seth) over your fathers kingdom of Osiris, I went to Hormanouthi, i.e. Hermoupolis, the town of Hermes, the town of the Holy Technique of Egypt and stayed there for some time."

The Holy Technique (hiera techne) refers to alchemy. This is a reference to Horus in the battle with the evil Set, and a connection to Isis and alchemy. To go on, "After a certain passing of the kairoi and a necessary movement of the heavenly sphere." The kairoi is our objective here, and to explain it and connect it we visit Zosimos. A theory of his, and how he described it was thus "chemical processes do not always happen of themselves, but only at the astrologically right moment." The astrological constellations must be taken into consideration. The alchemist is the man that must consider these moments along with knowing the holy technique. This tells us that the stone has to be made according to the passing of time, and that each step is done in conjunction with what is happening outside. What is happening is the movement of the stars, the sun and moon. The process works when it is done with and attached to the seasons of the year. There-fore Isis says "That according to the passing of these moments, one must consider one moment after another (one has to choose the right one), and according to the movement of the heavenly sphere, it happened." These comments come from Isis, and is from a discussion of her and some angles that want to unite with her. She is willing to unite with them, but only if they will tell her the secret of the holy technique. As she wins out from a promise of her favors, the technique is given and explained. " go to the Acheron (pheasant) and watch and ask. The secret is that like produces like. A man can reproduce a man, a seed of corn can reproduce corn, gold can reproduce gold. The whole of Creation is of this way. Nature enjoys nature, nature impregnates nature, and nature overcomes nature." This though was only a part of the mystery. To go on, " having part of the divine power and being happy about its divine presence, I will now answer their questions about sands. "Sands- which one does not prepare from other substances, for one must stay with existing nature." Now sands has to do with shapes! And so as one must stay with nature, one must to know and consider the mystery, like produces like, and gold reproduces gold. Shape is involved. Gold reproduces the gold, and to the ancients the sun was considered gold. Now the explanation, "the sun in your glass pyramid oven!" What this means, is the "gold is in sand." Which means, "The sun is within your oven." Other things are needed as we have and shall see. More is within the oven. the pheasant Acharontos, Aker, and Rwti.

"Just before the resurrection of the sun god takes place, he is shown in his tomb, phallus erect, and surrounded by the arborous." The inscription says " this is the corps, You see therefore that in the underworld when the sun god has reached the moment of death and resurrection, he is surrounded by this snake." Now, Aker or Akerou. This is the two lions, back to back. The sun between the two backs. This is called Rwti. Now Aker means 'that movement.' I have shown prior to this, is September, when the sun is in equilibrium, and the moment is when it crosses the equator. This is when the Djed piller is/was raised, and when death is overcome. This in alchemy is Septembers Child. This is when Osiris was born again under the constellation Virgo, and was considered the 'Virgin Birth.' Now in alchemy we see the practical application of this symbolism. We take our matters and return it to a substance that would be 'like' the substance of the creation. This is after the rotting stage. With our process covering the three hottest months of summer, the ouroborous, we regenerate this matter. Then with the constellation Virgo, we continue and bring it to the point of being a pure white substance. Now this is Osiris newborn. We have not pure matter in September, we have the base matter for the stone. Now, with the spiritual, and with Aker, the double lion, he is represented as the 'door to the beyond.' The double lions become the doorkeepers to this beyond. In the spiritual aspect, this is the place where the soul of the departed will start his passage in the underworld spanning the seven, to go on to heaven, my understanding. And so we have the physical on earth, (seven months more of purification) we have the spiritual in the other world. This is considered an admixture of two ideas. We purify with the lights in the process, the matters here considered anybody's dead body, had to go through the seven areas in the underworld to get to heaven. Lion is also the sign before Virgo!

To explain this in another way, sometimes the double Lion was replaced in many of the tombs by Anubis's jackals. and so why a dog head on Anubis? Why dogs, or jackals? Simply as a way to explain a principle found in nature. Dogs, jackals can and in many places live on rotted, or rotting meat. They turn the rotted or rotting meat into something good, food for themselves. It is the principle of turning the rotten bodies into something good that is considered the principle. Anubis is to turn their (the dead) rotted bodies into another good spirit body. The inscription found by these two, within some of the tombs is, "these are the openers of the way, the agents of resurrection." The way is explained by the principle. This is also explained in some of the tombs that Aker, and Shu (air god) are the two creators of the world, and so, rotted matter and air. Consider again now what is found within the oven. Just remember that air is only a carrier between the above and the below. Rotted material, air, and vapor to carry the energy of the two lights to the below. The Egyptians always were as was said, puzzled by the creation, and of matter. As we consider the making of the stone, we are also working with matter and trying to remake it. If we can resurrect the matters of the stone, then the problem of resurrection is worked out. Man had found how matter could be reworked by man, and also, more importantly, by god. With the finding of the stone, man had found, he believed, how god could eventually resurrect his body. Remembering the double lions, and the double idea, I can't say if they ever believed that the body buried would be resurrected, but I can see and understand how they connected it to the resurrection of the spirit or glorified body, that could unite with god in heaven.

To continue, and show some more information of why I work with an egg. Not only did they see all from the creation as from an egg, but- " I have seen the mysteries, my sun disk and Geb, the earth god, are those whom I carry on my back. Chepera is now inside his envelope." "Chepera is the resurrecting form of the sun god who is now in his egg, he is in his envelope." The rotted within the oven is Osiris showing only his face (outside of shell) It is Chepera within his envelope.

From all this, and from the book of the dead, and from alchemy we find that the matters, the people, the bodies, all must undergo this process of destruction and rebirth before they can be resurrected. Consider again the compost pile, all matters we destroy and return to a black substance.

The matters are inert! They can be nothing. But the matter can become anything or, correctly said a part of anything in nature that can use that material. I believe the compost pile, or something like it is where the ancients got the idea that after resurrection, the man could again walk the earth, but as man or women, man or beast.

To continue with more on Osiris and his tomb and his matters. 'Oracles,' of the past have also said things about the process. The oracel comments, "Osiris is the suffocated coffin in which are hidden his limbs and whoes face only is visible to mortal beings." "Hiding the bodies, nature is astonished." "He, Osiris is the original principle of moist substances." "He is kept down as a prisoner by the sphere of fire." "He, therefore, has suffocated all the lead." Now the lead is described as the egg, sometimes connected to the four elements. The egg is suffocated. The face is the outside of the egg, all that can be seen by mortals in the oven, or in the sand. He is kept down by the sphere of fire, which means simply he is kept warm so that the process works. Now, why is nature astonished? I would say because things now happen because of sand, and because of time within the oven/sand. Nature is used with nature as was said with the understanding of Like! Shape is used in a controlled place where the matters are returned to a base matter like that matter the world and all in it were created. "Nature is astonished because she cannot do this by herself." The compost pile is a good way to understand, but the matters of the compost, and the matters of the oven are different. This compost is what nature can do. What is within the sands, nature cannot do by herself. Olympiodoros speaks of the substance and says. "this is the original substance, and is the material called prima materia." "It is not black when it starts out, and it is not lead, but a different lead." "It is a substance you must experiment with, a more basic substance, to understand what earlier writers meant." He goes on to say that "this is Osiris in his coffin." "This is the beginning of all moist substances, basic matter, original matter, the starting point." And it must be caught in the sphere of fire. This sphere of fire is also connected to a 'male water.' The male water is sulfurous, or mixed with the sun. This is as we continue with the process, and is, with the start of what we know as the third day of creation, when the waters above and below come together. As I earlier explained, the air is a carrier of the vapor and a place for the fire and air to meet and mix to be carried into the tomb. This sphere of fire, this light of the sun is which will eventually give the perfection. All comes from the 'good light.' Flamel spoke of this in his work, The soul and spirit (sun and moon) was around the tomb in the graveyard but could not enter the grave. The body (water) could come and go within the tomb.

This information I post as the most important information ever connected to the understanding of alchemy.

ANCIENT EGYPT: THE LIGHT OF THE WORLD

A WORK OF RECLAMATION AND RESTITUTION IN TWELVE BOOKS

by GERALD MASSEY

AUTHOR OF "A BOOK OF THE BEGINNINGS" and "THE NATURAL GENESIS"

It may have been a Million years ago
The Light was kindled in the Old Dark Land
With which the illumined Scrolls are all aglow,
That Egypt gave us with her mummied hand :
This was the secret of that subtle smile
Inscrutable upon the Sphinx's face,
Now told from sea to sea, from isle to isle ;
The revelation of the Old Dark Race ;
Theirs was the wisdom of the Bee and Bird,
Ant, Tortoise, Beaver, working human-wise ;
The ancient darkness spake with Egypt's Word ;
Hers was the primal message of the skies:
The Heavens are telling nightly of her glory,
And for all time Earth echoes her great story.

VOLUME -1-

London
T.Fisher Unwin
Adelphi Terrace
1907

EDITION LIMITED TO FIVE HUNDRED COPIES

PREFATORY

I have written other books, but this I look on as the exceptional labour which has made my life worth living. Comparatively speaking, "A Book of the Beginnings" (London, 1881) was written in the dark, "The Natural Genesis" (London, 1883) was written in the twilight, whereas" Ancient Egypt" has been written in the light of day. The earlier books were met in England with the truly orthodox conspiracy of silence. Nevertheless, four thousand volumes have got into circulation somewhere or other up and down the reading world, where they are slowly working in their unacknowledged way. Probably the present book will be appraised at home in proportion as it comes back piecemeal from abroad, from Germany, or France, or maybe from the Country of the Rising Sun.

To all dear lovers of the truth the writer now commends the verifiable truths that wait for recognition in these pages.

Truth is all-potent with its silent power
If only whispered, never heard aloud,
But working secretly, almost unseen,
Save in some excommunicated Book;
'Tis as the lightning with its errand done
Before you hear the thunder.

*For myself, it is enough to know that in despite of many hindrances
from straitened circumstances, chronic ailments, and the deepening shadows of encroaching age, my book is printed, and the subject-matter that I cared for most is now entrusted safely to the keeping of John Gutenberg, on this my nine-and-seventieth birthday.*

This document is a publication of the
Canadian Theosophical Association (a regional association of the Theosophical Society in Adyar)
89 Promenade Riverside,
St-Lambert, QC J4R 1A3
Canada

http://www.theosophical.ca/AncientEgyptIntroduction.htm

It was said by Mr. Tompkins that Mr. Massey was the 'Greatest of Minds' with the ancient of Egypt. I believe with reading this book that is true. It to me was the answer that all my adult life I looked for. In the past though I would have not known the information it contained, even like those mysteries Mr. Tompkins mentioned with his work. None has ever connected the past of Egypt and the discussion of alchemy. None has known that the life and times of Osiris is those of the stone of alchemy. Not only the times, what was said, how it was celebrated Also the structures they used during those ancient holidays. What I have done is to take from Mr. Massey's work, those things he has found and understood within his work, and to connect them to the steps of the alchemical stone. Mr. Massey had said, from Mr. Tompkins work, that all of this had to be based on something. I with what could be called my life's work, found the steps of the stone, and the times of the steps of the process. Never, though reading parts in many book, ever did I see the connection of the two works. It was first Mr. Tompkins work, and then through a friend who led me to this work that it all came together. Here though the material is different. It is not bits and pieces picked apart by some author that knew not what he was reading, here from Mr. Massey is a through discussion of what was known and how it was celebrated during the times. If you will learn the steps I have laid out for the stone, and how it is described by past master achemists, with what I point out with this work, you will know that the understanding of the one, is from the other. There is so much information I will not here point out I can only say, I included the book address as to where it can be seen. As you understand you also can go back in time and learn all. It is of a long time in ancient history. I still can only surmise how long it must have taken for all this to be found by the ancients. I would say many thousands of years. Why is it we don't know our past?

What my intentions are with this part of the work, is to copy from the paragraph what is said that is important, explain and connect it to alchemy, a step, and to then let you read it in the paragraph. In this first paragraph, Mr. Massey discusses how long, by observation that it must have taken to find what it was they were searching for. Here first, it was the 'Procession of the Equinox.' Not known even to them. You decide from what is written here, how long it would have, by observation, to find. Concerning alchemy, it was a result of this study, not of just the stars, but of all that was seen. The process of the stone, and the naming of the constellations had to be done together. What happened in the below was a result of what happened over time in the above. Close cycles like that of the moon, longer cycles like that of the year, and then long periods like the procession of the equinox. All were brought together. Concerning alchemy, even a greater length of time need be considered.

"The Egyptian founders of astronomical science did not begin with mathematical calculations. They had to verify everything by observation through all the range of periodic time, and this was the only method that was fundamental or practical at first. It was by direct observation, not by calculation, that the wise men of Egypt and Meroë attained their knowledge of precession. By ages on ages of watching and registering they perceived that the backward movement of the equinox, as immense in time as it is slow in motion, had to be reckoned with as a factor of vast magnitude; and that this long hand on the face of the eternal horologe was a determinative of the hugest cycle of all, so far as they could measure periodic time. By imperceptible degrees the movement itself had become apparent, and the point of equal day and night was observed to be passing out of one group of stars upon the ecliptic into another; which sometimes coincided with a change of polestars."

In the following, and with much of the information to come, one has to somewhat know the procession of the Equinox's. Why? Here, I will say I have discussed I think the 'Seven' enough to show you originally what it was about. In alchemy it is the last seven months of the process. It is tied to the above, and as each month passes and another constellation is referred to, what is in the below is seen in another fashion. Also, one here must start to consider that, in the Long Measure of Time, as the procession continues, each two thousand years here in the below, another time of the procession is occurring. This I can relate to you with a song of our time, "This is the Dawning of the Age of Aquarius." The last age had to do with the fish! The age of Pisces. Consider the fish, and how it was connected to religion and Jesus Christ, and you will be on your way of understanding. Each age with the ancients caused a Great Change in how it was seen, and how things were changed with them and their religion as far as how shown in the below. To them it was a religion, to us a mythology. All based on the fact of the alchemical process, the times of Osiris, and how the all worked together.

"One of the most perfect illustrations of fulfilment attained by the mythos may be studied in a scene that was copied from the Roman **[Page 737]** Catacombs by De Rossi (*Rom. Sott.*, 2, pl. 16). In this the seven great spirits appear in human guise, who are elsewhere represented by the seven fishers or the seven lambs with Horus, ignorantly supposed to be an historic personage. These seven are with the fish in the sign of the two fishes, who are figured as the two fishes laid out on two dishes. Moreover, lest there might be any mistake in reading the picture it is placed between two other illustrations. In one of these the lamb is portrayed as the victim of sacrifice; in the other a fish is lying with the bread upon the altar. So that *the central picture shows the result of the transference from the sign of the ram to the sign of the fishes.* In another scene the seven who were followers of Horus are portrayed together with seven baskets of bread (Bosio, pp. 216, 217). In relation to the group of seven spirits in the Roman Catacombs it must be noted that the company of twelve, as followers of Horus, or disciples of Iusa, was not a primary formation. It was preceded by the group of seven, the seven who were with Horus, the leader of that "glorious company", from the beginning; the same in the eschatology as in the astronomical mythology. They are the seven with Horus in the bark of souls or Sahus that was constellated in Orion. In the creation attributed to Atum-Ra, which opened on the day of "come thou hither", otherwise upon the resurrection day, the seven great spirits are assigned their place in this new heaven; they are called the seven glorious ones "who are in the train of Horus" ; and who follow after the coffined one, that is Osiris-Sekari, whose bier or coffin was configurated in the greater bear. They who followed their lord as his attendants in the resurrection were also grouped as seven khuti in the lesser bear. In his various advents Horus was attended by the seven great spirits termed his seshu, or his servants. So Jesus, according to Hebrew prophecy, was to be attended by the seven spirits called (1) the spirit of the Lord; (2) the spirit of wisdom; (3) the spirit of understanding; (4) the spirit of counsel; (5) the spirit of might; (6) the spirit of knowledge; (7) the spirit of the fear of the Lord (Is. XI. 1, 2). These, as Egyptian, were they who had originated as the seven elemental powers and who afterwards became the Khuti as the seven great spirits. But in their Hebrew guise they are evaporized and attenuated past all recognition except as a septenary of spirits. The seven with Jesus as a group of attendant powers or followers may be seen in the seven doves that hover round the child *in utero*; the seven solar rays about his head; the seven lambs or rams with Jesus on the mount; the seven as stars with Jesus in the midst; the seven as fishers in the boat; and lastly, the seven as communicants who solemnize the Eucharist with the loaves and fishes in the mortuary meal of the Roman Catacombs. There are various pictures in the Catacombs which can only be explained by the pre-Christian gnosis. This alone can tell us why the divine infant should be imaged as a little mummy with the solar halo round his head, or why the so-called "Star of Bethlehem" should be figured with eight rays. Such things are Egypto-gnostic remains belonging to the Church in Rome that was not founded on the Canonical Gospels, but was pre-extant as gnostic; the Church of Marcion and of Marcelina. Several of these pictures contain the group of the seven great spirits who were with **[Page 738]** Horus of the Resurrection at his advent in the sign of Pisces, as they had been with him in the previous signs when he was the lamb, the calf, the beetle or the lion. Two pictures are copied by Lundy, one from De Rossi's *Roma Sotteranea Christiana* (vol. 1) and one from Bosio (*Rom. Sott.*). In the one scene seven persons are seated at a semicircular table with two fishes and eight baskets of bread before them. In the other scene, seven persons are kneeling with two fishes, seven cakes and seven baskets of bread in front of them (Lundy, *Monumental Christianity*, figs. 169 and 171). Now, there is nothing whatsoever in the canonical Gospels to account for or suggest the eight baskets-full of cakes which are somewhat common in the Catacombs. These we claim to be a direct survival from the Egyptian; the eight loaves or cakes which are a sacred regulation number in the Ritual. According to the Rubrical directions appended to chapter 144 it is commanded that *eight* Persen loaves, *eight* Shenen loaves, *eight* Khenfer loaves, and *eight* Hebennu loaves are to be offered at each gate of the seven arits or mansions of the celestial Heptanomis. These offerings were made for the feast of illumining the earth, or elsewhere (ch. 18), the coffin of Osiris, and therefore for the festival of the Resurrection and solemnizing of the Eucharist."

Alchemically one must realize that the eight connected to the stone has to do with the eight months of work leading up to what we call 'Septembers Child' which is Osiris in his resurrection during the next month of September. Seen astrologically, it is the eight stars connected to the dippers above. Seven in the constellation, the eight is Osiris which is the north or Polaris. The little dipper never sets, the big dipper, or the Great Bear, the Plough, however you see it does set from the viewpoint of Egypt. Thus the Little dipper gave stability. The seven is everywhere, and so not needs to be discussed again here. As you consider the procession of the equinox, and that the fish was a sign used in 0000 AD, it was the star searched for by the three wise men. It was the constellation Pisces, of the constellations repeated as you will read, repeated every two thousand years by the procession. This is shown and proved by the various names of Osiris connected to these constellation in different tombs found and studied. Had the religion continued, it would have been Osiris connected to the fish, not Jesus Christ.

"The seven persons present with the Lord are identifiable with the typical seven followers of Horus as the seven khuti or glorious ones. The speaker, who personates the lord of the seven, says "I am the divine leader of the seven. I am a khu, the lord of the khus". The Osiris Nu thus celebrates the monthly festival by offering eight loaves or cakes at each of the seven halls. The khus were seven in number or eight with Horus their lord, in whom Osiris rose again from the condition of the dead. The chapter is to be repeated over a picture of the seven sovereign chiefs, which we now claim to be the original of the seven personages that keep the sacramental ceremony in the Catacombs when the eight cakes are figured on the table of the seven personages who have been termed the "*Septem Pii Sacerdotes*" (Northcote and Brownlow, *Rom. Sott.*, vol. 2, pl. 17, p. 68). "

So alchemically one must see the eight, as prior months to the resurrection, and seven as the work to be continued after the new birth or first resurrection. The ninth month is not spoken of here other than as of the resurrection of Osiris. We work for eight months with the matters to make a substance that can be resurrected as , alchemically, Septembers Child which is Osiris, seven more months of work are needed to totally purify the matters into the stone. Seven more months are needed for Osiris to be made totally perfect so that he can in April, his second resurrection be joined to the gods

"But to return, our starting-point for tracking the movement in precession was with the vernal equinox in the sign of Leo, on the birthday of the year that was determined at the time by the heliacal rising of the star which announced the birthplace of Horus, now figured in the solar zodiac, nigh where the evil dragon Hydra lay in wait to devour the babe as soon as it was born. This was about

11,000 years B.C., or 13,000 years ago. During these eleven thousand years, by the changes in precession and the continual rectification of the calendar from old style to new, July 25th at starting had receded to December 25th in the end. That is, the birthday of the coming child Iusa or Horus in the Lion sign, celebrated on the 25th of July, came to be commemorated on the 25th of December at the end of this period, by those who kept the reckoning, and this, as will be shown, is precisely what did occur in the evolution of the Jesus-legend.

According to the decree of Canopus (B.C. 238) the date of Osiris's entry into the moon at the annual resurrection had then receded to the 29th of Choiak, equivalent to December 26th, *in the Alexandrian year*, which was established in the reign of Augustus, B.C. 25. "The entry of Osiris into the sacred bark takes place here annually at the **[Page 739]** defined time on the 29th day of the month Choiak". In this way the Christmas festival, by which the "Birth of Christ" is now celebrated, can be identified with the yearly celebration of the rebirth of Osiris (or Horus) in the moon. Moreover, we can thus trace it, following the course of precession, from the 17th of Athor (October 5th in the sacred year; November 14th in the Alexandrian year), mentioned by Plutarch, to the 29th of Choiak, our December 26th. The next day, December 27th, was the first of Tybi, and this was the day on which the child-Horus was crowned, and the festival of his coronation celebrated. If we reckon the 25th of December (28th Choiak) to be the day of birth, the day of resurrection and of the crowning *in Amenta* is on the third day. In the month-list of the Ramesseum, Tybi is the month dedicated to Amsu, the Horus who arose from the dead in Amenta, and who was crowned as conqueror *on the third day* — that is, on December 27th=Tybi 1st. There are several symbols of this resurrection on the third day. First, Osiris rises on that day in the new moon. Next, Amsu figures as the Sahu-mummy risen to his feet, with right arm free, as ruler in Amenta, the earth of eternity. Thirdly, Horus the child is ruler in Amenta, the earth of eternity. Thirdly, Horus the child is crowned in the seat of Osiris for another year. Fourthly, the Tat was erected as a figure of the god re-risen, and a type of eternal stability in the depths of the winter solstice. Thus the resurrection on the third day was in Amenta and not upon this earth."

To understand alchemically, it is easiest just to know where the sun is according to the times of the year and the position of the sun overhead. December, as above, is the starting point of the stone. It also is (because it overlaps) the next December. Above, the resurrection in Amenta, is the stone below during the second December. It is or has gone through three of the seven months of purification. It is raised in the oven (important to understand) from the below position to the above position, so that now it can unite with the sun. Alchemically, it is now is worked on totally by the sun to become 'like' the sun. To become perfect, and if Osiris, understood connected to him, also to be able to join with the God above as he also is now perfect. The physical process below became the philosophical religion of the past. What they found with matter and shape and time, they believed to be the way of god and man, and with the matters of man being likened to Osiris and to the stone, they believed they had found how god could resurrect all men. Also to be understood, the three days mentioned above, and ending in December. This was to me the three months, but is also linked to the sun as it seems to stand still at Dec. 21, the day before, that day and one after. Based in alchemy, the three days above are the three months from the conjunction of alchemy to the end of December. These three days I have shown in many places. This is where the understanding, along with Genesis comes from.

The next work, first is the dove. In alchemy, we see a white goose. Easiest for me to show is in those pictorial allegories of October, and what we know of as the conjunction. The white goose of alchemy represents the dove spoken of in this part of the work. It is tied to the moon, and to soul alchemically. White is the color of purity, of the moon, of soul, and of the white stone. In alchemy and at the conjunction, (which starts in September) it is the start of the work for both stones. That is usually what is indicated by the pictorial allegories of this stage. The goose is usually shown in the background, biting herself. What this signifies, is it is a work of like. The white work is like, meaning only white, which is the white pure substance (Septembers Child) only the moon (white), only soul, and only water. Some would tell you also only silver, this is something I have yet to know well enough to say. Also, in the below work, it is mentioned that the one has his head "within a triangle." This means that actually, that person is within heaven. This is shown in some pictorial allegories where it shows a Master Alchemist praying to God, and it also shows the head of God enclosed within a triangle, which again means he is praying to God in Heaven. More at the end of this part. As so many things were changed to hide the past, this ancient understanding of showing God with his head within a triangle, may be where painting saints, with a halo over their head came from. I don't know but it seems a possibility to me.

"The Egyptians celebrated their festival of the resurrection every year, called the feast of Ptah-Sekari-Osiris, in the month Choiak (November 27th, December 26th, Alexandrian year). The rite is otherwise known as "the erection of the Tat-pillar". Erman recovered a description of the festival from a Theban tomb. Of this he says: "The special festival was of all the greater importance because it was solemnized on the morning of the royal jubilee. The festivities began with a sacrifice offered by the king to Osiris, the 'LORD of Eternity,' a mummied figure, wearing the Tat-pillar on his head". It lasted for ten days, from the 20th to the 30th of the month Choiak, the 26th being the great day of feasting. The royal endowment of the temple at Medinet Habu for the sixth day of the festival included 3,694 loaves of bread, 600 cakes, 905 jugs of beer and 33 jars of wine. This was the great day of eating and drinking, corresponding to our Christmas gorging and guzzling, but on the 22nd December, instead of the 25th, of a somewhat later period. The festival was devoted to the god Osiris-Ptah-Sekari, who had been dead and was alive again; cut in pieces and reconstituted with his vertebrae sound and not a bone of his body found to be broken or missing. The festival of the sixth day is clearly the Ha-k-er-a feast that was celebrated on the sixth night of the Ten Mysteries. Moreover, the ten days of the festival that was sacred to the god Osiris-Sekari are also in agreement with the ten nights of the mysteries (Rit., ch. 18). In the scene copied from the Theban tomb the "Noble Pillar" of the Tat-cross is to be seen lying pronely on the ground where it had been overthrown by Sut and the Sebau. The object of the festival was to celebrate the re-erection of the Tat and turn the Cross of death once more into the Cross of life as the symbol of resurrection. The king, as representative of Horus who reconstitutes [**Page 741**] his father, with the aid of the royal relatives and a priest, pulls the pillar upright. Four priests bring in the usual table of offerings and place them in front of the Tat. So far, says Erman, we can understand the festival. But the further ceremonies refer to mythological events unknown to us. Four priests with their fists raised rush upon four others, who appear to give way; two more strike each other, and one standing by says of them, "I seize Horus shining in truth". Then follows a great flogging scene, in which fifteen persons beat each other mercilessly with their sticks and fists; they are divided into several groups, two of which, according to the inscription, represent the people of the town Pa and of the town Tepu. This is evidently the representation of a great mythological fight, in which were engaged the inhabitants of Pa and Tepu, *i.e.*, of the ancient city of Buto, in the north of the delta. "The ceremonies which close the sacred rite are also quite problematic; four herds of *oxen and asses* are seen driven by their herdsmen, and we are told in the accompanying text four times they circle round the walls on that day when the noble Tat-pillar is re-erected. Raising the Tat-pillar was typical of Horus in his second advent raising the dead Osiris from his sepulchre and calling the mummy to come forth alive. The gods in Tattu on the night of the resurrection, symbolized by this re-erection of the Tat, are Osiris, Isis, Nephthys, and Horus the avenger of his father. Thus in re-erecting the Tat, Amenhetep III, with his queen Ti and one of the royal princesses were personating Horus the avenger and the two divine sisters in the resurrection of Osiris. (Rit., ch. 18.)"

"The death and rebirth at Christmas, or New Year, and the resurrection at Easter can only be explained by the Osirian mysteries, and these are still celebrated throughout Europe, precisely the same as in Asia and in Africa. The Ritual also has a word to say concerning the Jewish Sabbath of Saturday, and the Christian Sabbath sacred to the sun. The ancient Egyptians celebrated festivals on the first, the sixth, the seventh, and the fifteenth of the month. The feast of the first and the fifteenth was a festival of Ra and the day was dedicated to Horus, who represented the earlier sun, and whose Sabbath was the seventh day, or Saturday in the earlier cult. It is said in the Ritual, "I am with Horus on the day when the *Festivals* of Osiris are celebrated, and when offerings are made on *the sixth day of the month*, and on the Feast of the Tenait in Heliopolis" (Rit., ch. 1). This Tenait was a feast associated with *the seventh day of the month*. Here then is a feast of *the sixth and* [**Page 747**] *seventh*, or night and day, corresponding to the Jewish Sabbath. Osiris entered the moon on the sixth day of the month. The seventh was the feast-day, when "couplings and conceptions did abound". This was celebrated in Annu, the city of the sun, and thus far the day was a sun-day. The word *tenait* denotes a measure of time, a division, a week *or* a fortnight. A feast-day on the seventh, dedicated to the solar god, would be the sun's day, or *Sunday once a month*. Now, two great festivals were dedicated to Ra, the solar god, upon the seventh and fifteenth of the month. Here, then, is a fifteen-day fortnight, or solar half-month (fifteen days), which was correlated with the half-month, or *tenait*, of fourteen days in the lunar reckoning. The sixth of the month was a moon-day, on the night of which the love-feast of Agapae began with the entrance of Osiris, earlier Horus, into the moon, or the conjunction, say, of Horus or Hu with Hathor. This was on Friday night. The next day was a phallic festival in celebration of the celestial conjunction; it was the day assigned to Sebek=Saturn in conjunction with his mother. The festival was luni-solar; hence it was celebrated on the *sixth and seventh of the month*, like the Sabbath of the Jews, which is *repeated later on the sixth and seventh days of the week*. Now, if we start with Sunday as the first of the month, the tenait festival fell on Saturday as a Sabbath of the seventh day. The second festival of Ra, that of Sunday, was on the fifteenth of the month, which would be eight days after the Tenait-feast upon the seventh of the month. The tenait on the Saturday and a feast of the 15th on a Sunday show the existence of a Sabbath celebrated on Saturday, the 7th, and another, *eight days later*, on Sunday, the 15th of *the month*. These, however, were monthly at first, as the festivals of Osiris or Ra, and not weekly, as they afterwards became with the Jews and the Christians. The festival of Saturday as the seventh day of the month is Jewish. The Sabbath of Sunday, the day of Ra, is a survival of the festival celebrated on the 15th of the month in ancient Egypt as the sun's day, or Sunday, once a month.

It was the custom at one time in Rome for the mummy, or corpse of the dead Christ, to be exhibited in the churches on Holy Thursday, the day before the Crucifixion, and if the symbolical corpse is not now exposed to the public gaze, the Holy Sepulchre is still exhibited. This has the appearance of commemorating two different deaths, the only explanation of which is to be found in the Egyptian mythos. Osiris was the *Corpus Christi* at Christmas or in the solstice. He died to be reborn again as Horus in various phenomena on the third day in the moon; also from the water in his baptism; after forty days in the buried grain; and at the end of three months, in the Easter equinox. In the Kamite original the night of the Last Supper, and of the death of Osiris, and the laying out of his body on the table of offerings are identical. It is the "night of provisioning the altar" and the provender was the mummy of the god provided for the mortuary meal. That was the dead Christ, or *Corpus Christi* (Rit., ch. 18).

Holy Thursday is especially consecrated by the Roman Catholic Church as a commemoration of the Last Supper and the institution of the eucharistic meal, at which the corpus of the Christ already dead was laid out to be eaten sacramentally. It is similar in the Gospels. **[Page 748]** The Last Supper is there celebrated, and the body and blood of the Christ are there partaken of *before the Crucifixion has occurred*. This, in the Egyptian original, would be the corpse of Osiris, the karest-mummy of him who died in the winter solstice three months before the resurrection in the equinox occurred at Easter. Seven days of mourning for the burial of Osiris were also celebrated at the end of the month Choiak. This was known as the "*fêtes des ténèbres*", which, according to Brugsch, commemorated the "*sept jours qu'il a passé dans le ventre de sa mère, Nût*" — equivalent to Jonah being in the belly of the fish, only the days of darkness in this phase are seven instead of three. These seven days of mourning are the prototype of Passion week in the rubrical usage of the Roman Church, during which the pictures of the cross (and Crucifixion) are all covered up and veiled in darkness. Here the funeral ceremony followed the burial of Osiris, whereas in the Christian version the *fêtes des ténèbres* precede the death and burial of the supposed historic victim.

But the early Christians never really knew which was the true Sabbath, the seventh day or the eighth, so they celebrated both. As now demonstrated, according to the record of the mystery-teachers in the astronomical mythology of Egypt the legend of a child that was born of a mother who was a virgin at the time is at least as old as the constellation in the zodiac when the birthplace (in precession) coincided with the sign of Virgo some 15,000 years ago. The virgin, in this category, was the goddess Neith. The child was Horus-Sebek, the great fish of the inundation that typified the deliverer from drought and hunger, and was, in other words, the saviour of the world. Thus, by aid of equinoctial precession, the origin and development of the Christian legend and its festivals can be scientifically traced in the pre-Christian past from the time when the virgin birth of the divine child and the house of birth were in the sign of Virgo, or in Leo for the present purpose, reckoned by the movement in precession

We have evidence from the pyramid of Medum that from 6,000 to 7,000 years ago the dead in Egypt were buried in a faith which was founded on the mystery of the cross, and rationally founded too, because that cross was a figure of the fourfold foundation on which **[Page 750]** heaven itself was built. The Tat-cross is a type of the eternal in Tattu. But whether as a fourfold, a fivefold, or a twelvefold support it was a figure of an all-sustaining, all-renewing, all-revivifying power that was re-erected and religiously besought for hope, encouragement, and succour, when the day was at the darkest and things were at the worst in physical nature. The sun apparently was going out. The life of Egypt in the Nile was running low and lower toward the desert drought. The spirit of vegetation died within itself. The rebel powers of evil gathered from all quarters for the annual conflict, led by Apap and the Sebau in one domain, and by Sut and his seventy-two conspirators in another. At this point began the ten mysteries grouped together in the Ritual (ch. 18). The Tat for the time being was overthrown. The deity suffered, as was represented, unto death. The heart of life that bled in every wound was no longer felt to pulsate. The god in matter was inert and breathless. Make ye the word of Osiris truth against his enemies! Raise up the Tat, which portrayed the resurrection of the god; let the mummy-type of the eternal be once more erected as the mainstay and divine support of all. It was thus that the power of salvation through Osiris-Tat was represented in the mysteries. Fundamentally the cross was astronomical. It is a figure of time, as much so in its way as is the clock. It is a measure of time made visible upon the scale and in the circle of the year instead of the hour. A cross with equal arms ✠ denotes the time of equal day and night. Hence it is a figure of the equinox. Another cross † is a figure of time in the winter solstice. It is a modified form of the Tat of Ptah ⵜ SYMBOL on which the four quarters are more obviously portrayed in the four arms of the pedestal. This was re-erected annually in the depths of the solstice where the darkness lasts some sixteen hours and the daylight only eight — the measure of time that is imaged by this Tat-figure of the cross. These two are now known as the Greek and Roman crosses, and under those two names the fact has been lost sight of that the first is a type of time in the equinox, the other a symbol of the winter solstice. The two crosses are scientific figures in the astronomical mythology. They were symbols of mystical significance in the Egyptian eschatology: and they formed the ground plan of the Ka-chambers of King Rahetep and his wife Nefermat in the pyramid of Medum (Petrie, *Medum*)."

In discussing the above, one must know well what is involved with the process of the stone. The cross with four arms was raised when all was in equality, September. The four priests, as described represent these four months of work. -Dec. to Jan. to Feb. to March to April. The completion of the seven. You have seen the first three of these months leads to what we call in alchemy 'The Crowned Androgynyn" although described the same, but differently by Mr. Massey. With the above, had he known of the stone, and the workings of matter and shape and time, I know he would have explained it much more clearer, in fact totally as he would then have had all the information. Please note again, the times mentioned always are connected to the movement of the sun, the moon, and the days of the year. Also, compare the crosses with what is found in the oven, and the movement of the matters within the oven. Always all the same. The scale also is mentioned above, and I have already explained that. But again, it came into being at the end of September. This alchemically was the start of the work in October, the sign, the scales. In the above, the 'Two divine Sisters' are mentioned. This has to do with the moon, and the constellation Virgo used to resurrect the matters during September, Septembers child, or the Virgin birth. The 'Baptism' is mentioned. I believe this comes from the physical work where we always are using water to wash the matters in the below of the oven. The resurrection in Easter is mentioned, please note that it was Flamel who said, "It was during Easter that he transmuted to gold with the red stone." The cross above Mr. Massey describes, with four arms I believe is also known as the Djed Pillar. I have described this earlier, and explained what the tit and lion cloth are connected to. The stone, Jesus, and Osiris all said to resurrect perfect in April. Also, the four bulls that are driven in a circle. This also represents the four months ending at 'Bull in Ram' time of year, and why bulls are used. Always, if you know what is happening alchemically, you will be able to connect to the numbers mention and what is linked to those numbers. The 15, it takes 15 months of process to get to the finish. I can't say why the one group was beating the other.

The following I termed in part, 'why an Egg.' There are many connections of the past tied to the use of an egg for all things tied to the creation. "The origin of the innocents that were massacred by the monster Herod can be traced in accordance with the ancient wisdom. A primitive soul of life was derived from the elements; the soul of Shu from wind or air; the soul of Seb from the earth; the soul of Horus, son of Ra, from the sun, which became the supreme source of the **[Page 770]** elemental souls that preceded a human soul. When the solar force was looked upon as the highest soul of life in nature, the souls of future beings were considered to be emanations from the sun as a source of life in external nature that was superhuman. This gave rise to the class of beings known as the Hamemmat, which originated as germs of soul that issued from the sun. They are described as circling round the solar orb in glory. The word hamemmat signifies that which is unembodied or not yet incorporated. We might say the hamemmat were pre-existing souls when souls were derived from the elemental forces in the germ, and the highest of these was solar. They are the germ-souls of future beings which originate as children of the sun portrayed in a human form. As offspring of the sun, they are called the children of Horus, who, as the child-Horus, is one with them; and if they can be destroyed in the germ, or, as the Ritual has it, in the egg, the devourer of souls may succeed in slaying the divine heir himself, who is destined to bruise the serpent's head and win the victory over all the powers of evil as the lord of light and link of continuity of life. Being at enmity with the sun, the reptile of darkness seeks to devour the new-born child of light. For that purpose he lies in wait till the woman clothed with the sun shall bring forth. He seeks the life of the young child-Horus, and other lives are involved in taking this. For Horus is the head of the solar race, the hamemmat or future beings that issue from the Eye of the sun. These future souls are called the "issue of Horus". They are the Innocents of the legend that are supposed to suffer, whereas the child of light, the divine offspring of the solar god, is sure to escape from the coils of the monster who has been rendered anthropomorphically as the ruling tyrant — the monster Herod in a mortal guise. Thus, if any little children were murdered by the Apap-monster, the dragon of darkness, these would be the offspring and issue of the solar disk in the domain of physical phenomena — little ones that were neither human nor spiritual beings, but the seed or germs of souls about to be. The parallel to the slaughter of the innocents can be traced in what is termed "the slaughter which is wrought in Suten-Khen"; that is, in the khen or birthplace where the young child-Horus was reborn as the royal Horus. Each one of the manes or the "younglings of Shu" had to pass through this place of rebirth where the Herrut-reptile lay in wait. Chapter 42 is the one "by which one *hindereth the slaughter which is wrought in Suten-Khen*". Here the manes speaks in the character of Horus the babe. "I am the babe" is said four times. As human manes, he is one of those who may be destroyed, but is safe so far as he has become assimilated to Horus. He tells the reptile, the herrut=Herod, that he is not to be seized or grasped by him, and that neither men nor gods, neither the glorified nor the damned can inflict any injury on him who is Horus the divine child, born and bound to fulfil his course as the ever-coming One, who "steppeth onward through eternity" (ch. 42). Sotinen, "a certain city on the borders of Hermopolis", is the dreaded place in Amenta, where the slaughter of the innocents was periodically wrought. The would be destroyer of the child is addressed in one of his reptile-forms, "O serpent Abur!" (the name rendered "great thirst" is **[Page 771]** equivalent to that of the dragon of drought), thou sayest this day "the block of execution is furnished (Rit. ch. 42), and thou art come to contaminate the Mighty One". In another chapter Horus exults that in making his descent to the earth of Seb for putting a stop to evil *his nest is safe*. 'Not to be seen is my nest. Not to be broken is my egg. I have made my nest on the confines of Heaven" (Rit., ch. 85). He rejoices on account of his escape from the slaughter of the innocents which followed his descent into the earth of Seb. Thus in the Osirian mythos the child-Horus was with the widow in Suten-Khen, and in the Gospel of the Infancy it is the child-Jesus with the widow in Sotinen."

Now above we see in several places, 'my egg, not in my egg.' I consider it as meaning the same thing. We might say the hamemmat were pre-existing souls when souls were derived from the elemental forces in the germ, and the highest of these was solar. They are the germ-souls of future beings which originate as children of the sun portrayed in a human form. As offspring of the sun, they are called the children of Horus, who, as the child-Horus, is one with them; and if they can be destroyed in the germ, or, as the Ritual has it, in the egg. In ancient Egypt, all came from an egg. Osiris came from an egg. The 'Great Cackler' laid an egg for the sun. In other words, to the ancients all came first from an egg. This is from the study of nature. Does not all start out somehow from an egg or seed? Even in the creation epic, they called the 'firmament heaven.' Heaven was first created with the earth, to understand it the heaven and earth should be understood as an egg, heaven the shell. In other works I have shown "Osiris in his envelope" or, "Only the face of Osiris is shown" All indicates Osiris was regenerated within an enclosure. Within the tomb that only he could fit! Now in Genesis, I have shown in that part of the work that the tomb, the inner oven had to be like an egg shell, why? The waters came together 'within' it. or, in one place which depicts an oven within an oven, and so the inner oven had some sort of transparent walls so that the light could shine through. This is what we have with an egg shell. Also, it is mentioned above of the four quarters, and the fifth, or the five supporters. This would be over the moat, (an alchemical description of the oven). You will see the Tat cross that looks like the Christian cross with only drawing in one line from the side view. Also, this same cross, if you look further you will see with imagination, the balance, the lower pyramid shapes form the scales.

The below work discusses how and why the child is brought forth only from the two females as I mentioned, or, simply put, brought forth by the white Dove, and the female. How to understand? The white dove, represents actually the moon alchemically. In many of the pictorial works at this time, which is the time of the conjunction, the white dove has been changed to a white Goose. And so there again is two females, the moon or goose, and the virgin which is 'Virgo the Constellation.' As the dove was used as we have come to know it, and as ones life may be in peril by such a copy, a white goose or swan was then used by alchemists to show that part of the work.

"This birth of the eternal in time was astronomical. But it was humanized for the birthday of Amen-hetep in Egypt, for Alexander in Greece, and for Caesar-Augustus in Rome before the era that was designated Christian. The virgin-mother in mythology, and there never was any other, is she who made her proclamation in the Temple of Neith at Sais that she proceeded from herself and bore the child without her peplum being lifted by the male. The myth reflects the matriarchate from a time when the fatherhood was not yet individualized. The mother with child, the great or *enceinte* mother, is at the head of the Kamite Pantheon as the mother of life and a figure of fecundity. This type of the mother and child retains its position in the Christian iconography when the child Jesus, like Kheper, is exhibited in the Virgin's womb surrounded by the seven spirits as doves (Didron). The mother with her child *in utero* or in her arms was indefinitely earlier than the typical father and son whose worshippers were opposed to the more primitive representation of nature. Horus, at first, is the child of Isis only, with Seb as putative or foster-father, who was not the begetter. "On Horror's head horrors accumulate" in manufacturing history from the mythos. Horus, the fatherless, was the fecundator of his own virgin mother, but neither as the human Horus nor the divine **[Page 762]** Horus was it presented that he was other than the typical figure in a mystery, or that the doctrine came the human way. Jesus in the same character, called the Mamzer ממזור SANSKRIT by the Jews, is the same fatherless fecundator of the virgin mother when the two are Jew and Jewess. To the truly religious sense this is a most profane parody of the sacred Osirian drama. Thus the fragments of a great complex in dogma and doctrine were collected together in relation to the conception of the Messianic child. First, the virgin mother was the insufflator of a soul. Secondly, there is a begettal in which the offspring fecundates the mother — this of course is in the mythical representation. Thirdly, according to Matthew, the divine child was *either* conceived or begotten of the Holy Ghost.

It is the type that tells so many secrets of the non-historical beginnings: and nothing has been bottomed, nothing could be fundamentally explained with the Egypto-gnostic wisdom still unknown. The dove that aid the egg is pre-eminent as a type in the conception and the birth of Jesus. At first the insufflating spirit of life, whether called holy or not, was female. This was demonstrated by the Mother-nature. In the Gospels the Holy Spirit as female suffices for the miraculous conception of the child-Jesus who is generated without a father. But *Pistis Sophia* witnesses that the gnostic Jesus proceeded from the father in the likeness of a dove. And that the mystery of all mysteries, the first and final mystery, was this of the dove, considered to be the bird of God the Father. By this means the Holy Spirit is portrayed as male, whereas according to the secret wisdom the dove had been a female type of spirit from the first. The gnosis was so ancient as Egyptian that the dove had been succeeded by the hawk as the bird of Ra, the Holy Spirit as male. The hawk was now the symbol of the father and the son, that is, of Ra and Horus. Whereas the dove as mother-bird was primary. The female nature of the mystic dove is also shown by its co-type the pigeon, still employed in modern slang as a survival of sign-language. Thus the earliest human soul was insufflated by the mother, and the mother divinized was represented by the Dove, the bird of soul when soul was first attributed to female source. Lastly, the same bird was given to the Holy Spirit as God the Father, and as a type of the Trinity consisting of Father, Son and Holy Spirit, with the mother veiled and hidden by the dove."

But what does this have to do with Osiris at this point? It would seem to me there is more to the understanding that is available for me to find. I can make two stones from the matter, and so I understand why it is made by the female aspects. But it is understood by me only in the alchemical way. Perhaps it is tied to just how matter works at that stage, and so the mythology has to match what we can do in the below. As all of Egypt and how they thought had to do with male/female, this substance is surly also going to be tied to sex. I also understand we have already made an androgynous material by process with both lights up to this point, and so the material already has within it the possibility of all things here in the below. However, what is within this material, is not yet pure enough for Osiris to go on, we know that. But what of the other material, the other white stone that can be made? I don't seem to find how they considered it or used it, and perhaps they didn't! We can see how with the above explanation, originally the two aspects brought forth to the matters are female. We have with this material the ability of both stones, and so, is that the answer. I will try to explain it more clearly. Osiris at the stage of being brought forth as a child is like the understanding of the earth created. It was androgynous so all things will unite with it. Here the material at this stage is brought forth by the two females. Why? The matter as by being brought forth this way can go on and make the white stone that is connected to only the light of the moon. It can be made because we use like with it until finished. Probably in all that I have come to know alchemically, I must admit I have a small problem right here with what I have found. Flamel said that this white substance was where they hid all the secrets of alchemy. This white substance has everything available within it. Yes, it is Osiris reborn, and at the point where he can go on, but what of the 'other' material that we can make from the moon and the three months? Now the problem I have can come from what has been found, but all I have is what Mr. Massey has written down! It should be clear that what this is based on he didn't know of. They answers may have been there, but he didn't copy the material, he didn't understand and so it is lost? I don't know. I know the priests of the temples were all male, perhaps a female stone wasn't important to them, or it was made and used in other ways. Perhaps others will someday find.

Herself, the goose eats herself you could say, as she drinks her own blood. This is the same as 'again.' The earth also is eating itself every time it evaporates moisture and it raises again! What this signifies alchemically, is like again. That stones can only be made by the use of like forces and matters. As Mr. Massey said, this material is so ancient! Concerning the creation, this is or would be the matter that in Genesis is called 'The Dry Land called Earth.' all seed could be brought to it to reproduce. In Genesis this would be the end of the purification of the matters, with Osiris, and with the stone we go on. What is below is not 'like' what is above. What is below is maintained and slowly it seems being brought forth, or nearer to the above over time. It would seem if the above does perfect over time, why is it being done that way? The only answer is that it is gods Way of bringing man forth.

With the above, the trinity is mentioned. This has to do with the androgynous material formed. It is three in one because it was formed, (refer to Genesis) by both sun and moon, and has a body. To me it becomes easy to understand when I just say, They found this material. They found this way to purify it! To make sense of it all, concerning the All, they had to explain it as they did! They found after eight months of work that they could change the matter into a pure white substance with the moon. The effect was caused by those conditions, and by the stars and planets and moon above. If the below is connected to the above, then the above had to be connected to what they had. The material was pure, and formed by the constellation and the moon. The moon was seen as female! Probably this is also linked to the fact that female brings forth all living things here on this planet. Could it be any different with this material? Therefore, the above at that point had to be female, both the moon, and the constellation above it. They also found that even that matter, though in a pure state could be further augmented. They found it could be further augmented by either light above. Thus the two stones. You have to figure, if the material could be augmented above what is found here in the below, it to them became 'Divine.' This is in part why I say they were looking for god! Why is the 'light good?' Why is it connected to god? Why Osiris and a religion? The matters were it seems augmented to the point that they must do what we have understood that the stones do! They must somehow purify what they touch! They must be the medicine that cures all! They also should cure the metals by changing them to gold. It can be the only reason why we have the religion. It still remains to be seen if it works, but that time is not far away. Osiris became divine because he was linked to these matters, and because they were different than anything found in the below! They became linked to god, and the proof they wanted to know they had somehow found god! Lastly, I said that what is below is not like what is above. What to consider? Is man slowly being brought forth to become like the finished stones? Seems an odd question, but look to what man was a few million years ago, will we continue to grow and adapt, will Genesis continue to bring us forth? If you understand, you should know that we are getting better, we are moving forward. What will the end point be?

"It may be noted in passing that the dove was not necessarily a type of sensual desire although it became associated with Venus in Greece. There was nothing licentious in Hathor or Iusâas. The earliest Venus was a personification of the *enceinte* mother, not a goddess Lubricity provocative of lust, but in all simplicity and seriousness a type of tenderest maternity. The dove had been the bird of Hathor as the insufflator of a soul of breath. In this character it is portrayed with brooding wings extended on the bosom of the mummy as quickener of the spirit for a future life. On the tomb of Rameses IX the dove appears in place of the hawk as a co-type of Horus at the prow of the solar boat. Also, in a statuette of the 19th dynasty there is a human-headed dove which takes the place of the hawk as a zootype of the soul. It is seen hovering over the bosom of a mummy. The divine Horus rises again in the form of a dove, as well as in the shape of a hawk. "I *am the* [**Page 763**] *Dove: I am the Dove*", exclaims the risen spirit as he soars up from Amenta, where the egg of his future being was hatched by the divine incubator (Rit., 86, 1). Here the bird of Hathor is also the bird of Ra, and thus the dove became the bird of the Holy Spirit, female in the mother, and male in the divine child Horus, and finally in the Father. In the Councils of Nice and Constantinople, the fathers condemned Xenora, who derided the imaging of the Holy Spirit by the dove. And to show how the type will persist, in *The Catholic Layman* for July 17th, 1856, there is a Papal picture of the Christian Godhead that was extant in that same year, as the trinity of the Father, Son and Holy Spirit. In this, God the Father and God the Son are represented as a man with two heads, one body and two arms. One of the heads is like the ordinary pictures of Jesus, or Serapis, the other is the head of an *old man* surmounted by a triangle. Out of the middle of this figure is proceeding the Holy Ghost in the form of a dove (*Catholic Layman*, July 17th, 1856).

Note the triangle!   A sign of god being in heaven! Also, the alchemical material is always expressed in a hidden fashion. Can you understand, if in the conjunction, a white dove was drawn?

Only questions would arise. The dove, then, as an emblem of the 'Holy Spirit,' also shows the gnostic nature of the beginnings in the gospels termed 'Canonical.'

"Now the birth of the Christ was on this wise. When his Mother Mary had been betrothed to Joseph, before they came together she was found with child of the Holy Ghost," or, as rendered in sign-language, with the dove as emblem of the Holy Spirit. Hence, in the Iconography, child-Jesus is represented in the Virgin's arms or womb, surrounded by the seven doves as symbols of the Holy Spirit (Didron, fig. 124).

We might say that the dove of Hathor-Iusãas came to Rome on board the papyrus-boat, in which the mother Isis crossed the swamps to save her little one from the pursuing dragon (Plutarch, *Of Isis and Osiris*, 18). For the papyrus-boat is obviously the bark of Peter in the Roman Catacombs (Lundy, *Mont. Christ*, fig. 139). Iusãas, the mother of Iusa=Iusu, the Egyptian Jesus, was a form of Hathor-Meri, and was brought on in the cult of Rome as Mary, the mystical dove and mother of Iusu, now believed to have become historical. A dovecote was the dwelling where she brought him forth in Rome. As Cyprien Robert says, "The first basilicas, placed generally upon eminences, were called *domus columbae*, dwellings of the dove, that is, the Holy Ghost" (Didron, 1, 439, Eng. tr.). Now Atum was the holy spirit in the eschatology of Annu; the first who ever did attain that status in theology. His consort was Iusãas, who, in the character of Hathor, was the female holy spirit, as the dove. Their child was Iusa, the Egyptian Jesus. This was he who says, on rising from Amenta as a spirit, "I am the dove, I am the dove" (The "Menat". Rit., ch. 86). Thus, the gnostic mystery of the dove is traceable to Atum as the holy spirit, and to Iusãas-Hathor as the Mother of the Coming Son (Iusa), he who emanated from them as the dove. This mode of incarnation is followed by a second descent of the holy spirit in the baptism of Jesus. "Lo, the heavens were opened unto him, and he saw the Spirit of God descending as a dove, and coming upon him; and lo, a voice out of the heavens saying, This is my beloved son in whom I am well pleased". Thus, the child that was conceived of the virgin in the first descent of the spirit is authenticated as son of the father at the time of the second [**Page 764**] descent of the holy spirit as the dove. And this, as Egyptian, is the doctrine of the dual Horus, who was born of Isis, the virgin, and afterwards begotten in spirit as the beloved son of Ra, the holy spirit. Jesus when *mothered* by the virgin-dove, whether at On or Bethlehem, is Iusa the coming child of Hathor-Iusãas; and Jesus when authenticated by the bird from heaven is Iusa as the son of Atum-Ra, the holy spirit who is *fathered* by the dove. This fatherhood of Jesus in his baptism is vouched for by the writers of the Canonical Gospels. And in "the Gospel according to the Hebrews", Jesus speaks of His "Mother, the Holy Ghost". He says, "the Holy Spirit, my mother, took me and bore me away to the great mountain, called Thabor". Which can be understood as a saying of Iusa, the Egyptian Jesus.

Can you see here what is meant by the alchemists that said, "You must turn the wheel again"?

"At the birth of Horus the life of the young child was sought by the evil Sut. The mother was warned of the danger by Taht, the lunar god, called the great one. He says to her, "Come, thou goddess Isis, hide thyself with thy child" ; and he tells her it is well to be obedient. She is to take the child down into the marshes of lower Egypt, called Kheb, or Khebt. There, says Taht, "these things will happen: his limbs will grow; he will wax entirely strong; he will attain the dignity of prince of the double earth, and sit (or rest) upon the throne of his father". Then the child and mother make their way to the papyrus-swamps. It is said that the plants were so secret that no enemy could enter there. "Sut could not penetrate this region, or go about in Kheb". Nevertheless the child was bitten by the reptile, as the story is rendered in the sorrows of Isis, the pre-Christian *mater dolorosa* (Budge, *The Gods of the Egyptians*, vol. II, ch. 14). "Horus in Kheb" (Egypt) was a title of the divine child. Kheb was in the north of Egypt, and it was there that Horus passed his early days, and was reared in secret by his mother Isis. Horus lands upon the earth of Seb at eventide. He sits upon the seat of Ra, which is on the western horizon, and receives the offerings upon the altars. He says, "I drink the sacred liquor each evening, in the form of the lord of all creatures" (Rit., ch. 79). The descent of Horus, as a child, to earth was daily or yearly according to the mythos. Every night the sinking sun was received by the mother in the breeding-place, or Meskhen, of the western mount, where she prepared him (or he her) for his new birth daily in the East. The point at which the god descends to earth at evening is well portrayed in the oblong zodiac of Denderah. In this the child-Horus is seated *on the mount* of the western equinox in the sign of the Scales. The sign of the Scales, Makhu, was once the sign of the autumn equinox, and at that point child-Horus touches earth for his descent from heaven. In this sign the child is portrayed sitting on the mount in the disc of the full moon. As seen by night, the mount of earth, or the horizon, is the mount of the ecliptic, the meeting-point of earth and heaven. The full moon is the mother who is Virgo in the previous sign, and in the sign of the Scales she has brought forth the child."

This indicates the start of the conjunction in alchemy. The physical steps of the stone tie to and explain what and why things that are being done can be understood. Mr. Massey did not know of the physical. I believe the total explanation of what the scholars have said will be somewhat different with what I have found with the physical. After it is known. This 'Mother Child' and what is said, "Come, thou goddess Isis, hide thyself with thy child" are words we read tied to Jesus while on the Cross.

"In vain do we try to make out the doctrinal mysteries of the eschatology, whether it is called Egyptian, Hebrew, Coptic, Gnostic, or Christian, until we have mastered the mythology. Without this foundation there is no foothold. Neither is there any help in an exoteric version of the esoteric wisdom. The group of powers was seven or eight, nine or ten, before it included the twelve. And the character is the same in the mythos when the group is twelve as when it was ten or nine, eight or seven or four — that is, it was astronomical."

Authors Note. In consideration, now, if it be eight, seven, nine or ten, it can be understood, and tied to the physical works of the stone. By understanding exactly what happens to the matters of the stone, all this mythology can be understood and linked. It can be no coincidence!

The following is to show the Two! What alchemically we term Androgynyn. Androgynous material simply means both male and female. This is a principle male female from the lights we receive with the matter we work on as I have explained as the process goes through its steps. Then after the rebirth of Osiris as a babe. He then is further processed by both lights "turn the wheel again " to become now the Crowned Androgynyn. Each stage makes him more perfect, and more like the Perfect God he is to become. Crowned Androgynyn is though what makes him divine. The following shows some of this aspect. Also, a new number here to consider, the twelve and the connection of them to light. Our process is 16 months long, 4 of them in darkness, and then 12 months of light. Those twelve months give us the 12 and their connection to light.

"Thus *Pistis Sophia* shows the physical foundation of the mysteries. Astronomical science was taught as matter of the mysteries, but the science being physical these were classified as the lesser mysteries, whereas the greater mysteries were eschatological. The twelve on earth, or in matter, were the companions of elder Horus, the son of Isis, the suffering saviour. The twelve in Amenta are the associates of Horus, the triumphant saviour, the beloved only-begotten son of God the father. The twelve with Horus or Jesus risen from Amenta are freed from the environment, the darkness, the stains of matter, as pure spirits to be wholly perfected. They have attained the beatific vision, as the children of light. They have passed through death and the purgation of matter to become clear spirit when risen to the status of Horus the immortal. With Horus or Jesus, in the character of the young sun-god, the twelve were astronomical powers, rulers, or saviours of the treasure (light) in the physical domain. With Horus or Jesus, the saviour as son of God the father, they are the twelve glorious ones or gods of Amenta, the twelve who as spirits are the children of Ra the holy spirit; in short, they are the twelve in the eschatology who were the chosen twelve with Horus on earth as sowers of the seed, and the twelve with Horus as reapers of the harvest in Amenta."

Please note this is connected to 'matters.' This agrees with the use of an egg. Within the shell are just 'matters.'

"It was a saying of Philo's that "the logos is double". This it is as the double Horus, or as Jesus and the Christ, who was dual as manifestor for the Virgin Mother and afterwards for God the Father: double by nature, human and divine; double in matter and in spirit; double as child and as adult, double as the soul of both sexes. But when the word 'logos' comes to be used for the divine Reason we are in the midst of Greek metaphysic and doctrinal mystification. These two, blended in one person, constituted the double Horus who was that double logos spoken of by Philo, the figure of which was founded, as Egyptian, on the two halves of the soul, or pair of gods in the mystery of Tattu (Rit., ch. 17). Horus in these two characters was Horus with the tress of infancy, and Horus who becomes bird-headed at the transformation in his baptism. In his first advent Horus is the sower in the seed-field of time; in his second he is the lord of the reapers in the harvest of eternity. In the astronomical mythos Horus was the king of one year. Naturally that was as ruler of the seasons in the annual circuit of the sun. As the prince of eternity he was the typical adult of thirty years, and lord of the Sut-Heb festival, who is called "the living Horus, the powerful bull, lord of the festivals of thirty years," which are termed "the years of Horus as King" (*Rec. of the Past*, vol. 10, 34). This was the royal Horus in whom the child that was destined to be a king attained his manhood and assumed his perfect sovereignty.

As already shown, the genesis of the double Horus is portrayed in the Ritual (ch. 115). In this description "two brethren come into being." One of these was the wearer of the female lock, as the child-Horus. His birth was mystical. He was both male and female in person, or, as it is said, "he assumed the form of a female with a lock," the sign of pre-pubescence in either sex, and hence a type of both. He is also called "the Afflicted One," which denotes the mystery of the Virgin's child. The second is "the active one of Heliopolis." He is "the heir of the temple." The first is also called the heir, and the second the heir of the heir. He has the divine might of "the son whom the father hath begotten." This was "the only-begotten of the father." Thus the "two brethren" were Horus the child who wears the long tress that is the sign of either sex, and Horus the adult who images the power and glory of the father as the god in spirit."

Please note, this is where we receive two stones from the one base material. There are not many places where I can connect two stones from this ancient work. This validates the two stones of alchemy.

"Iusa, the Jesus of On, like Horus in the Osirian cult, was born bi-mater. His two mothers were Iusáas and Neb-hetep, the two consorts of Atum-Ra. These two mothers were at first two sisters in the mythos. One of them was the mother in the western mountain, or later in the winter solstice; the other gave birth to Horus on the horizon in the eastern equinox. It follows inevitably that the Gospel-Jesus has two mothers who were sisters, and two places of birth and rebirth. When [**Page 787**] the mythology was merged in the eschatology, and Ra became the father in heaven, he is described as having two companions who are with him in the solar bark. In this text the two sister-mothers with whom Ra consorts in the "divine ship" are Isis and Nut, who are the bringers-forth of Iusa or Jesus in his twofold character: child-Horus at his first advent being the son of Isis (Har-si-Hesi) the earth-mother, and in his second advent, or rebirth in spirit, the son of Nut, the heavenly mother. Such is the origin of the two mothers who were two sisters, and two consorts in two places of birth and rebirth represented in the "historic" narrative by Nazareth and Bethlehem as the birthplace of the shoot or natzer in Virgo, and the house of bread in Pisces, which two places of birth corresponded to the two seasons of seedtime and of harvest in the old Egyptian year."

This two places of birth may be tied to the two stones we make. Some of it I agree with Mr. Massey and what he has said, but I think also it is tied to the two androgynous materials we make and the two times of the year that we make them.

"The elder Horus came to earth in the body of his humility. The younger came from heaven to wear the vesture of his father's glory. The first was the child of a baptism by water. The second is Horus the anointed or Christified; the oil upon whose face reflected the glory of the Father. This was the double baptism of the mysteries which is referred to in the Ritual by the priest who says, "I lustrate with water in Tattu and with oil in Abydos" (ch. 1). The duality manifested in Horus is shown when he is said to come into being as two brethren, the same that *Pistis Sophia* describes as "the Saviour-twins"; also when the transformer Kheper takes the form of two children - the elder and the younger (Litany of Ra, 61). Again, in the seventy-first chapter of the Ritual, Horus divinized is called " the owner of twin souls, who lives in two twin souls," now united in the eternal one. It is the potential duality of sex in the child-Horus that will account for Queen Hatshepsu being designated Mat-Ka-Ra, the true likeness of the solar god, called the golden Horus. She assumed the habiliments of both sexes in token that the divinity was **[Page 788]** dual."

Please note the 'Double Baptism' as I understand it is in the alchemical process, the two times the matters are flooded with water, after the May Day, and again after Septembers Child. The duality again is because of work with both lights. The two souls of sex are male and female, it is the work of the two lights, male and female with the baptism that gives this effect. As it seems so much other material of our religions are tied to this, I am only assuming that the baptism is also tied to those times I mentioned, but it seems a great possibility to me.

"this duality was reproduced in the golden Horus whose various phases of twinship included the two souls of sex. The golden Horus was a supreme type because of the twofold nature of the soul. It was this duality of Horus that is referred to by Hatshepsu when she says "the two *Horus-gods* have united the two divisions (south and north) for me." "I rule over this land like the son of Isis" ; "I am victorious like the son of Nut" ; which two likewise constitute the double Horus (Inscription: *Records*, vol. 12, 134). It is said of the Osirian Horus in his twofold genesis from matter and spirit, "Horus proceedeth from the essence of his father and the corruption which befell him" (Rit., ch. 78). That is in the incarnation or immergence in matter as the opposite of spirit, according to the later theology. Matter was at this time considered to be corrupt, and matter was maternal, but spirit was paternal and held to be divine. This will also explain the language of the Ritual applied to Osiris when he is spoken of as suffering decay and corruption, although inherently inviolate and incorruptible. The Osiris is embalmed in the divine type of him that never saw corruption. Yet Horus the child is born of Isis into the corruption of matter in his incorporation, and all the evil that was derived from matter or the mother-nature has to be purged away in becoming pure spirit like Horus at the second advent, when he has become the glorified, anointed, only-begotten son. These were the two halves of a soul that was perfected in oneness, when Horus the child was blended with Horus the adult in the marriage-mystery of Tattu, but not till then, and not otherwise. "The two Horus-gods" is a title of the dual Horus in the Pyramid-texts of Teta. The Olive is there said to be "the tree of the two Horus-gods who are in the temples." Horus proclaims himself to be the issue of Seb (or Earth) whose spouse is Isis, and affirms that his mother is Nut (ch. 42). That is as the double Horus. Horus the human soul on earth, and Horus as a spirit in Amenta; Horus born of two mothers who were two sisters, and who in the different theologies may be Neith and Sekhet; Iusáas and Nebhetep; Isis and Nut; or two Marys, the two Meris who were at first the cow of earth and the cow of heaven. The child of Isis, the virgin heifer, was imaged as the calf, the red calf of sacrifice, also by the golden calf. After his death he rose again as the bull in the likeness of his father, Osiris, the bull of eternity. In the solar mythos he was born as a calf in the autumn equinox that became a bull in the Easter equinox when this occurred in Taurus. The type was repeated in the eschatology, when the manes is baptized to become the anointed in the character of Horus, who says, "I am the divine bull, son of the ancestress of Osiris" (Rit., ch. 147).

Please note here that the calf born would be Septembers Child, and the bull would be the stone after April, perfected Osiris, or the perfected stone. I believe bull is used to represent the sun and that work performed at the end of process.

"So in Egypt the earth-mound led up to the pyramid with steps, (NOTE) the steps would be seven. that culminated in the altar-mound of stone. The Chinese still call the altar a mound. Because of its being a figure of the earth amidst the Nun, the altar-mound was raised immediately after the deluge in the Semitic mythos. In this way the teachers who first glorified the storied windows of the heavens, like some cathedral of immensity, with their pictures of the past, are demonstrably Egyptian, because the Sign-Ianguage, the mythos, the legends, and the eschatology involved are wholly Egyptian, and entirely independent of all who came after them. The so-called "wisdom of the ancients" was Egyptian when the elemental powers were represented first as characters in mythology. It was Egyptian when that primeval mythology was rendered astronomically. It is also Egyptian in the phase of eschatology. Speaking generally, and it would be difficult to speak too generally from the present stand-point, the Egyptian mythology is the source of the märchen, the legends, and the folk-lore of the world, whilst the eschatology is the fountain-head of all the religious mysteries. that lie betwixt the earliest totemic and the latest Osirian, that were ultimately continued in the religion of ancient Rome. The mysteries were a dramatic mode of communicating the secrets of primitive knowledge in Sign-Ianguage when this had been extended to the astronomical mythology . Hence, we repeat, the Egyptian urshi or astronomers were known by the title of "mystery teachers of the heavens" , because they explained the mysteries of primitive astronomy. "

Note also, with the alchemical pictorial allegories, always where steps are used, and that is in many, seven is the number of steps. Seven is throughout alchemy, and right here you see part of the reason. Always it is about the seven months just shown in many ways.

"For one thing, a later theology has wrought havoc with the beginnings previously evolved and naturally rendered. And we have consequently been egregiously misled and systematically duped by the Semitic perversions of the ancient " wisdom" . There was indeed "a fall" from the foothold first attained by the Egyptians to the dismal swamp of the Assyrian and Hebrew legends. In Egyptian mythology compared with the Babylonian the same types that represent evil in the one had represented good in the other. The old Great Mother of Evil, called the Dragon-horse in the Assyrian version, was neither the source nor the product of evil in the original. The serpent-goddess Rannut, as renewer of the fruits of earth in the soil or on the tree, is not a representative of evil. We hold that moral evil in the mythical domain is an abortion of theology which was mainly Semitic in its birth. The Kamite beginning with the Great Mother and the elemental powers which are definite and identifiable enough in the Egyptian wisdom became confused and chimerical in Babylonian and Hebrew versions of the same Sign-language; the dark of a benighted heaven followed day. Elemental evils were converted into moral evil. The types of good and ill were indiscriminately mixed, pre-eminently so in the reproduction of the old Great Mother as Tiamat. Originally she was a form of the Mother-earth, the womb of life, the suckler, the universal mother in an elemental phase. But the types of good and evil were confounded in the later rendering. The creation of evil as a **[Page 272]** mis-creation of theology is plainly traceable in the Akkadian, BabyIonian , Assyrian, and Hebrew remains. The Great Mother, variously named Tiamat, Zikum. Nin-Ki-Gal, or Nana, was not originally evil. She represented source in perfect correspondence to Apt, Ta-Urt, or Rannut in the Egyptian representation of the Great Mother, who, howsoever hideous, was not bad or inimical to man; the "mother and nurse of all" , the "mother of gods and men" , who was the renewer and bringer forth of life in earth and water. Nor were the elemental offspring evil, although imaged in the shape of monsters or of zootypes. As Egyptian, the seven Anunaki were spirits of earth, born of the Earth-mother in the earth, but they were not wicked spirits. The elements are not immoral. These are a primitive form of the seven great gods who sit on golden thrones in Hades as lords of life and masters of the under-world. Moreover, the seven *Nunu* or Anunas can be traced to their Egyptian origin."

"In the later Semitic legend it was said the earth was founded on the flood, as if it were afloat upon the water of the abyss. But according to the primary expression the earth stood on its own bottom in the water, at the fixed centre, with the tree upon the summit as a figure of food and water in vegetation. The mythical abyss of the beginning was the welling-place of water underground where life was brought to birth by the Great Mother from the womb of the Abyss. In the Ritual this is described as the tuat, a place of entrance to and egress from the lower earth of Amenta. It is a secret Deep that nobody can fathom, which sends out light in the dark, and "its offerings are eatable plants" . It is the birthplace of water and vegetation, and therefore, more abstractly, of life. The bottomless pit is a figure that was derived from this unplumbed deep inside the earth itself. From this abyss the Mother-earth (as womb of life) had brought forth her elemental progeny as the perennial renewers of food to eat, water to drink, and air to breathe.

This is called the work of "Ansar and Kisar" , Who " created the earth", *i.e.*, when "creation" had been rendered cosmogonically. But "the heaven was created from the waters" which were firmamental and uranographic. The non-Semitic legend of Cutha describes the beginning with a condition of non-entity or pre-entity; there was nothing but an amorphous world of water. As it is said, "the whole of the lands were sea" ; "the abyss had not been made" below, nor was there any seat of the gods above. There was no field of reeds; no tree of life had been planted in the midst of an enclosure. There flowed no stream from the abyss "within the sea" of the celestial water (Pinches, T.G., *Records of the Past*, 2nd Series, vol. vi. page 107; Sayce, *Assyrian Story Of Creation*, New Series, vol. i. pages 133 to 153). This, when bottomed, means that configuration of the signs in the astronomical mythology had not as yet begun. But as space the firmamental water was extant, and dry earth itself had stood for ever in the midst thereof; earth and water were the uncreated substance which had no beginning, any more than they had in the Egyptian Nun. The monsters born of Tiamat had their home in the ground of earth. It was there she suckled **[Page 282]** them. Earth as the natural fact preceded the abyss in the astronomy. As Professor Sayce observes, somewhat naïvely, "There was already an earth by the side of the deep" (H. L., p. 377). No. Earth was the ground to go upon in the deep, and this was the Mother-earth which brought forth in and from the deep that was depicted as the abyss, or as the Great Fish in "the water" of the southern heaven. It was in the extreme south that the Babylonians also placed their entrance to the under-world or the abyss. That is where the Egyptians had already localized the *outrance* from this mysterious region whence the inundation came. Here was the "Ununait" or place of springing up that was first applied to water in the pre-solar mythos, the water that was pictured in its rising from the fish's mouth."

This mention of a prior time, before the constellations is important to consider as to the age of the stone. It is my understanding, and I have noted it, that first the stone was developed, and then from that process the constellations were named and understood. Consider the definitions that also are linked to the constellations. As I have explained, the 'earth' is the base matter for the stone, the earth in the creation. The stone is that matter further purified by the lights. Truthfully, I wish I could find other references that explain the stone, but I haven't been able to so far. It was not my wish or intention to mix up the fact of alchemy with what we call Christianity. The information of the past should be known by us, and it is not? Why? Had this information been available, whatever the stone is, it would have been found and understood long ago. Even now it is not my wish to use this material, but when again looked at by our scholars, and compared to the alchemical material, there can be no misunderstanding that the one process, is tied to the other mythology. The first mythology resulted from man's desire to find and to know if there was 'One God'! Our past in many ways, and with many sciences are all tied together. As it was about Nature and the search for god, can we not see how it is also tied to our religions?

"The power of perennial renewal was perceived in nature. This was manifested by successive births. Hence the child-god of Egypt became a type of the eternal, ever-coming by rebirth in time and season and the elements of life and light, which in the character of Horus was at first by food and water. This was the eternal, ever-coming, ever-renewing spirit of youth. In the illustration from a Theban tomb the Great

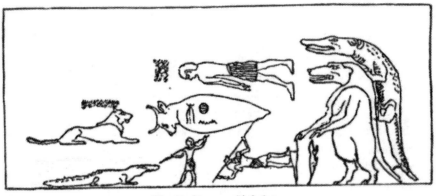

The Meskhen, or Birthplace.

Mother, who in one form is a crocodile, has just given birth to her child, Horus, Har-Ur, as the young crocodile poised on end in front of her. It is a picture of the young child that was brought forth annually from the water by the mother, who was constelled as the Crocodile or Hippopotamus at the northern centre of the planisphere. The history of Horus is depicted in the heavens as if upon the walls and windows of some vast cathedral of immensity. This was the subject of subjects in the astronomical mythology. He was conceived of a virgin mother in the sign of Virgo. His birth or advent was announced by the star Phact in the constellation Columba. The **[Page 290]** earliest mother who conceived as a virgin in mythology was represented by the sacred heifer of the immaculate Isis. Also by the white vulture in the cult of the Virgin Neith. She was the dove of Hathor in the worship of Iusãas, the mother of Iusa. The human only comes in as a challenging element when the mythos is related as history. When the woman took the place of the heifer, the vulture, the dove, or other zootype of virginity - that is, when the type was humanized and Horus imaged as a child - the doctrine of incarnation, or the incorporation of a spirit of life in matter, had entered into the human sphere. Thus the mystical virgin and child in human guise, whether in Egypt or in any other land, was a result of doctrinal development, and the doctrine itself could not be understood without a knowledge of the earlier phase. When the type of the Great Mother and her youngling had been changed from the totemic zootype to the anthrotype, and the goddess was imaged as a woman, a child became the figure of a superhuman power that was ever-coming, ever-renewing, ever-repeating, ever-incorporating or incarnating, ever-manifesting in phenomena. Then- the youthful god was naturally born as a child. This was Har-Ur, the child of Isis or the Virgin Neith. Horus the child or shoot, on the papyrus or on his mother's lap, is representative of the resurrection and renewal of life for another year. Horus came to Egypt as saviour of the people from the dreaded drought. He came, invested with "the power of the southern lakes" to drown the dragon in the inundation. In one phase Horus is the saviour as the bringer of the water. In another he is the child of light. In both he comes to wrestle with the enemy of man in various natural phenomena on earth, and likewise in the internecine struggle which is represented by the astronomical mythology as the war in heaven, and which maybe summed up as the war of Horus and the dragon. Horus brings the water of the inundation which is the source of life to Egypt. The little one is cradled on the Nile in his ark of the papyrus reed. He is assailed by Apap, the dragon of drought, who lies in wait to destroy the young deliverer when he is born. As bringer of the waters Horus slays the dragon of drought, which would otherwise have drunk the inundation dry. He also treads the serpent of darkness under foot as the renewer of light. Under the name of Iu-m-hetep, Horus came as the proverbial "prince of peace" . The word *hetep* denotes peace or rest, plenty of food, and also good luck. His coming in this character had a very tangible significance, for the inundation brought the season of rest to Egypt, which was celebrated by the Uaka festival, when the prince came out of Ethiopia as the giver of rest to the weary, bread to the hungry, water to the thirsty, and wine for the periodic wassail. In the solar mythos Horus became the lord of light, but food and drink were first, according to the human needs.

When the sun was in the sign of Aquarius the moon at full had taken up the leadership by night in heaven, as the mother-moon. This was she who fetched the water of life from the lower regions and gave re-birth to vegetation in the upper-world. The great goddess **[Page 299]** that renewed the light above was also the renewer of the waters from the springs of source in the abyss below. In one legend which, like several others, is common to Egypt and Babylonia, the Great Mother, as Isis, also as Ishtar, descends into the under-world in search of the water of life, otherwise represented as her child, who was Horus or Tammuz according to the cult. The "Descent of Ishtar" is dated in the Aramaic-Akkadian calendar by the month *Ki-Gingir-na*, "the errand of Ishtar" , which was dedicated to the goddess with "Virgo" as its zodiacal sign. This descent in search of the vanished water, the lost light, the disappearing child, was obviously made by the goddess in her lunar character. It was as the moon that Ishtar passed through the seven gates on her downward way when she was stripped of all her glory. (Talbot, *The Legend of Ishtar; Records of the Past*, vol. i.) This search for the water of life occurs some five months earlier in the Babylonian calendar than in the Egyptian year. Plutarch, in speaking of the mysteries, tells us that "on the eve of the winter solstice" the Egyptians "carry the cow seven times round the Temple" , which is called "the seeking for Osiris" . (Isis and Osiris, 52.) This in the pre-Osirian mythos was the elder Horus as the mother's child. Plutarch adds that the goddess who in one character is the earth-mother was in great distress from want of water in the winter-time. The lost Osiris of the legend was not only signified by the loss of solar potency that Isis went to seek for, it was also the renewal of water that she sighed for and wept in the first drops of the new inundation. The disappearance of the water in Egypt was coincident with the sinking of the sun in the winter solstice; both were commemorated in the mourning of Isis. The journey of Isis in search of the water of life was about the time of the winter solstice; when the water disappeared from Egypt and the coming time of drought began. The season coincided with the sun in the sign of Aquarius when the lost Osiris or Child-Horus was re-discovered by the weeping mother seeking for the water in the nether-world. The same errand is ascribed to Ishtar in the Babylonian version of the mythos. But in the re-adjustment to the change of season in the Akkadian calendar, the search is given to the month *Ki-Gingir-na* when the sun was in the sign of Virgo

The walls and windows of the house on high have been emblazoned like all Italy with pictures of the Virgin Mother and her child; the **[Page 302]** Virgin Mother in one character who conceived, and the Great Mother as bringer-forth in the character of gestator. The planisphere contains a whole pantheon of Egyptian deities. They are the gods and goddesses of Egypt, the mythological personages and zootypes that make up the vast procession which moves on for ever round and round according to the revolutions of the earth or the apparent revolution of the sphere. Taking the same order in which the signs on the ecliptic are read today when Aries has become Princeps Zodiac: we can identify at least a dozen deities of Egypt with the twelve signs.

(1) The ram-headed Amen with the constellation Aries;

(2) Osiris, the Bull of Eternity, with the sign of Taurus;

(3) the Sut-Horus Twins with the Gemini;

(4) the beetle-headed Kheper-Ptah with the sign of the Beetle, later Crab;

(5) the lion-faced Atum with the sign of Leo;

(6) the Virgin Neith with the constellation Virgo;

(7) Har-Makhu of the Scales with the sign of Libra;

(8) Isis-Serkh, the scorpion goddess, with the sign of Scorpio;

(9) Shu and Tefnut figured as the Archer with the sign of Sagittarius;

(10) Num, the goat-headed, who presided over the abyss with the sign of Capricornus

(11) Menat, the divine wet-nurse with the sign of Aquarius;

(12) Horus of the two crocodiles with the sign of Pisces.

The following I have posted to show more the link between the above, and how it is and was all tied together over time. I consider Genesis as to be about the yearly cycle, and it is. This material helps to show the ancients were always concerned about these cycles for many thousands of years, and how they related to the yearly cycle and how to understand the All. The connections to the alchemical process should now be easier to see and know. Also, how it was connected to nature, by the use of animals, or creatures because of what they termed "principle." It was their way of showing how to understand, and also our way to understand them and the alchemical process.

If you the reader will spend the time with outside, learn the constellations, and know what is happening to matter outside as the year progresses, all this will become very plain. I mention the 'All.' You're a part of and produced over time by this all. Myself I believe it is by the hand of God that it works as it does. I believe it is the system (Genesis) that he set up for us so that we could live here. I connect to this system, but I have lived now for a long time trying to understand all of it. It does give me Great Pleasure because through out the year I am involved with just looking at outside as I call it, and trying to touch it in some way. I believe it was Thomas Paine who said, "We can only know of God what we can observe in Nature." There was another that said something like, "By studying and knowing nature it is like touching the hem string of God." It is the American Indian that finds 'The Great Spirit' by worship outside! I would like to say that to me they are all Brothers.

The case for Charles Darwin, and his Theory.

Darwin's theory for those that aren't familiar with it, basically states that species arise naturally through a process of evolution. That a species is not created -forever immutable- by God. What this means is by a process of natural selection, the species best suited for the conditions it lives within will survive and adapt to those conditions over time. Eventually becoming the species that would coexist in those conditions in the natural way. We have now many examples of the statement, be it about Polar Bears in the far north of the planet, or serpents that live in our deserts. Most species of any particular area are or have become what those conditions have caused them to become over time. But, there is a problem. Mr. Darwin in his day did not know or understand Genesis and it's application to the species, or it's connection to the yearly process. Not only is it a yearly process, it always is a changing process through out the year depending on things that happen naturally. Volcanic activity could increase on the planet and change the condition in an area, or planet wide that would eventually change the species that live here or there. An outside effect as we know, an asteroid, could also cause these changes. And so Darwin's Theory should have read that God in his wisdom created a species, always and forever adaptable to the ever changing conditions around them. Had Darwin of known Genesis as it should be known, linked to our yearly cycle, I am sure he would have said something similar to this.

By a study of alchemy, and by finding it also is about conditions of nature, and how to use those conditions to our advantage. The ancients had to have studied many things. Alchemy ends up a science about what happens to matter with controlled, conditions. Controlled by being subjected to those conditions of nature through out the yearly cycle. Obviously to find how to control matter. Shape, conditions and time, must have covered a wide range of subjects studied. It also must have covered a study of nature and how and what the effect of those conditions were on basic matter. Did they know of effects of living species as well as we know they found of the dead matters? I am sure, as I mention the compost pile, and how they must have used and studied that part of natural recycling. How could they have studied the one without the other? How can we even say what they studied, or for how long it must have taken them to find those things they discovered about as they termed it, 'The All.' One thing is evident, conditions of nature, and the effects of these conditions were studied to the point of being able to control the end point of natural processes. They are given credit for developing some of our Cereal grains! Also, it was they who domesticated several of our animals. I am including with this part of the work, copies of beliefs they had concerning matter. If one consider the development of matter, of cereal grains, of domesticating animals, of finding and figuring the movement of the constellations. What is it we can say that over time, if it connected to nature, they didn't know or study? As they were so involved with what we call Genesis and condition and how they effected matter, can we say that what they knew was never about the species? If they found and mentioned how matter evolved, connected it to the development of their gods, and so evidently to themselves. If we accept what Mr. Massey said about the study of constellations, 'that by observation,' is how they had to have learned, and so over a 'Great Period of Time.' As I can also say, finding the stone also took or must have taken a considerable amount of time. To them a study of nature is all that mattered, and time had no meaning as to how long they would study a thing to know of it. They studied until all they could know was known! Surly they knew, over the thousands of years they looked, that those conditions of nature, changed all they touched. If stability was of importance to them, was it also about things that could and did happen, that caused chaos? They existed long enough to know of both sides of nature. I am sure they studied both aspect and what happened with the bad as well as the good!

Now Darwin found that a species was the result of these same conditions. Is not the study of the one, tied to the other? Is the only thing that separates the two sciences, if they are two, is a long period of time? Had it been common knowledge that conditions change matter, us, our surroundings, and all within those boundaries. Wouldn't his study of species only served to extend the known things at that time? All of it is tied together, and all of it must be understood in that way. I commend Darwin for being able to see when so many things were against his finding his answers. I commend him for being brave enough to start a new look to nature in his time. I am sure that in many a way it created problems for himself. Even today, those discussion in our time are discussed, and sometimes in an unpleasant way! All those concerned need now take another look, learn about our 'All.' Also learn how our all is exactly that, tied to what exists here in its many forms. Man is the one thing not so concerned about conditions as we alone in the creation have the ability to create our own environment to live by. Over time man has adapted in his own way, clothing, insulation, modern conveniences, all supply us with our needs, all in an unnatural way. It has become our way of life. Again there is a problem, man is now altering those conditions, and man should be concerned with what the long term outcome will be to himself. To those species he seems to want to discuss as to how they change and why. Man is a result of these conditions over time. These conditions over time is still Genesis. Our sciences have proved that, at least to me. I think man might just start to consider where it is he might be taking himself with the changes he is causing. Genesis we say comes from Moses. The fact is that Moses was educated in the temples of Egypt! I don't know what they, the Egyptians called outside, or the yearly cycle, but I am sure that they had a name for it. Perhaps it was Genesis, why not? The thing is I believe I have shown enough in this work to show all is about nature and how she effects matter over time. Is that not the crux of Darwins theory? It is not right for us to take a thing and rename it and call it ours, not if we find those of the past knew and used it. Now I can't blame Darwin for his work or what he has caused to happen from it. I commend him as I said, but he just didn't know!

The part of being adaptable connected to the species, also concerns plants on our planet. Obviously as you travel around on our planet, the plant life is different and changing. It also we know is adaptable always, to those conditions. Now I read somewhere that the ancients in Egypt developed some of our cereal grains. How did they do this? To me it is a proof that more was in their study of nature than dead matter. I have found that the pyramid oven may be the answer to this question. Within is what we know of as a controlled condition. Within I could make it the best conditions for a plant to exist, warmth, moisture, more than outside, and a place where the plant was happy and just grew exceedingly well. As the oven becomes a place where natural forces seem to be concentrated, it then become a place where cereal grains could have been developed! I wonder, what happens to those conditions, and the plant if I used, for example, brackish water with the plant? Could I speed up evolution and bring out what the plant would be in a long period of time under those same conditions? Could the oven again serve mankind and work such wonders as to develop a cereal grain that would grow happily with brackish waters? I think it needs to be researched and found out. Our growing population, and the polluted and brackish waters that surround us deem it necessary to find a way to feed ourselves with other than good or excellent growing conditions. Maybe the oven is an answer. Perhaps it is a part of what was done in the past. If I can conceive of this idea, did they?

Whatever happens with this understanding, Genesis and conditions, one must realize that as we see changes in matter from changes in conditions. We need realize we are not exempt from some type of change ourselves. Darwin showed us what was going on, obviously it was known by the ancients thousands of years ago. Shouldn't we as a people become concerned, again?

This is from the Papyrus of Nesi, preserved in the British museum.

"In the third section of this papyrus we find a work which was written with the sole object of overthrowing .Apep, the great enemy of Ha, and in the composition itself we find two versions of the chapter which describes the creation of the earth and all things therein. The god N eb-er-tcher is the speaker, and he says,

"I evolved the evolving of evolutions. I evolved myself under the form of the evolutions of the god Khepera, which were evolved at the beginning of all time. I evolved with the evolutions of the god Khepera; I evolved by the evolution of evolutions-that is to say., I developed myself from the primeval matter which I made, I developed myself out of the primeval matter. My name is Ausares (Osiris), the germ of primeval matter. I have wrought my will wholly in this earth, I have spread abroad and filled it, I have strengthened it [with] my hand. I was alone, for nothing had been brought forth; I had not then emitted from myself either Shu or Tefnut. I uttered my own name, as a word of power, from my own mouth, and I straightway evolved myself. I evolved myself under the form of the evolutions of the god Khepera, and I developed myself out of the primeval matter which has evolved multitudes of evolutions from the beginning of time. Nothing existed on this earth then, and I made all things. There was none other who worked with me at that time.

I performed all evolutions there by means of that
divine Soul which I fashioned there, and which had
remained inoperative in the watery abyss. I found
no place there whereon to stand. But I was strong
in my heart, and I made a foundation for myself, and
I made everything which was made. I was alone. I
made a foundation for my heart (or will), and I created
multitudes of things which evolved themselves like
unto the evolutions of the god Khepera, and their
offspring came into being from the evolutions of their
births.

Budge, pg. 41, 42, "Egyptian Religion."

"I created
multitudes of things which evolved themselves like
unto the evolutions of the god Khepera, and their
offspring came into being from the evolutions of their
births. "

Things which evolved themselves"! There are many examples of this , but all within this book
should show that what Darwin found was no more than an ancient understanding of how nature
works. And all of it was linked to what we understand as Genesis, which is also from them. It is very
simple, God Created Life with the ability to survive and if necessary evolve with the conditions here
if they for some reason over time changed. What Darwin could deduce by observation, the ancients
had also seen and understood. God in his wisdom never created the "fittest." God Created life, and
within it gave to it the ability to survive those conditions it found itself within. You have now seen
from the text that to the ancients, there was "Two Earths." The north and the south. The creation
worked in both areas, and so was the original understanding of the "Six Days of Genesis." Those six
days in each hemisphere gave the year we know. This understanding was many thousands of years
old before Darwin.

More.

Pg. liv   INTRODUCTION." Book of the Dead", by E. A. Wallis Budge.

"Osiris the god of the resurrection Represented by such works as " The Book of Respirations,"
The Lamentations of Isis and Nephthys,   " The Festival Songs of Isis and Nephthys," The Litanies
of Seker," and the like, the hymns and prayers of which are addressed to Osiris rather as the god of
the dead and type of the resurrection than as the successor of the great cosmic god Tmu-Ra. He
is called " the soul that liveth again, " the being who becometh a child again, "the firstborn son of
unformed matter, the lord " of multitudes of aspects and forms, the lord of time and bestower of
years, the lord

" of life for all eternity." He is the" giver of life from the beginning;" life

" springs up to us from his destruction," and the germ which proceeds from him engenders life in both the dead and the living."

Thou shalt exist for millions of millions of years, a period of millions of years.

In the LXXXIVth Chapter, as given in the same papyrus, the infinite duration of the past and future existence of the soul, as well as its divine nature, is proclaimed by Ani in the words "I am Shu [the god] of unformed matter. My soul is God, my soul is eternity."

When the deceased identifies himself with Shu, he makes the period of his existence coeval with that of Tmu-Ra, *i.e.,* he existed before Osiris and the other gods of his company. These two passages prove the identity of the belief in eternal life in the XVIIIth dynasty with that in the Vth and VIth dynasties.

But while we have this evidence of the Egyptian belief in eternal life, we are nowhere told that man's corruptible body will rise again; indeed, the following extracts show that the idea prevailed that the body lay in the earth while the soul or spirit lived in heaven.

Authors Note: Throughout the Book of the Dead, there are many references to matter, formed and unformed. As above, "multitudes of aspects and forms, the lord of time and bestower of years." We can see that possibly for thousands of years matter and forms were studied proving Genesis is about (to them) more than just a yearly cycle. All was considered over time. Surly they knew of evolution as they studied conditions and how it effected the below. Their society was much longer lasting and much older than ours! God did not create a species 'best able to adapt." God created all species with the ability to adapt. The 'fittest' does not always become the survivor. The fittest may be the species that was destroyed. And in all likelihood it was! Darwins theory is not a theory! It is a known fact, and that fact for a great period of time was known. Perhaps the way to see this is also tied to the All. If you know the all, you simply would know Genesis and how it works, as the creation is about knowing the all. Now in all actuality, the ancients worked with and knew the All!! I would say there is more to it than we even know today. More about how to use those forces, more about how to create! More to the oven and how it brings forces together to remake matter. As you learn about and try to experience outside, I am sure that it will in time become Genesis again, only seen as it was so long ago! Darwins Theory can be taught to our children or to whom ever wants to understand it, thing is, Genesis will always have to be taught along with it. Genesis is what was the original!

Questions and Answers

This section is about questions and points to Ponder! Things I have been asked, comments, information I haven't mentioned from other books. It is hard to explain one so called world mystery, here we are dealing with many. I could repeat with each connections from the other works. But, I actually have tried not to repeat. You cannot explain alchemy without discussing Genesis. You can not understand where the stone came from without the information of Osiris. Alchemy cannot be explained without showing allegories tied to Jesus Christ. The oven is tied to the creation, the list of ties goes on. The creation is tied to Genesis, outside is Genesis! One would think this is a book about Genesis, but it is not. This is supposed to be a book explaining the stone. Originally I did not know that it would get to some of these subjects. Thus, I want to make a few comments, and then go on with questions and answers. I want to cover the subject in such a way as to eliminate questions and misunderstanding of the material. Also, some of the other writers covered alchemy in such a way as to show exactly what I am explaining. Obviously, even those that did explain well, it is questionable if they knew of this stone. I make the exception with Delmar Bryant, it would be my opinion that he knew everything I have found, and more. This section is then, things they said in their books, but not linked to Genesis or Osiris. If I point this out in enough places tied to my explanation, then it will be evident it is not just a coincidence. Even this material, one might have to think about.

Genesis, I figure if there is a person living that is an expert with Genesis, it is me. It, that statement, needs to be clarified. I only know the first lines of Genesis, those first days of the Creation. Lets say the first six. I have tried to explain them, as I have been considering them for many years now. I am sure I have thought about them more than anyone else on this earth. I say consider and think, read the material, and reread it again after you have considered it or found something that connects. So, here some comments about Genesis. "And a gentle moisture rose up all about the garden and watered it, for God had not caused it to rain upon the earth." I think a message here about how the process is worked. In my oven, this is exactly what I do. The vapors raise up, mix with the above lights and condense to descend to water the earth. I have pointed to that mixture in many places.

The cross with equal arms, I believe it is the river with four heads that many have looked for. I don't believe there ever was such a thing naturally. My explanation, how does this happen naturally. How does four rivers to go out in four directions, where is the supply from? It would have had to be a massive source of water exiting from a hill, evenly balanced so that the flow would produce four rivers going off in four directions! I am not saying this could not happen. I just have never seen such a thing, and don't accept it as being anything other than tied to man's imagined creation. How he thought it happened. I believe the oven is a part of that imagination, it is easily explained and tied to past beliefs. It also satisfies those descriptions of the garden we know of. Again, each must decide what he wants to accept and believe.

Jesus Christ. It was never a consideration of mine to ever discuss Jesus as a part of the alchemical explanation. But, it was many an alchemist of the past that linked Jesus to the stone. This to me was a sort of puzzle, why did they do this? They did things in a hidden fashion, all knew what they were showing, why use Jesus? Now, I can answer that question. Here again, my thoughts based on consideration of this material over long years. It will be evident to those that read this work, or it should be, that at 0000 AD Jesus replaced Osiris and the old religion. Why do I say this? Through much study I know this to be a fact. The past has been lost! The religious beliefs of the past has been lost! What needs to be done is a book explaining the ancients beliefs still around at 0000AD. How they were used but slowly lost as time went on with the new religion of the Christians. Much of the past was absorbed, but in a fashion that lost the origin meaning of those symbols. The understanding of those symbols have slowly been changed. The new understanding has been claimed as original. To me this is wrong. We have lost much of the heritage that belongs to us. Those symbols and signs should be known, and their origin accepted as original, or as to leading to what we have accepted today.

I believe everyone that has an interest of why 'Jesus and Alchemy,' should see the film recently made called, 'The Lost Tomb of Jesus.' I saw it several times and believe it is the tomb of that family. On the entrance to the tomb is a chevron, with a small circle or oval within it. The oval to me is egg shaped. To me the chevron is the sign of the firmament. The egg design is too close to what I do. There was another tomb in that movie they had checked out. Found within the other tomb, the same sign, but this one was a chevron with a small line drawn within it. Now if the oval is of the egg, or of an oval, I can understand the small line drawn, If it was of a circle, I believe the small line would have been made as a point to represent a circle. How does a line represent a circle? Each should see the film, and look very closely at what they call a circle, if you do you will see it is oval in shape. Neither was explained, and I doubt either ever will be. Those commenting did not know of this information I point out.

Also, it was shown in this film that Jesus used the Tau Cross as a sign for their group or following. This was of course before he was crucified. I should also like to point out to you, Jesus was connected to the fish, another secret way followers showed they were part of his group or that they were a follower of that belief. What is the fish? Now, for thousands of years, the constellations as they moved over head, the sign was tied to Osiris. If the religion had not been destroyed, lost, covered up, forgotten, at 0000 AD Osiris would have been tied to the fish, the sign of Pisces, and the Tau Cross. That cross was tied to Osiris thousands of years before Christ. What does all this mean. To me there are too many connection to Jesus and the past to not consider that Jesus knew of this ancient religion, and in some ways was connected. They (writers of the past) also discussed the following of Jesus. Too many followers, too fast, the following grew at an incredible rate, why? Consider that in 0000 AD, many knew of the constellation connection to a messiah! Many were looking again, perhaps for Osiris or someone to be that Messiah, and Jesus became that to them. The 'Star' that was seen in the heavens was no star, it was the constellation. The sign of the fish, and it's connection to Pisces, I believe proves that. Lastly, from the film I found that the family of Jesus, on both sides were not just common persons, but descended from a long line of people that probably were better educated in these things than the common man. It is very possible, and very probable that

Jesus knew of the past religious beliefs. Again, each must consider and accept what he or she feels is for themselves. I am sure there would be many more ties to the past connected to Jesus, but, sadly most of that information has been lost and needs to be searched out. I believe it could be found. At least for me, I believe I understand at least in part why they (the alchemist) tied Jesus to the stone. They saw him and Osiris in a similar fashion. And Jesus had simply replaced the old ways. As we continue now, things said and written by others to help with a full understanding.

How to understand the allegories, those that are in a series. My explanation comes first from the Abraham and Flamel series. Abraham used seven tablets. Flamel used a similar but a linear way of describing. First Abraham's, to clear thing up. I told you there were seven tablets, but also, the first three were used twice. This I call the overlap. I just said, Flamel used a linear way of showing the same thing. Two ways on one page. What matters is that there are ten connections to making the stone. I have include a page with Flamel, that just says step #1, etc., and do all ten to be sure it is clear. If you will learn these ten steps, and how they show them, then you can go to a series and figure it out most of the time. I said most of the time because there are many false stones described out there. If you cant find the basic steps, move on and forget that series. Now, why an overlap? In part because the path of the stone is a copy of the trials of Osiris. In actuality it is Osiris copied to the stone! Can you imaging trying to make and follow a process that was set up in this way, how would you ever figure it out? To you the first tablet was only the first step! The second was only the second. Never would you or could you follow that way and find an answer. Now Flamel those tablets with Abraham, is linear. Flamel used a lot less steps than many. Why did they use many? Again, to show the same process, but in a different and hidden way. If they all used ten steps, it would quickly become a clear process. When I come to a series where there is 150 steps, I just look at it, say, "that's nice," and move on. If it is a series that I think I can figure out, or want to, I look for those steps I can recognize first and label them. Is there an overlap? Many but not all have it. How to tell? If you know the last few steps, and see them in the first part of the series, there is an overlap based on the Abraham series. Is there another way to figure a series out? Yes is the answer. Count! If there is anything in number, count it. Now flowers are used a lot. I have also showed stars, and castle ramparts. So anything can be used. Is there a problem with counting? Yes. You have to know the process was divided in many series at Septembers Child. September is nine, but there are 16 months, and so the division is always between nine and seven for the most part. With this division, one must see a step to recognize where he is at, and then count. Seven is the last number of the last seven months, and is tied to April. Nine I mentioned is tied to Septembers Child. Now some of the alchemists just counted to 16 based on the number of months of process. So if you see 13, it is the following January, or the 13th month. Abraham, if you will look at April, the garden, there are 16 squares on that garden floor, they represent the 16 months it took to get there. Yet, it is the third picture? See how the overlap works? Now there are many series out there, or just a pictorial allegory that shows the last seven months. Why? Many of the alchemist I believe just figured the first nine months as making a base matter of the stone. The last seven actually make the stone. And so, to hide yet show, they showed the last seven only. Many times, colors of the allegory show what happens during that time. I know the designer of this type of allegory had the stone, as would any master alchemists that saw the work. The colors are very the only way that shows the material is being at that time treated right. This is also why I believe that most, many, different organic material can produce the correct matters of the stones. In the knowledge I have now, I would tend to agree that all organics are destroyed by nature in the same way, if so, the destroyed mater would then advance in the same way as the egg material if treated in the same manner. To me this means eventually I am going to try to make a ton of this stuff at once! Also, at the end it grows, it reproduces itself! If it is a medicine, all will have it in one way or another. 221

What I want to point out is, the 'good' light seems to continue to augment the matter below as long as we do it in the correct fashion, that is the important thing to know. Consider here as I said, that matter has no seed, but the light tries to make something out of it! When we reach the point that the light can no longer improve it, then you have the stone. They considered it perfect as they felt a part of the light was. They ended their search with the red stone. If at that point it is perfect, what else could nature add! Who knows what we will do with it today, with our abilities, there may be more. By reading for example, The Book of the Dead, you will find many more connections to what I have said. It will help to show you the understanding in a clearer fashion than I can present. Also, read the other books I will discuss may help. I have picked material that emphasizes my points.

I mentioned seed! The matters are augmented by the lights, but there is no seed. Now, consider what the ancients said about the light. The sun is gold, and the seed for gold. Now if I make that below substance 'like the sun,' the red stone, would it not contain the seed for gold within it? Would it not be like that good we have been collecting for so long? That good is supposed to be something of God. If God is perfect, the good of the light is perfect, then also the red stone is perfect. The white stone is made from a reflection of the good light of the sun. It is a lesser light, and so, a white stone, and one of silver for the same reasons. Now, I did not miss the fact, that it seemed funny to me, two lights and sure, they are tied to the two special metals we hold dear here in the below. Seemed a pretty good coincidence don't you think? But then I though about it, how do we know that silver was always such a thing? Perhaps it became a metal we desired because it was a result of this alchemical process? Who can say why some things happen? I also found the electron spin on the metals, silver and gold seem to be different. It may be somehow tied to the spin, or that the stone so creates the same type of thing in another metal, and so that makes the changes. This is above my abilities to explain at present. As is if it is a medicine, how does it work. To me, all in the below is from the above. The stone becomes concentrated above! Why wouldn't it help me?

The Ouroborous, The serpent biting it's tail. What does it mean. It is used in alchemy, but myself I never really understood exactly what it meant or stood for. I always considered it as the symbol they used to take the matters back to primordial. And so I thought it was over when the May-Day was started. This I now see in another way. The serpent was painted on the coffin or tomb of Osiris, it was there until he rose again as Septembers Child. In other words, the matters were taken back and then brought forward to a base substance. This completes the circle of the matters and of Osiris at that stage. This ties into what Flamel said about this step, "as before we called it death, now we can, to continue the metaphor, call it life." He saw this part of the process as one, and that one is the circle of the serpent. So, the Ouroborous is the matters from the time you pick up an egg, until you pull from the oven a white substance nine months later. Normally I see the Ouroborous painted a green and a red color. Now again Flamel said, "that it stays green longer than any color." Now the three hottest months of the summer, while process is going on, it is of a greenish color. That is the longest time. What is the red? I know that eventually it ends up red, but I don't see why a red and green color. Myself I would just have it green and white! It could be connected with generation! Nature when growing is green! Nature gets that way from the sun which is red! God, the power in the sun as good, Jesus, all is about generation or this force the ancients found. I have said it another way, it is the 'Power of Creation,' or 'Creation Energy.' What else could it be called, and why is it we don't know of it?

Smell and the stone. Flamel said that the stone "had the stench of graves." He also said that he soon knew it because of the strong smell. I always wondered how he could know a thing by the smell, that he had never known or smelled before? Believe me when I tell you this, it is about the strongest worse smell I have ever been around. It does last a long time, about three months, and then again it will smell while those three hot months are going on. Not as bad because it then is outside, and so vented. I have also said, consider the past and try to see things as they did. Now in "Art of Alchemy " by Adiramled, Delmar Bryant, said that in the past people knew how good or bad, (rotten) a thing was because of the smell. I had never considered that. In the past, no refrigeration means a lot of spoilt food. I am sure that a lot of it was eaten that way. I am sure there was a lot of smelling going on with each meal to see just how bad it was, or, how good it was. In fact I am sure the world was a smelly place back then. So, the point. Why did Adiramled say such a thing if smell is not connected to the stone? Smell is connected, and it is as Flamel said, as the stench of graves. This is a smelly process. If you do not have a place well ventilated to do the work in? When the oven is opened after the dark time at the start, all you will smell is ammonia. Now that seems strange to me, as I never smell it until I open it. I worked in an ammonia plant for some time and so I do know the smell. The smell goes away by the time it is dried in moonlight, and a base matter for the stones is produced. And so, how would Flamel know it by the smell? I figure it smelled so bad he knew he must have had a substance that was being taken back as no other substance he had ever smelt, and so was on the right track for the stone. That can be the only answer.

Moving toward the Light. As we start this process, we work in the dark. Adiramled said that the only Hell was when we moved away from the light. Now as you work for this substance if you pay attention, after the dark you are always moving toward the light. Cleopatra (an alchemist) said that at the end of the work, "let there be a union between the greatest and the smallest." This is the last step for the stones, and only then can there be such a union. I don't care if your 15 months into the process, and you shine the light on your substance the wrong way, start again! If it is put in one time wrong, you can not,   (easy to understand) take it out. This was a hard lesson for me!

Mercury, our mercury as compared to the vulgar mercury. First the name itself. In consideration it is the name of the messenger of the gods! The gods we can connect to as far as alchemy is concerned is the two lights. Sun and moon. From ancient Egypt, and all of this is from there The lights are said to be the two eyes of god. The sun being the greater. Now the messenger has to do with water as I have explained. If you understand, the only way we can capture the above is by the lights being or shining into our oven setting outside. And so mercury (water) absorbs these lights, something of these lights, and carries it to the below. That is why the alchemists called the substance mercury in many places. But, they said it was not the real mercury until it had reached a certain stage, and that stage is Septembers Child. The other part of this explanation for mercury I want to blame on 'metallic principles.' Many alchemists work with metals because of this term. Even Flamel said something about metallic principles. Now I have told you principles come from nature, because of a lack of terms to express ideas. Things in nature were used to give an understanding. Now the sun is the seed of gold. The moon is the seed for silver. The sun and moon produce these two stones, and so if I can get gold from a substance made by the sun, can you see to express this, the sun would become a metallic principle for gold? The moon for silver? They are the metallic principles, and no metals are ever used. Another way to say this is, if I want to make something that will grow gold, I need to use the sun which produces the seed for gold! Now Adiramled said about this. From "Art of alchemy" Pg. 14 "First, the honey is the white substance that forms out of the carcass by the operations of these hidden principles. This white substance is what the sages term our Mercury and is virtually the mother of the stone." Now below, pg.14 The honey of this moon is the same that Sampson ate, and the real truth is that it is not perfected for about nine moons (months). Adiramled also said, pg. 16., in mentioning the Rhine Gold. " a certain divine essence coming from the sun and pierces the soil and the rocks and vitalizes the seed of gold that slumbers there. This agent is the active agent for transformation." This agent, essence of the sun is the agent for transformation.! How much clearer could it be? Adi also said, "No great knowledge of natural science as now understood is necessary. In fact technical training of this kind is apt to blunt the facilities to a perception of the true natural principles." I only want to point out, 'Natural Principles.' On pg. 15 he said, "Man cannot do this by any known chemical process. This wonderful Adamic earth is actually made by God, in the air, or as we may truly say in heaven, for heaven is every bit of the ground above the earth." Pg. 16, "The object of earth is to afford a place to conserve the astral influences." Pg. 16, The alchemists who is constantly molding earth into higher forms of expression." Pg. 16, " We find the substance into which two opposite principles of expression are brought to the highest perfection possible found in nature." All say as I understand it that the above, sun and moon are the two principles, and they are captured and absorbed by the below. Now Adiramled said many things in his book, and I want to use many of them here as we proceed. Thus it is not my words, but his that say the same thing. If you understand those steps I pointed out, all this should be clear.

We go on. " From these ashes, Moses death, there follows a resurrection which is attained in O (Capricorn, having the symbol of the goat) (it also is the symbol of the sun). (consider Osiris and December end, and the stone at this time), the end of 120 (three times 40) more days. This points directly to the Crowned Androgyny, and Osiris as he becomes of the earth, Perfect man and woman.

"At this time, X (cross) will have effected and the Snowy Splendor will greet the gaze of the enraptured artist." Here he speaks of the 120 days, four months, 120 days of the matters in the darkness. Then there is a resurrection of sort as the waters come together. Then, at this time, X (cross) will have effected and we see the snowy splendor. Now the cross, X (equal arm cross) is tied to September, and so Septembers Child, and so that is when we see the snowy splendor. Even Adiramled could mix up the steps to tell yet hide!

On pg. 4. Speaking of mercury, the mercury in the first tablet of Flamel. " In his hand he hold a caduceus, formed of a rod with two serpents entwined, - expressive of one substance containing two principles, i.e., fire and water." And so as I described, the rod is the fire, and the two serpents are the sun and moon. Mercury is water. The one substance having two principles. To express it another way, all of the creation is male and female! Everything conceived is made this way. Now the ancients recognized this, and Adiramled points it out in many places. So, the stones, if you understand is a separation of nature! The one substance or all, as all is, was divided and made into two separate stones.

"This principle, apprehended as energy actively expressed is creation, is mercury, Christ, God, or anything else we choose to name it". Pg. 4 "Alchemy alone explains the true meaning, mercury is the mystery of magic." "Alchemy, science, religion, if properly understood are synonymous terms, since they all express a mental recognition of the one great central fact , or principle of existence." " The word alchemy, itself goes further back to Chaldea and Egypt where Al or El meant God, and Cham the sun. The word virtually means the power of the divine solar Influence expressed in nature," (the good light). Ida, here goes on to say that the term alchemy is from the middle ages (few knew the past understanding), but that it is as old as the world itself. Pg. 5, Speaking of earth, " This earth then , must contain all other elements. In the one, therefore, there are four. But the only visible is earth and water, the others being invisible and only recognized as inner principles or formative energies." Now here again consider compost naturally, and then consider our own earth as we remake it within the oven, taking it beyond what nature can do. We don't see the sun or moon within the substances, but they are there. And, as far as our organic substance is concerned, I mention because many believe that an organic substance cannot change an inorganic substance. On pg. 6 Adi said of this, "organic and inorganic, the division is entirely arbitrary and unreal." How do we explain and understand this? I will say it this way. If I take an organic egg, and change it naturally and it will mix with a base metal and change it to gold, an inorganic substance, what does that mean? It means that the matters on this planet, from the simple to the complex, gold, are all the same. No difference as we have chosen to describe them in present terms. It also means, if you consider, for Adi to say this to me means that the stone he made does as I just expressed. He made it out of organic, and it will change the inorganic! And so, no difference.

Another way to explain this is from another understanding I have about things said by alchemists. "Visit the interior of the earth, go down into a mine and see what is happening." Now many have done this, and gone into a mine and what did they find? Sulfur, and minerals. And so many have worked with vulgar sulfur, and vulgar minerals. Is that the message of the mine? No it is not. How to understand this part is that first you consider the earth as it was created. A big ball of substance as I have described it, being androgynous. That is how it was though to be made. It would combine with anything and so anything would grow upon it. What about within it? It was considered the same matters? And so, as time passed, as it rained upon the earth, as the above slowly filtered down into this matter it slowly is changing it to gold. Now it doesn't go directly to gold, it advances mineral by mineral, but the aim of nature is to slowly turn what is in the below into what is in the above. The message of the alchemists is to repeat this natural work, but we do it in such a way as to assist nature to the end substance. We don't go through each mineral, we go directly to gold, or directly to the good that is causing this to happen. Another allegory that is similar is 'vitroil.' What it means is to visit the inward parts of the earth, by changing the stone is found. Here the alchemists are speaking of earth (water) which becomes earth. By visiting with light, we change the inward parts of water, and by this action we will eventually find the stone. Now Adi. Said that, "The earth is being formed above the earth." This is the same thing. Above the earth, in heaven the vapor and the light is mixing and forming earth! Heaven was that space above the earth, as the earth is under the firmament and so this work is being done in heaven! " But the water loved the earth and returned to it again and again, each time purifying and refining it a little". Pg. 12. Now, is this not similar to the Emerald Tablet where it says, "It rose from earth to heaven and descended again. You see, both speak of this circulation of the vapors in light, and descending to earth to purify. Pg. 17, In fact you must know that Saturn, Jupiter, Mars, Venus, Mercury, are merely successive stages of the one work, each exhibiting a different color." Flamel, saying "Gods Procession," means the same thing. The colors that come and go do so with the changing planets mentioned in the above. Pg. 19, All writers are unanimous in saying the substance of our stone is the same thing. "As concerns the matter, it is one, and contains within itself all that is needed. Its birth is in the sand. It is the distilled moisture of the moon joined to the light of the sun and congealed." Now, did you see that it's birth is in the sand? Do you remember that sand, has to do with shape, and is a very old word for shape! And so it's birth is within a shape! Adi goes on to say that nothing truer was ever spoken of the stone. "It is called a stone, not because it is a stone, but because finally it becomes a stone capable of resisting the fire." Did I not say to never let the sun shine directly on it? Did I not say that as Cleopatra said, at the end let there be a joining of the greatest and the smallest! If there is a joining before the stone is finished, it will not resist and it will be destroyed. Always there is more to know, or more to be said about your matters. Pg. 20., "Though I say only one thing is required, one seed. it is to be taken for granted that you must have a soil in which to sow the seed. Nor is it possible to raise it in more than one soil, because in only one do we find the rays of the sun congealed in just the right proportions." "I trust you will be able to understand the scientific application of the term, congealed solar rays." Now what is he saying here. This points again to first matter of the earth in the creation. The same base substance used then you must use now for it to work. Now as we have seen, we must make this One substance. Also, congealed solar rays. Some of the alchemists used a burning glass as a metaphor in alchemical allegories.

Now the burning glass concentrates the solar ray of the sun, and will cause a fire. Some have felt this is the secret fire, and it is, but it must be understood somewhat different than it is shown. We concentrate the rays of the sun, but over time, not at once! And so it is a good metaphor if you understand. They never show you a thing directly as it is, but what they show usually points to something you should figure out as to what it is they are showing. Pg. 22., Adi, a quote of another writer, " To some foolish and shallow persons I have several times expounded this art in the simplest manner and even word for word, but they despised it and would not believe me that there is exhibited in our work a two-fold resurrection of the dead." Now this is true, and I have shown it with the Mythology of Osiris. He is first resurrected as a new born child, Septembers Child, he is again resurrected as a God in April! Each a different level of purity. The same for the stone exactly. Pg 22., And important, but no more so than any other of this material. Lamed represents the beginning of spring, the sign of Pisces or two fishes which are united in one sea, a sea as dark as Erebus. The soil is now prepared by nature in which the philosopher is to sow his golden seed. This soil is the sulfur, which is the philosophic earth containing the seed within itself (Gen. 1. 11) mercury the maiden is our symbol, the developer of this seed, now becomes united in close embrace with sulfur, or as the ancients expressed it, sol and luna are in conjunction. You should recognize this now as our substance going into the oven and into the dark to become this soil. What soil? The soil that will absorb those lights we use when we bring them together as in Genesis, and here as we do so in the May-Day. He mentioned the conjunction, and I wanted to point this out as it is not the only conjunction. October, when we "turn the wheel again" is also seen as the conjunction in alchemy. As two resurrections, there are also two conjunctions. Pg. 23., "For remember, that a chemist burns with fire, alchemists perform all their operations with water, all that need be known is to find how to infuse this with natural heavenly virtue."

Water! I have mentioned it, very important to alchemy. How would we work our process without water? Answer, we would not be able to. It is not though my words that mean so much, and it is my way to use the words of other master alchemists. It is my belief that Adiramled was a master alchemist. I wanted to read him because he was a near time alchemist. His book is a little very inexpensive book to be had. But as far as information it is a great book. I couldn't believe it when I first found and read it, as what I do I found within those pages. I have said, "I could have written that book!" But it is not true. I can use and reference his work, but I never could write as well as he. Now, he speaks of water. Important for me to bring this information to you, as the more you know and understand, the better you will understand how to do this work. So, Adi and water. Pg.25, The zigzag lines in the character represent the sign Aquarius. It represents the zigzag lines or ripples found on the surface of water". I showed these zigzag lines on the second tablet of Abraham, the two dragons! There January, but astrologically, this is the dawning of a new age. The new age of Aquarius. This age is different than many of the last ages past, I leave it to you to figure out why! "Aquarius is the man. His origin is in aqueous. Water may be termed the mean element. It contains potentially all the elements, Hence it is called the mother, being shown in Genesis as the primal element, or first matter of the world." Now I have considered first matter, and what I finally understood it to be was the combination of the water vapor and the light mixture in the air. This combination I showed as Adi said, "the earth being formed above the earth". And so in alchemy, when they mention first matter as something you should understand, it is from this combination, and is the first matter ever produced. " Water is the vehicle of eternal, creative energy, Inseparably associated with water therefore are ideas of fertility and formation." Adi goes on to say that we cannot, in our world consider creation though without destruction. Life and death are both tied together, are a part of one eternal sphere of being, which, despite the manifestation phenomena of change, leads the mind to the conscious recognition of the indestructibility of universal substance, and to the knowledge that life is for-ever is." Now what I have said along these lines, is that the matters are never dead, only in transition. All outside is in transition. If the matters were truly dead, could they ever be used again? The same thing was said about Osiris, that he was born a new born babe, but first, came death! Even when the matters are returned to a base, I question if death is the proper description. Even then they are moved forward by the light! Always it gets back to the light, and so perhaps why in the past it was termed, 'The Good Light.'

The thing about all this is, it is always tied to combinations with water! Nature is this water, matter and seed. Nature's actions are always positive, always generation of the matters. Now for example, coal would be different. It is pent up light, but it is going nowhere as it is out of reach of nature. Now man controls nature and works with nature, or man holds nature back. Nature works with means, and man can find and know those means, that is alchemy. Nature is positive, and will always try to produce. If there is no seed, then the energy goes into the matters and they become a way of collecting and augmenting those things of nature that normally produce. Now important to understand, we see nature all around us producing, but what about metals? What about within the earth? " It is not generally known that minerals are formed like vegetables from seed, but it is a fact, nevertheless. Not seed separated and encased in distinct coverings or sheaths but essential , vital seed-- so fine of course that it cannot be seen any more than the living principle of other seeds." Adi uses Philalethes to explain this. "The seed of all things has been placed in water by God. This seed some exhibit openly like vegetables, some keep in their kidneys, like animals; some conceal in the depths of their essential being like metals. The seed is stirred into action by a certain celestial influence, coagulates the material water, and passes through a series of formative principles." Sendivogius says, "seed is nothing but congealed air, or a vaporous humor enclosed in a body; and unless is be dissolved by a warm vapor, it cannot work." This metallic seed, hidden in water is able to penetrate the rock, and to develop various minerals. This seed in time will transform the rock into a higher form of existence. Although the process of this seed is vastly different than a seed placed in the soil, it is the same. Both seeds are composed of the same substance. Nature alone determines the different outcome. People have not searched for this metallic seed, because they were not aware of it." Now consider what I said about the alchemist saying to you to visit a mine and see nature in action. It is the above seed penetrating to the below. It is the seed absorbed in the vapors that condense and trickle down into the depths. It is what they believed, one must consider why. As many of them said the same thing down through the ages, either these master alchemist had a similar understanding of nature, or they all read the same book.

"And so man walks over the magic Argil and beholds the Golden River flowing over the whole earth, totally unconscious of the fact!"

"Fermentation means a chemical change in constituency, it means decomposition, it means putrefaction; it means death. There is no change of vital conditions, no resurrection of life , without this death."

St. Paul says, "That which thou sowest is not quickened except it die."

"All that death ever means is the freeing of atoms of an organized body by the process of dissolution. Death is thus the initial step toward a new life-expression." As I work with my egg, I do to it as he describes. I always wondered though, when a chicken is setting on the nest, and the substances are warm? How is it the matters know the difference in construction and destruction? I know it is because the egg is alive, and so nature does as the seed within directs. Now I destroy. "The Slaughter of the Innocent." But it is something I think about. It is as he say's, "the right conditions so that the matters resurrect and growth taking place out of the decomposed mass."

"Nothing ever is or can be permanently destroyed" Siva and Brahma, destroyer and builder always work together for one end, expression, more expression." For the reason that this wonderful phenomenon of death and birth takes place in the earth, through always, the medium of water."

"The ram has always been the symbol of this divine fire." In Egypt Ra or ram was the sun, which the Py-Ram-ids symbolize." In alchemy it is said that the house of the ram (Aries) cunningly conceals the transmuting fire." The pyramid shaped oven contains this fire! Consider again, Artephins, he said, That only one thing is necessary to perfect the work, that there is only one stone, only one medicine, only one vessel, only one regimen, only one method of making the red and white. Through the scent of water, it will bring forth boughs like a plant."

I have quoted here quite extensively Idaramled. In many books, and from my collections many thing are used to help one understand the making of the stone. Those little things said have been never explained or connected to any one process. Here though, I think I have brought together enough information to show what it is about, and that it again can be accomplished, the work. Yes,

I have done it and presently I am working to do it again with many members of my forum. Many will have it around the world. Many are well educated in ways that the material whatever it is will at last be checked out and so understood as never before. There are other stones! The thing is, is this the original stone, and to me, yes it is! It matters not what I say about the stone, what matters is if this material I present, and all these things said by others sufficiently described the process I have found. It does. After a while, one has to say it is no coincidence! How many facts, how many descriptions and colors of a thing could be the same?

As now I have mentioned this fire, and the pyramid oven, I want to continue with Adiramled and his practical lesson six in his book.

Lesson Six

In lesson six of "Art of Alchemy," Adiramled is going to discuss 'Ayin' hebrew Letter and it's meaning. First meaning is that it is the eye and here it means The All-seeing Eye. The second meaning he attaches to a fountain. He states that the alchemist that finds this fountain will also find the hidden eye, the light of the fountain. This fountain becomes the goats fountain, and is tied to Capricorn. For certain reasons this goats fountain was tied to, by myth makers to the 'Magic Fountain of Life.' The word goat, and god according to the "etymological derivation of the words are exactly the same." Mythically it is tied to the omnipotent universal energy. Summing it up, Adi says, pg. 62, The point in a circle, the eye, the fountain, Iod, god, goat- all are one. When we find the one, we have found them all!

The goat is significant in many ways. It is to be tied with the Tropic of Capricorn. It is tied to the sun when it reaches it's lowest point, the winter solstice. The real meaning though is not to be found in astronomy, but astrology. At this time the sun is said to be in Capricorn, alchemically we would say that the sun, sol is in the goat. Adi goes on to say, "corresponding to the sun, we have the principle of fermentation, which is practically fire, solar fire- held in captivity by the sun." "Fire is not merely flame. Fire is an invisible principle in all things. Properly speaking it is no element but a phenomena." Now I ask you to remember the last step of Osiris. He was blended from work below in or on earth. This is where the body disappears, and goes to heaven. This is late December, and the matters of Osiris are now tied to the god, goat above in Capricorn. In the upper part of the oven. This is tied to second resurrection of the matters previously mentioned. To continue, as explained by Adi, he goes on speaking of these matters, pg. 66 and 67, as ash, and aish. Ash meaning fire, Aish meaning man. I had said that Adam was created as androgynous material, my understanding, and is the reason or past understanding of how a women could be made of his rib. Asha, (Eve) the offspring of ash is really the product of a natural sexation- an interaction of the natural duel fire animating the human furnace. The natural sexation is androgynous material as was believed created in the creation epic. Adam was created duel, of both sexes so that his seed also would blend with whatever seed that came to him. Those words, "Who's seed is within itself," have a much deeper meaning form the past than we ever discovered or considered. The alchemists brought this originally to my attention by saying that "Adam was made of a different material than the rest of us were." Now we all come from a man and a woman, but we come from the joining of a man and a woman, Adam was created of a material that had both principles within. All Ida said here of the Goat (December), the fountain (oven), eye of god (above in oven or in heaven), all tie to the matter at the last stage when it is moved to the upper part of the oven in end of December.

Like Alchemy, Adi goes on that the true meaning of Capricorn had been lost to man. Note that I said, 'had been lost to mankind.' Last about the goat, Adi goes on to say, "How can the goat be called a fountain", and states that , "simply because it is water, not common water- but a water that does not wet the hands." Now alchemists have searched for this dry water for many years, and by many means attaching it to many substances. Here I hope they realize is the answer. It is vapor, it is light, it is the combination. It is found only within the oven. Consider again, the design found on the back side of the American dollar. It is about the 'eye of God within the goat!' It is about the place of work for Osiris at the end, and also for the stone. It is about the original astrology. Not the astrology man has made it today!

Also the Alchemical Citadel. This is a pictorial allegory as are many another. It was described as having 21 doors, 21 ways that an alchemist could go astray. Now, at this point in the game, although it was some time ago when I considered, 21 must mean something. Also, it describes a drawbridge, one that spans the broad moat! Always I find that whatever is in an allegory, pictorial or written, it means something. What did 21 mean, and what has a broad moat? As you look at the oven, see that it is made of five pyramids. There is one large covering all, which is of four pieces and four small, little mountains within which is 16 more pieces. When we put a base under these shapes, we have 21 pieces. What is the broad moat? Consider now, there is an upper place to work. A piece of glass that hold the egg during the cooler months of work. It sets on the four small mountains. And so spans the river below, the moat below, the place where the waters come together. However you want to express it, it does as they say in the allegory. And so, the alchemical citadel becomes the description of the oven. If it does not, then it is again just another coincidence but I am convinced this is the answer. Now I know we have a base below, but that is separate and so not part of the description. You consider. I also want to point out that originally I had my ovens made perfect! They were cut glass done as well as could be done today, even the sides of the glass was beveled. The cost was quite high, and that was now 15 years ago. I admit I have been having problems with the process the last several years, and I am working that out. I have considered temperature, size of oven, now even the perfection of the cut, and, lastly, the size of the egg. Trying to save money I have resorted to having the local in town cut my ovens and pieces for me. I can't believe that all alchemists had ovens that were butter built than what I try to do. I do now, with backtracking to see what I am doing wrong, believe that part of the problems I am experiencing is from the egg size. I always complained to myself that I must be wrong, as I just didn't have enough material to work with. I ended up with a half a teaspoon of material! I however didn't figure on the multiplication at the end. Always I considered Flamel who said " I had enough when I did it once, but did it thrice, always trying to figure out the workings of nature within the vessels." If he had enough with one process, surly what I was doing is wrong. So, I started working with jumbo eggs! The ratio of air within the oven changes a heck of a lot when switching between a large, and a jumbo egg.! Don't do it unless you use a larger oven. The eggs will turn black, but you won't see the rainbow. If it is not there, start again. When considering the egg, I laughed at myself, as I have said many times consider the past to understand. Lets consider the size of the chickens in ancient Egypt? Lets consider if they even had chickens. I mention this because as you read Massey's Book on Osiris, it was the dove that was spoken of, dove eggs? Not so big at all. Also, Flamle in his wisdom gave us the color of the substance when he painted himself, in his fresco, rrange, black and white. Orange is the color of the substance used. What is orange. Now for many years I considered the yolk of the eggs I was using. They could be called orange, wild bird eggs are orange, but the hen's eggs I was using are more yellow than orange? Also, a lot of problems as many of them exploded within the oven, or cracked apart as the shells are just too week. I never considered that today's eggs are fed, to the chicken, antibiotics! How would this corrupt or alter the rotting process. Anyhow, I found that if you use an egg from your local farmer, the shells are tough, the yolks are orange, no medicines to deal with, and just be happy we can still find a normal egg somewhere. All things have to be considered. Especially, the ratio of the matters and the volume of the air inside. I made 6 inch ovens because the alchemists said that having the top equal to the width of the hand was about right. A six in. oven when made gives this ratio fairly close. I use a 2 inch base beneath, however now I am experimenting to find what works best ever time if that is possible. Simple process, yes! hard to do, extremely! If you don't succeed first time, try to remember, I didn't for over 25 years. There is more about dead matter and process. As that is presently being worked on, see the answers on my forum.

A Poem, pg. 72, Art of alchemy.

> Blessed be Seh, the God of Seven
>> Who broods the egg of Night,
> Praised be Ma-at the Goddess of heaven
>> Queen of the Living Light
>
> Osiris sinks in Capricorn
>> And Isis seals the Tomb---
> Horus the prince of Love is Born
>> And Joy dispelleth gloom
>
> O, sweet was the joy of the heavenly One
>> But sweeter the joy of mine Own.

One thing, remember Osiris is 16 months, and so sinks is the start. Capricorn is twice known! Anything I find connected to Osiris I feel must be used to show where this all came from.

"The Visible Universe contains the source of its Divination in itself." This is the force that dispenses the essence of Life which gives it the means of perpetually renewing its creation after destruction." pg. 75 Creation after destruction, within the oven! "Nearly all root words beginning with "P' bear some occult relation to our mercury, or mystic Pe. For example Pur (pyr) is the old Egyptian word for fire. The pyramids are monuments revealing to us the fact that the Egyptians were masters in the use of this sacred Fire, which meant to them unlimited wealth and power. Pg. 80. Now one must consider right here, did the Egyptians use a stone oven to bring the forces together, to capture this sacred fire? Or, did they as I have said, have a working model. Consider what the design must have meant to them to cause them to build such a thing as they did to be sure the idea and information would not be lost to mankind.

I realize I have quoted quite a bit of information from Adiramleds book. Actually, I have used very little of what it contains as an explanation of what I have said alchemy is. Probably within his book is found on ever page something that a student should know and understand.

This shape is found throughout nature, and there are many ways to use the forces connected. I want here to briefly mention Rudolf Steiner. A Mystic for sure. He has written several books, but is also known for his biodynamic fertilizer. I consider him an alchemists that gave mankind something of the science, and perhaps a consideration of what might be the benefit for mankind if or when all is known. Mr. Steiner produce a substance from rotted cow manure and a cows horn. He gave instructions that a cows horn was to be filled with manure, buried over the winter months, dug up and then a "pinch" of the matter mixed with water made an excellent fertilizer. Now to many this seems a crazy thing to do, but it works! Can you see how it and Mr. Steiner are tied to alchemy? The horn contains the shape, the manure is the rotten matter, burying gives the time for it to work, and a substance is produce that makes things grow well! I can't explain it, but I understand it and now perhaps you can also. He also suggested stirring water in a bucket in sunlight to energize it. It somehow works. It needs to be stirred for a length of time, and stirred well enough to make that small whirlpool that we can see in our sinks as water is drained. The base of that whirlpool somehow energizes the water, and so is good for you to drink. Myself, during the summer months where I live, I have set out quart jars. I fill them half way with pure water and I let the sun shine on them. After a week, I drink one a day. I don't know if it helps me, but I don't believe it hurts. Now this year I have constructed a 12 inch glass oven, with a fairly large base, and I am going to drink from that as it also sets in the sun and at night, moonlight. Not designed after the oven I use for my matters, just four sides and a large base. The 12 inch circulated continuously, raising and falling, and mixing the above to the below.

I want to now spend a little time with the "Book of the Dead, by A.E. Wallis Budge. I might say that when I purchased this book, some 30 years ago, I often wondered why I had done so. There was not much that I read that had any meaning to me. Now, I need to purchase another copy as this one is too full of my notes and marks. Always we need get back to ancient Egypt to understand, and remarks are few as connected with the alchemical process. Like Mr. Massey, Mr. Budge did not know of the alchemical connections to this work. But here also is a collection of and from the past that is our heritage, not that we need to know this book, but we should know enough to know ourselves. It is our past, and we live today based on the life they found and lived many thousands of years ago. Again, some of this material comes from a time so remote, we just don't know where or when it is actually from. The name we have is 'Book of the Dead,' but it is variously translated to mean 'manifested in Light.' We start right out with seeing that light is what the book is about, and so it is how we understand. It is the light of God, and how we are to connect with this light, how to live so that we can get back to it. Another title for the book, "the chapter of making strong (or perfect) the Khu." As Mr. Budge says. "We probably wont ever know the exact meaning it had for the early Egyptians." But I think some of that will now change. What they have said for their understanding I have explained and connected, or very close. Pg. 28.

Pg.31, chapter XVII. "and of changing into any form which he pleases." This is the body of the individual coming forth from Amenta, the underworld. Evidently this is a soul, a person who's heart has been weighed and he has been found good in the balance an so has gained eternal life. They believed they could come back as male or female, man or beast. By the alchemical process, and by the Osirian understand of being formed androgynous, we can see how he could come back as male or female. As you consider this is about the transformation of matter, and that matter has the possibility of all things, then he is of this transformed matter. He could also come back as man, or animal. I link this as to why the sphinx is both man and beast, it is a grave marker and a understanding of the matters gained by this process with the after life. This is also found on pg. 37. Chapter LXXVI, "The chapter of a man changing into whatsoever form he pleases." Pg.53 - Concerning Osiris. On the day he was born, "and at the moment of his birth a voice was heard to proclaim that the 'Lord of Creation' was born." Now this is explained more on pg. 58. And necessary to connect to the alchemical process. "He is called the soul that livith again, the being that becomes a child again, the firstborn son of the primeval god, the lord of multiples of forms and aspects, the lord of times and the bestower of years, the lord of life for all eternity. He is the giver of life from the beginning, life springs up to us from his destruction, and the germ which proceeds from him engenders life in both the dead and the living." Please note, from his destruction, and that he was a child born again. Now on pg. 83, and pg. 84 it speaks of Osiris as "When Osiris of a man has entered heaven as a living soul. He is regarded as one of those that has 'eaten the eye of Horus.'" He walks among the living ones. Three Ankh's follow. How does Osiris eat the eye of Horus? The last step of his purification, when he is moved to the upper section of the oven, to join with the above god is this time. It is the sign of the egg setting on the top of the Tau Cross. Remember what Adi had said about the oven, "god, goat, whatever we want to call it, it is the upper area of the oven where the substance embraces and absorbs the principle of god." From the side view of the oven, the ankh (with egg in place) is what you see on this last step. He is eating the Eye of Horus.

Pg. 99, The word "Neter" The understanding is that the creation and all in it was given this name by the Egyptians. The word has been translated as holy, god like, strong, force, mighty, etc. Mr. Budge says that the exact meaning is probably lost. On the same page, a Dr. Brugsch defined the word to mean "the active power which produces and creates things in a regular recurrence; which bestows new life upon them, and gives back to them their youthful vigor." I want you to consider Genesis as we call it. It is, neter connected to nature, and it does as has been described by Mr Brugsch. I think this understanding shows where Genesis comes from, and that it is so ancient we really don't know just how old it is. Mr Brugsch, along with Champollion, Figeac, deRouge, Pierret all came to the conclusion that the dwellers along the Nile from earliest times believed in one god. Nameless, incomprehensible and eternal. The word neter referred to this god, and if the word was plural then it might refer to different classes of gods. I understand it today as being similar to god, and the saints. They believed this one god was self existent, was one being, and had created man with an eternal soul. He is eternal and infinite and endureth forever, and no man can know his form. We can know of him through nature (Neter), and Genesis (All).

Some facts collected from this book that we need to tie to the alchemical process.

Pg. 114 "The first act of creation was the sending forth from Nu the ball of the sun, the creation of light." This is important because many have believed the light of the creation was a special light. It was not, it is as we have outside, always was and always will be always renewing on a yearly basis.

Pg. 118, At this time, the beginning, nothing existed except a vast mass of celestial waters containing the germ within of all living things.

Pg. 119, He made a second eye, the moon of which he gave a part of the splendor of the first eye, the sun.

Pg. 119, The First act of creation was the formation of an egg, out of the primeval water, from which emerged Ra, the immediate cause of all life upon the Earth.

Pg 137, The Theben Recension of the Book of the Dead contains several chapters dealing with Osiris. From these several facts are derived. The CXLIVth chapter states there were seven halls or mansions that the deceased had to pass through before he could see the god. Compare to the last seven months of process.

Pg 174, The four pillars raised up of the same in the firmament,

Pg. 175, The four Pillars of heaven. Pointed out as compared to the design of the base of the oven and divided into four sections.

Pg. 184, The name of Tehu, the name given to the moon as a measurer of time. This shows a day of the creation based on the moon going through a cycle is one day.

Pg. 235, On the upper part of the Tet are the 'Two Utchatcs' or eyes of the sun and moon with the symbol of good between them. Compare to Genesis where it said, "The Light was Good."

Pg. 282, Chapter LIV, the chapter of giving air to the scribe. Ani identifies himself with the egg of the Great Cackler, that is to say with the egg of the sun which was laid by the great god Keb. As the embryo inside the shell obtains air and grows to maturity so the embro of Ani spirit body lives and grows inside the tomb, which takes the place of the shell of the egg. I believe this quote shows they did work with eggs and substance inside of the shell. I myself have considered many times this problem as to how does the chick get enough air while maturing?

Pg. 293, "Ani also identifies himself with the Moon-god who was a form of Osiris and the symbol and a type of the New Birth or Resurrection. This shows Osiris is tied to the Virgin Birth by the moon and constellation Virgo. Note the New Birth was also seen as a resurrection. The Favor of the God of the moon allows Ani to make his way successfully to the other world and to the relm of Osiris and this is one of the oldest spells in the Book of the Dead."

The book of the Dead contains many references to the creation, and to this process we can work within the oven. Many of the facts stated and copied with some misunderstanding if connected to this process can now be totally understood. Again I have hardly touched on a book here that is full of connections and proofs. It is up to the individual to read and study as more or all really can be found among these pages. I reread many of them, many times a year. This and others, as it is like they said, read, read and reread those same books. You like I have indicated will not be able to understand the information that is there until you have a good understanding of how it all fits together. As you read, and then reread, you will be amassed as to how things appear, and you will wonder why it is that you didn't see it before.

Another Book I wish to use in part is by A. E. Waite. Noted as an alchemical expert of the past.

There were a few in our near past that spent a considerable amount of time with alchemy, and one of them, A. E. Waite spent most of his life looking for answers. I have several of his books, and wish now to spend a little time with one of them, 'Brotherhood of the Rosy Cross.' Another book I have had for over 30 years, read it many times, and for many years, had a lot of facts, but felt somewhat dismayed as I do believe Mr. Waite was himself. Those facts though, with what I have been trying to point out will make your understanding deeper as they do point to the ancient past. They also connect to a great extent to religion, to Christianity, and to things about us we don't know or connect to as where it originated. My feelings of Mr. Waite is thankful for all he brought out in this book, but I also felt the frustration I believe he felt with not understanding what it was really all about. At least, I will say that for all the secrets he touched on, he never explained the connection as to how it all worked together. This would seem to indicate he never knew of the physical process of the stone, and so, how could he? IMO, and so a large book for only those that want the whole story. One they can have by only knowing that it is all based on the ancient religion of Osiris, based on the stone. Mr. Waite describes the brotherhood as a society concerned with alchemy, and that the theory of transmutation may have been pursued within those and their circles. Pg. 3 "It is our task to learn if we can, and so also whether the Philosophers Stone in the light of the Rosy Cross was a Mystery of Spiritual healing and Divine Tincture, an ethical art of contentment or a method of raising so called base metal into the perfect form of gold." Originally the order seemed to be occult, and that if it exists today, it still would be. Occult to me simply means unknown. What they do is unknown, some of their ceremonies are unknown. I point this out because many will see the word occult and think the order evil as the word by the unlearned is thought of in that way. To me it simply means that behind closed doors, I don't know what they do! My interest is in the facts Mr. Waite has presented, and how you may now see and understand them as to the process and information newly explained. Everything of all this information is tied together in some way, and my purpose is to present that understanding. And so, let us review some of what has been said.

Pg. 5 "It postulates a founder of the Rosicrucians in a certain Ormesius or Ormuz and affirms that he was converted to Christianity at Alexandria by St. mark A.D. 46. He is said to have purified the Egyptian Mysteries and married them to the new faith. He established the society of Ormuz or of the light. The sign of membership was a Red Cross worn on the person. Essenes and Therapeuta entered the ranks of this sodality, in which the Hermetic Secrets were preserved and transmitted." Now, "Essenes" is a name that should get your attention as to what and who was involved. We still today hear of this group. Also, in the organization of the United States, those Masons! Tied to the writing of our constitution, and to some of our symbols, like the dollar bill with the pyramid shape on the back, the Eye of God at the top. Is this then the same Eye of Horus of the ancient Egypt, the one that Osiris had to swallow to become God like? "Book of the Dead, pg. 83, 84"

Pg. 38. "It is an exceedingly mixed instruction which postulates Zoroaster as the fountain source of Gnostic doctrine, but he derived apparently from India. It was after this manner, if I understand it rightly- that Christianity itself came into the world, a Gnosticisation of the Ancient symbolism." The Templars arose in their day and received Gnosticism at the feet of the Persian Sufis. Being destroyed in due time, the Pure Gnostic symbolism was inherited and preserved by the Rosicrucian Order." "The two orders subsisted in close alliance"

pg. 86. (9) "That the Rose in Ancient Egypt is said to be a symbol for regeneration. I have not found adequate authority on this statement." The authority was a Mr. W. S. Hunter of the Society Rosicruciana in Scotia. Now after long contemplation, I explain this thusly. The Rose we always see as a flower. Try to see it as a design! We have rose windows, rose cut on a gemstone, etc. rose we know in the ancients was "sands" or shapes. Rose is just another name for shape or design. In the one oven, we see this design, and so the sand, shape, rose, however you want to call it, the design is necessary for the process to work. One Oven! In many places the drawings of Dalton and the rose are used as example, connected to alchemy. The rose he draws with seven petals, and I think I have explained and connected seven enough. But, in the background he draws a spider web! Other alchemists have drawn the spider web, to indicate the oven design. And so, the rose, the spider web design mean the same thing. What do we do in the oven, but regenerate matter!

Pg. 91, "Now I have connected the design of the rose to the design of the oven. I need now also to show how the ancient mystery has been changed by those that know, or, perhaps by those that don't know, you choose, and as to how the past is hidden. The Rose of Sharon has been attached in the Christian symbolism of Mary, Mother of the Divine Child. Also, Mary is Virgo, Virgin in all of Christendom. The Rose of Mary was more the White Rose, and it is said that the Red Rose continued for a long time to be connected to Holda, the Northern Goddess." Now I have shown alchemically the new birth of Osiris as Septembers Child came about because of two mothers, or two sisters. One of them being the moon, the other the constellation Virgo. This was a part of the ancient religion for thousands of years. And so the original understanding of the rose has to be tied to the rose of design. Tied also to those lights above at the time of year when the new birth was brought about. It was those lights shining on the matters within the oven that finished that part of the process and purified the matters, thus the virgin birth from the two. As understanding of most of the past, like 'Holda' the northern goddess has disappeared, Mary remains. The (time) place from whence this new understanding all came was known and understood. Around 00 AD - 50 AD   It was changed and in time so much so that the past is no longer known. Perhaps one can consider and understand what and why the Rose symbol was accepted and used. It may be tied to a meaning or an understanding that is lost as so much is. To us a rose is a flower. To me it has become a term connected to design. I can only present the past from what has been written down in places, as I have here concerning the rose as regeneration. That is all I do with the matters I work on within the oven, take it back to a base, and then regenerate it by steps until it is pure. Those of the past cannot be faulted because they saw the above, in this instance light being moon and constellation, as a part of the all. They believed that the combination from the above produced what they found in the below.

From Michael Maier, pg. 97. " He said, (1) that the Rose is the first, most Beautiful of all Flowers. (2) That it is guarded because it is a Virgin, and the guard is thorns. (3) That the Garden of Philosophy is planted with many Roses, both Red and White. (4) That these colors are in correspondence with gold and silver. (5)That the center is green and is emblematical and is of the Green Lion, a familiar emblem of the wise. (6) That even as the natural Rose is a pleasure to the senses of man on account of its sweetness and salubrity, so is the Philosophical Rose exhilarating to the heart and a giver of strength to the brain, (7) and as the natural Rose turns to the sun, and is refreshed by rain, so is the philosophical matter prepared in blood, grown in light and by these made perfect. Here of is the Rose in alchemy."

I think now one can understand the rose and where from, and why so revered. The reader should be able to see many alchemical connections from what was said by Mr. Maier! Why for example would he call the flower a virgin, if he had not known the connections to those facts I am presenting?

With this term, rose, we also had cross. The cross I believe I have shown and explained so that all can see and understand where it is from, but more than just the cross with equal arms, the Tau and Tet cross also. However, Mr. Waite did not know or understand the symbolism, or he chose to give that point of view. Pg. 98 "The cross of alchemy shall not detain us long." "That the symbol of the cross was reflected in the Order of the Rosy Cross and was a Cross with Equal Arms." "A Macrocosmic Cross, but there was no way of knowing." Mr. Waite describes different crosses and that there is no relevance to them. Either he knew not of the oven, or he chose to not discuss it. The cross with Equal arms, painted red and worn by many like those other symbols were known and understood in the past. All these crosses can be found in the oven design, they can be found throughout the alchemical symbolism, and on the walls of the ancient Egyptian Tombs. This would not be so if there was no, as with the other parts, some purpose tied to the symbol. It was more than a symbol of a machine that was used to hang things on, sometimes people. It was more than a cross of hope for the times to come.

Pg. 106. From the alchemist Robert Fludd. " affirmed that, (1) that the name of the order is not compounded of Rosa and Crux; (2) that this and other interpretations have been put forward by chemists themselves for the sake of imposing on others; (3) that the composed in reality is Ros = dew and Crux = Cross; (4) that the dew is the most powerful of all natural dissolvent; (5) that the figure of the cross exhibit's the letters of Lux = light, at a single view; (6) that Lux in alchemy signifies the menstruum of the Red Dragon, otherwise that crude and corporeal light which if properly concocted and digested produces gold; (7) That a Rosicrucian is there fore a Philosopher who seeks light by mean of dew, or otherwise the substance of the philosophers Stone." Here I think Mr. Fludd explains it very clearly. All these explanations need be considered together. As I pointed out before, here again we see light and dew! Before it was design and cross. Design, dew, light, all is needed is to know that to bring these things together, glass, design, oven, regeneration of matters, is the proper sand, shape, design of the place of work!

Now Pg. 109, and very important. "recent writers, Mr. Wigston whom I have quoted says that the crucified Rose of the Rosicrucian hints a the entire Logos legend in a mystical sense." Footnote 1, "It may be mentioned in this connection apart from Rose -symbolism, that the word Ros = dew - but no doubt in it's Greek form - was a Gnostic emblem of Christ. The Ophites, moreover , held that the dew which fell from the excess of light was -represented- wisdom understood- as a Hermaphroditic Deity." Now consider the process, we collect dew day and night, and so this statement of hermaphrodite is True! The lights being male and female. Hermaphrodite is what we produce in the process at two different times! All these statement by those that might have some knowledge of what it was about, must be considered.

'Wisdom understood' is just that, and has no meaning to those that do not know and so do not understand. All information could be presented openly, as it was without fear of others, (common people) even kings and princes understanding or knowing.

On the footnote pg. 111 Mr. Waite discusses the things Mr. Fludd has expressed. (4) Ros = that which is born from the corpse and exhales itself in sweet odours. " This Rose blossoms by following the example of the bird, I.e., nourishing it's own young by using it's own blood". Mr. Waite goes on to say "there is no analogy in symbolism between the Rose and the Pelican; while to speak of a Rose nourishing it's young is to confuse the image concerned." I disagree with Mr. Waite. If we say the oven circulates, "from earth to heaven." We are saying the substance produces the moisture that is to raise again and again to receive from the above, to condense and then to feed itself. If we understand rose to mean "regeneration" as from the old Egyptian understanding, how are we to produce this regeneration if not some form of circulation is not involved? The alchemists showed this work by metaphor, and so showed a pelican biting it's breast and so bleeding and feeding itself from itself. This is exactly a substance feeding itself from itself, and is exactly what is happening in the oven. "Ros =

that which is born from the corpse and exhales itself in sweet odours." There is more to it for a short review, like. Like is the sweet vapor from itself that must be used to augment the substance. Like is the blood of the substance, feeding the substance. A pelican or goose, biting itself and then drinking the blood is feeding itself from itself!

And so from this book, many One Liners that in all speak the Truth.

Pg. 149, "That the book of nature Stands free to all eyes, though few there are to read it." "There are secret characters and letters in the Sacred Scriptures, and they are inscribed also on all the works of Creation, the Heavens the earth and beasts."

Pg. 159, " the Great parable of the Hermetic Marriage is divided into seven books, representing seven days in the dramatic development of it's mysteries." Note Seven!

Pg.222, " Philosophy, Understood thus mystically, it is a key to the following lines:
" The matter, vase, Furnace, fire and coction- these are one thing only: The One thing and the sole one, the beginning, middle and end. It suffers no foreign substance and is performed without any alien thing. Behold, in mercury lies that which the Wise seek".

Pg. 287, " In alchemy the way of advancement is to realize that it's true work is a work of nature and that he who would co-operate therewith must use natural matrices in place of artificial furnaces, applying natural things to things which are also natural and species to their congruent."

Pg. 464. The dot within a circle! " The son of the sun is the product also of profoundly concentrated fire."

Pg. 622 " I am very sure that the great antique tradition of Egypt was, as to living essentials absorbed in Christ."

Pg. 626, " Moreover, the great central sign and symbol of the Rose placed upon a cross could never, as we have seen, have signified anything but a spiritual and as such a Christian Mystery." Right here, with the last two quotes we see how this subject has mystified those that searched it out. Mr. Waite was an expert in alchemy. He traced it back to Christ, and there the trail grew cold as it did with so many of those that searched this information. I have called it the Wall at 0000 AD! It seems that the past of Egypt is something that we as a society should just forget, as there never was anything there of interest. I for one am glad that seems to be changing, and with this work, perhaps it will be looked at more closely. It is so tied to all we are today, and to me it is something, their history and religion, that we today should know.

I still today cannot say what it is exactly that I have found. All the material now does have and hold meaning for me. That still doesn't prove I have totally solved the way of the stone. I have an explanation and I have some purified matter. I will have more, and with this work I know I will have, find a way to do more in depth work to see what it is. Slowly I gain friends all over the world, and so this work in total will be finished. As the friends are everywhere now, this information can no longer be hidden. That is the way of our world. I always disliked secrets, especially when they were kept from me! Now there may no longer be any concerned with this material. Whatever the outcome, in a short time we all will know. I never have seen proof of a transmutation, and from the training I have had I still have problems believing. However, I don't have much of a feeling for the word 'impossible.' But with my training, I can see a very pure substance made by nature, and art. Actually, who can say what it will do. We all in the below somehow are from the above, and this is pure above in a crystalline form! A shot of it in the arm just might be a good thing! I can surly believe it is a medicine.

And so, where do I go from here. I have considered all that I have written, and for me it is a good explanation. I realize though, it may not be for those reading the material. Why do I say this? In discussing with others interested in alchemy, I have found that the information I give is not always understood. Sometimes I give too much, too fast. I realize I have done this with this book. A good writer could have stretched this out for many more pages. A mechanic like myself, well, I just stick to the facts so to speak. I have forgotten what I said about myself when I started this search. I understood nothing, I knew nothing. I suspect many of my readers, if I get them, will be as I was back then. Without rereading, or a lot of study, much of this won't be understood! I didn't mean it to be that way, but it is hard for me to explain many different things connected as alchemy is. Explained in such a way as it is easy for all to see and do. So, I need another plan and have considered and I am implementing one. I had a forum in the past, and will again open that forum. The purpose will be to discuss this material with those that wish to learn more of what I have said. I suspect that the questions they will ask, will be similar to those anyone reading this material would ask. To be on my forum means that your question, and my answer will possibly be published. I will make all connected know of this fact. It will be my way of making this material understandable to all that want to know, or that want to know more. I think another connecting book will eventually be produced. The forum address will be with this material. You can join, speak, or just lurk there to read what others may say. If you do not see the answer you seek, you can always ask!

http://tech.groups.yahoo.com/group/ariadnes_thread/

I realize also that much needs to be done with what I have found with this process. The material that is produced is a very pure material, made by the sun. At the start of the process, it is about bugs and matter. It ends up being about matter and light. I don't know what it is yet, or what it will do. I have tried to give this material away to universities, and to other research centers. Most kind of snicker and ignore what I have to say. Hopefully, they will be sorry for the lack of interest. For those that are or want to try to make this stone, to do so successfully will truly take some work. Nature is a wonderful thing. Nature will do as you ask of her, but nature will also destroy your work as fast as she will help. 16 months is a long time to do a process outside, and it really has to be watched and protected all the time. A wind can come up anytime and blow your work away. It has to be outside and kept warm, a loss of power and it can freeze. Many things can happen, and all of them have happened to me. Also, if you do make it, things should be known. A pinch and no more! A small amount like a rape seed! In other words, the masters said, only a small amount mixed with a good wine. Evidently too much can be harmful. Many things can be involved, perhaps the purity matters as I am sure that it does. Maybe you think it is right, but it isn't. Whatever you do, if it is not right, and if it does not follow the color scheme as I have shown, I wouldn't use it. I have persons in several places working on this, but as of yet we don't know what it is, or what it will do. I believe in the near future, that will be explained and known. This is my way of the stone that I found, and still without the ending. You read and learn and decide. To me it is the lost Art found and restored to mankind. Time will tell.

As I learn and know, as with this book, all others also will know if I am able to tell. The purpose of the forum is to insure that others all around the world will know. That way, things that could happen will not cause this information to be lost again!

I am not sure if I believe that it will transmute metals, but I do believe that it is a medicine. What it will do remains to be seen. I also will say here, there are little tricks to the stone, but if you are on the right path, it will reveal them to you. What this means is I believe I have time to give you the proper answers before you find how to complete the stone in the proper method. Not that I have kept the steps from you, I haven't. But, there are some things I may not have explained as clearly as I could have. I want a little more time, but I have come to the point where I need a little help, and research. By going public as I am, I do believe I will receive what I need. The material proves what I am doing is correct or, it is the biggest set of coincidences I ever saw.

I wanted to point out that the ancients developed cereal grains in ancient Egypt. I believe the oven design is involved with that. I at one time grew wheat in a four foot glass oven. I had it raised above the ground so I could control the heat, and I kept it moist. My wheat was much better than what the local farmers were doing. My goal though was to try to develop wheat that would grow with brackish water. I never got to that because a storm ended that project! I told you about nature! However, I think there is benefit there for mankind. If you understand how the oven is a place that naturally focuses forces of nature, then you can see how this may work in developing new strains of wheat for example. You may say, that I am considering the survival of the fittest as Darwin would. I am creating a set of conditions, and the wheat I use may not be the fittest, but the oven may quickly draw out a strain that will survive within! I may never get to this, but by saying so here, I may cause it to happen somewhere in the world. It would be a cheap way to do research, and perhaps answer how the ancients developed our cereal grains.

I wanted also to say that within this book, there are subjects mentioned I never wanted to point out. Subjects I never dreamed would be connected! One cannot always pick and choose the information he needs to show for an understanding. Our past is a very colorful one indeed, and there are many things hidden and buried. I am sure some would like to keep it that way. I am different I would say. To me all things need to be looked at with an open mind. If one cannot do that, perhaps one shouldn't look too much. Always there will be things found one may not want to see. I, do not like secrets. Surly by reading this book, that is easily seen. I see us as all created equal, and I see all information as something all should be able to read and know. How you accept is your decision. Myself I believe all information comes from god, and so all information is for all men. I don't believe God has a favorite person, or a favorite people. Others may. I try to see god as a god, something I know little of. Something as others have said, "we only can know what we see in nature." I think this is what the ancients found, things in nature and felt that was enough. Today? We have a god I would say that is made in man's image! That may be so. Man is always trying to understand god, and so always it seems that god slowly becomes something so tied to us that he is like us. I am just not so sure. Again, each must decide what it is he wants to believe and how he wants to live. Alchemy was a science of the past. It was something that created a life style, a religion, an understanding of nature and how it works, many things. It tied man to all that was around him, from the Greatest to the Smallest! Much of it if not all was a good thing! I believe that by knowing our society can benefit, and it can be a good thing again.

I will at the end of this part of my work, include a few pictures of what I have seen. If you look you will see many design found in pictorial allegories. You will see insulated ovens that worked in the winter. You will see the green grass of summer. Also, you will see many of the colors of the stone. As you change a condition, you change what is inside! All one really needs to know, is what condition is next, and for how long! All one needs know is, Genesis, and 'The First Mythology!'

Peace!

A short explanation of the following pictures of my work!

A series of pictures. By looking closely you will see times of the year. The substance at different stages. Designs and shapes that are mentioned throughout alchemy. See also the mountains, and little mountains. The blue and yellow are of the rainbow. The orange is salamander. The black is the first color we see, and sometimes it needs cleaned. Yes, the final red is there, and, Septembers Child.

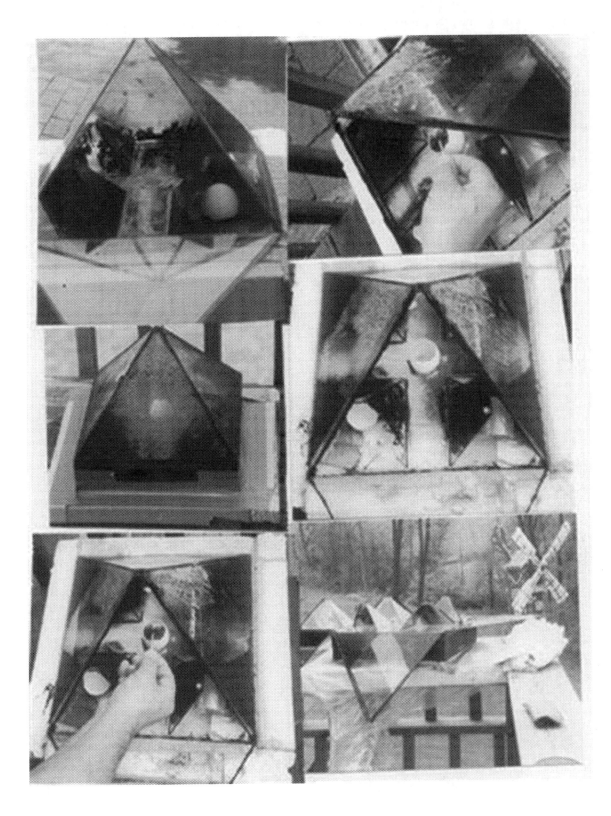

Several lists of Books used by the Author.

Those books I lived with for many years.

We Are Not The First, by Andrew Tomas. This book started me on this Path in 1972..

The Book of The Dead, Egyptian Religion, and Cleopatra's Needles by E. A. Wallis Budge.

The Magic of Obelisks, His Several Books on Pyramids, and those of Secret Life of Plants by Peter Tompkins.

Earth in Upheaval, Ages in Chaos, and Worlds in Collision by Immanual Velikovsky.

Alchemy, An introduction to the symbolism and the Psychology, by Marie-Louise Von Franz. - Very enlightening when the process is known!

The Alchemical Tradition, by Richard Grossinger.

Alchemy, by E. J. Holmyard.

Alchemists and Gold, by Jacques Sadoul.

Prelude to Chemistry, and Through Alchemy to Chemistry, by John Read. My favorite and most informative for many years!

The Royal Art of Alchemy, by Reinhard Federmann.

The Alchemists, by Hans Holzer.

Larousse Encyclopedia of Mythology, Batchworth Press Limited, 1959.

Alchemy, Pre-Egyptian Legacy, Millennial Promise, Richard Grossinger.

Atlantis, The Antediluvian World, by Egerton Sykes.

The History and practice of Magic, by Paul Cristian.

The Ancient Magic of Pyramids, by Ken Johnson.

Using Pyramid Power, by Wyckoff James.

Impossible Possibilities, by Louis Pauwels and Jacques Berger.

Pyramids and the Second Reality, by Bill Schul and Ed Pettit.

From Religion to Philosophy, by F. M. Cornford.

The Brotherhood of the Rosy Cross, by A. E. Waite.

Serpent In The Sky, by John Anthony West.

The Psychic Power of Pyramids, by Bill Schul and Ed Pettit.

Azoth or The Star in The East, by A. E. Waite.

Roots of Scientific Thought, by Philip P. Wiener and Aaron Noland.

The Story of Philosophy, by Will Durant.

Alchemy, The Secret Art, by Stanislas Klossowski.

Basic Teachings of the Great Philosophers, by S. E. Frost, jr.

Primitive Christianity, by Rudolph Bultmann.

The Bible as History, by Werner Keller.

Basic Christian Beliefs, by Frederick C. Grant.

Egypt and it's Monuments. by Amelia B. Edwards.

Ancient Egyptian Myths And legends, by Lewis Spence.

The Great Pyramid, by Piazzi Smyth.

A History of the Ancient Egyptians, by James Henry Breasted, PH.D.

Rosicrucian Manual, by H. Spencer Lewis, Ph.D., F.R.C.

Theurgy or The hermetic Practice, by E.J.Langford Garstin.

Edgar Cayce on Prophecy, by Mary Ellen Carter.

Albertus Magnus, by deLaurence, Scott & Co.

The Hermetic and Alchemical writings of Paracelsus, by Kessinger Publishing Co.

The Art of Alchemy, and The Light of Life or the Mastery of Death, Devine Symbols. by Delmar De Forest Bryant. Adiramled, referred by me as Adi in many places!

These are just a few of the Books I have now collected, but most of these I have had a long time. I have spent much time with them. Again and again I will read them as you cannot know the message until you have grown. I am always trying to learn and grow! When I started there were few books available without purchasing them, if you could know of them!

Printed in the United States
By Bookmasters